NON-FOOTBALL TABLES OF SOUTH WEST ENGLAND 1892-2015

EDITOR
Michael Robinson

FOREWORD

Since 2002, when we began to publish our 'Non-League Football Tables' series, we have considered introducting more regionalised books about various football leagues both past and present, and, at last, we have got around to doing it!

As this is the very first book in a planned series of six, we felt that it would be a good idea to start down in the 'West Country' and we hope that our readers will be satisfied with the range of Leagues which we have selected.

Those Leagues which currently form the apex of the 'Non-League Pyramid', namely the Football Conference (currently called the National League) and its three feeder leagues (Northern Premier, Southern Premier & Isthmian) will continue to be covered by our yearly 'Non-League Football Tables' books.

We are indebted to Mick Blakeman for providing tables for the various Leagues included in this edition of the book.

British Library Cataloguing in Publication Data
A catalogue record for this book is available from the British Library

ISBN: 978-1-86223-324-9

Printed in the UK by 4edge Ltd.

CONTENTS

WESTERN LEAGUE

The Western League was formed in 1892 as the Bristol & District League, changing its name to the Western League in 1895. For many of its 9 founder members, it was a first taste of league football although Wells City had already twice been champions of the Somerset Senior League.

Several of the published tables contained errors, principally in the goals scored record. Additional research has succeeded in correcting many of these but totals which still do not balance are shown below the relevant columns in italics.

Bristol & District League

1892-93

Warmley	16	11	3	2	72	19	25
Trowbridge Town	16	10	4	2	66	17	24
St. George	16	9	5	2	36	22	23
Bedminster	16	6	5	5	30	34	17
Clevedon	16	6	4	6	25	36	16
Eastville Rovers	16	6	3	7	36	40	15
Clifton	16	4	2	10	27	61	10
Mangotsfield	16	3	2	11	19	45	8
Wells City	16	1	4	11	14	51	6

Wells City left the league to return to the Somerset Senior League while Gloucester and Staple Hill joined, making a 10-club First Division.
A 10-club Second Division was formed by the Reserves of Bedminster, Clifton, Eastville Rovers, Mangotsfield, St. George, Trowbridge Town and Warmley plus the first XI's of Barton Hill, St. Paul's, and Waverley.

1893-94

Division One

Warmley	18	12	5	1	32	13	27
St. George	18	10	6	2	39	23	26
Trowbridge Town	18	9	4	5	54	33	22
Bedminster	18	9	2	7	41	36	20
Clevedon	18	7	5	6	34	40	19
Clifton	18	6	4	8	37	30	16
Staple Hill	18	5	5	8	23	33	15
Gloucester	18	6	1	11	32	45	13
Eastville Rovers	18	5	2	11	30	39	12
Mangotsfield	18	2	4	12	19	48	8
					341	*340*	

Warmley had 2 points deducted for allegedly fielding a professional player. Hereford Thistle and Swindon Wanderers both joined the league, increasing Division One to 12 clubs.

Division Two

Warmley Reserves	18	16	1	1	66	12	33
St. George Reserves	18	15	0	3	50	22	30
Trowbridge Town Reserves	18	11	1	6	47	22	23
St. Paul's	18	9	3	6	44	51	21
Barton Hill	18	7	4	7	40	32	18
Bedminster Reserves	18	6	3	9	35	42	15
Mangotsfield Reserves	18	6	1	11	26	41	13
Clifton Reserves	18	5	2	11	29	59	12
Eastville Rovers Reserves	18	4	2	12	23	45	10
Waverley	18	2	4	12	22	53	8
	81	21	78	382	*379*	*183*	

Trowbridge Town Reserves left the league but Willsbridge joined from the South Bristol & District League and Staple Hill Reserves also joined.

1894-95

Division One

Hereford Thistle	22	18	3	1	93	21	39
St. George	22	18	3	1	76	21	39
Warmley	22	14	2	6	74	30	30
Staple Hill	22	11	4	7	56	38	26
Gloucester	22	10	4	8	64	54	24
Eastville Rovers	22	10	4	8	46	40	24
Trowbridge Town	22	9	4	9	68	48	22
Clifton	22	8	2	12	47	55	18
Bedminster	22	7	0	15	39	73	14
Swindon Wanderers	22	5	3	14	40	63	13
Mangotsfield	22	5	2	15	22	68	12
Clevedon	22	1	1	20	23	136	3
					648	*647*	

Hereford Thistle left to join the Birmingham League and Clevedon also left. Cardiff joined the league and St. Paul's were promoted from Division Two.

Division Two

Warmley Reserves	20	17	0	3	75	20	34
St. Paul's	20	16	0	4	79	31	32
Willsbridge	20	15	1	4	48	21	31
St. George Reserves	20	14	1	5	69	33	29
Barton Hill	20	11	1	8	57	31	23
Bedminster Reserves	20	8	1	11	36	30	17
Eastville Rovers Reserves	20	8	0	12	45	45	16
Clifton Reserves	20	7	0	13	40	68	14
Mangotsfield Reserves	20	4	2	14	30	84	10
Staple Hill Reserves	20	4	1	15	32	79	9
Waverley	20	2	1	17	15	74	5
					526	*516*	

St. Paul's were promoted.
Mangotsfield Reserves, Waverley and Willsbridge all left the league. Cumberland, Eastville Wanderers, Fishponds and Frenchay joined.

Western League

1895-96

Division One

Warmley	20	16	3	1	65	13	35
Eastville Rovers	20	14	1	5	57	22	29
Staple Hill	20	13	3	4	48	19	29
Trowbridge Town	20	13	1	6	50	31	27
St. George	20	10	4	6	47	38	24
Clifton	20	8	3	9	44	50	17
Gloucester	20	6	4	10	29	42	16
Bedminster	20	6	2	12	36	41	14
Swindon Wanderers	20	4	4	12	22	57	12
Mangotsfield	20	3	3	14	17	54	9
St. Paul's	20	2	2	16	12	60	6

Clifton had 2 points deducted for a breach of the rules.
Cardiff were expelled in January 1896 for non-payment of fines and their record was expunged. Eastville Rovers and Staple Hill were declared joint runners-up, both clubs receiving silver medals.
Gloucester and Swindon Wanderers left and Mangotsfield were relegated to Division Two. Bristol South End joined. Division was reduced to 9 clubs.

Division Two

Barton Hill	18	15	2	1	45	16	32
Fishponds	18	11	4	3	33	14	26
St. George Reserves	18	11	3	4	52	22	25
Eastville Wanderers	18	10	2	6	34	23	22
Eastville Rovers Reserves	18	8	4	6	43	31	20
Cumberland	18	7	3	8	47	35	17
Staple Hill Reserves	18	7	2	9	34	58	16
Bedminster Reserves	18	6	1	11	35	38	13
Warmley Reserves	18	4	1	13	23	29	9
Clifton Reserves	18	0	0	18	10	84	0
					356	350	

Frenchay resigned during the season and their record was expunged. Cumberland, Clifton Reserves, St. George Reserves and Warmley Reserves all left the league and Division Two was reduced to 7 clubs.

1896-97

Division One

Warmley	16	13	2	1	42	9	28
South End	16	11	0	5	28	22	22
Bedminster	16	8	2	6	32	16	18
St. George	16	8	1	7	27	23	17
Eastville Rovers	16	7	2	7	25	23	14
Trowbridge Town	16	5	3	8	21	30	13
St. Paul's	16	3	5	8	29	31	11
Staple Hill	16	5	0	11	18	39	10
Clifton	16	4	1	11	19	48	9

Eastville Rovers had 2 points deducted for fielding an ineligible player.

Division Two

Eastville Wanderers	12	7	4	1	25	9	18
Barton Hill	12	7	3	2	28	7	17
Mangotsfield	12	6	3	3	23	14	15
Fishponds	12	4	5	3	17	16	13
Bedminster Reserves	12	6	1	5	19	20	13
Eastville Rovers Reserves	12	1	3	8	7	33	5
Staple Hill Reserves	12	1	1	10	8	34	3
					127	133	

A new 8-club Professional Section was formed for the following season. Eastville Rovers, South End (having changed their name to Bristol City), St. George (as Bristol St. George), Trowbridge Town and Warmley moved from Division One to this new section and were joined by three new members, Eastleigh, Reading and Swindon Town. Reading and Swindon Town also continued to play in the Southern League.
The original Division One and Two continued as the amateur section. Midsomer Norton and Radstock joined Division One while continuing to play in the Somerset Senior League and the division was made up to 10 clubs by the promotion of Eastville Wanderers, Barton Hill, Mangotsfield and Fishponds from Division Two.
Eastville Rovers Reserves and Staple Hill Reserves left Division Two but Barton Hill Reserves, Cotham, Eastville Wanderers Reserves, Fishponds Reserves, Hanham, Royal Artillery (Horfield) and St. Paul's Reserves joined, increasing the division to 8 clubs.

1897-98

Professional Section

Bristol City	14	11	1	2	51	16	23
Swindon Town	14	9	1	4	32	15	19
Reading	14	7	2	5	29	25	16
Bristol St. George	14	6	3	5	25	27	15
Eastville Rovers	14	6	2	6	38	25	14
Warmley	14	5	3	6	36	27	13
Eastleigh	14	3	2	9	22	55	8
Trowbridge Town	14	2	0	12	15	58	4

Eastleigh left to join the Southern League and Bristol City and Reading also left to concentrate solely on the Southern League. Southampton joined while continuing to play in the Southern League and Bedminster moved

from Division One of the Amateur section. The Professional Section was reduced to 7 clubs and the title was changed to Division One. Eastville Rovers changed their name to Bristol Eastville Rovers.

Amateur – Division One

Bedminster	16	15	0	1	65	11	30
Staple Hill	16	11	1	4	38	15	23
Fishponds	16	8	2	6	26	30	18
Midsomer Norton	16	7	2	7	23	33	16
Barton Hill	16	6	2	8	25	25	14
Radstock	16	5	4	7	17	28	14
St. Paul's	16	4	3	9	15	28	11
Eastville Wanderers	16	4	1	11	15	16	9
Mangotsfield	16	1	7	8	5	29	9
					229	215	

Clifton resigned early in the season and their record was expunged.

Amateur – Division Two

Hanham	10	9	1	0	32	8	19
Cotham	10	8	0	2	32	16	16
Barton Hill Reserves	10	4	2	4	20	14	10
St. Paul's Reserves	8	2	2	4	19	26	6
Bedminster Reserves	8	1	0	7	10	34	2
Fishponds Reserves	10	1	1	8	10	25	1

Fishponds Reserves had 2 points deducted for fielding an ineligible player. St. Paul's Reserves and Bedminster Reserves failed to arrange fixtures with each other so the League adjudicated that they had each lost both games. Royal Artillery (Horfield) and Eastville Wanderers Reserves resigned during the season and their records were expunged. At the end of the season, the two amateur divisions were combined into one and renamed Division Two. Radstock left to concentrate solely on the Somerset Senior League and Barton Hill Reserves, Bedminster Reserves, Eastville Wanderers, Fishponds Reserves, Mangotsfield, St. Paul's and St. Paul's Reserves also left. Bristol Amateurs and Mount Hill joined making a new Division Two of 8 clubs.

1898-99

Division One

Swindon Town	8	5	1	2	16	10	11
Bristol St. George	8	4	1	3	18	15	9
Southampton	8	4	0	4	18	15	8
Bristol Eastville Rovers	8	2	2	4	14	18	6
Bedminster	8	2	2	4	9	16	6
					75	74	

Trowbridge Town disbanded in October 1898 and their record was expunged when it stood as: 5   0   0   5   4   18   0
Warmley disbanded in January 1899 and their record was expunged when it stood as: 5   2   0   3   6   15   4
At the end of the season, Bristol St. George disbanded and Southampton left to concentrate on the Southern League. Bristol City joined while continuing in the Southern League. Bristol Eastville Rovers changed their name to Bristol Rovers.

Division Two (Amateur Section)

Staple Hill	14	11	1	2	55	15	23
Fishponds	14	10	2	2	42	15	22
Mount Hill	14	5	3	6	31	28	13
Midsomer Norton	14	6	3	5	20	32	13
Bristol Amateurs	14	5	2	7	31	32	12
Hanham	14	4	3	7	16	28	11
Barton Hill	14	4	1	9	14	31	9
Cotham	14	2	3	9	22	41	7
					231	222	

Midsomer Norton had 2 points deducted for fielding an ineligible player. Midsomer Norton left to concentrate on the Somerset Senior League and Barton Hill, Bristol Amateurs, Hanham and Mount Hill also left. Bristol East and Weston (Bath) joined. The Division was reduced to 5 clubs.

1899-1900

Division One

	P	W	D	L	F	A	Pts
Bristol Rovers	6	3	1	2	8	6	7
Bedminster	6	3	1	2	10	12	7
Swindon Town	6	3	0	3	7	7	6
Bristol City	6	2	0	4	12	12	4

Bedminster amalgamated with Bristol City but Millwall, Portsmouth, Queens Park Rangers, Reading, Southampton and Tottenham Hotspur all joined, increasing the division to 9 clubs, all of whom also played in the Southern League.

Division Two

	P	W	D	L	F	A	Pts
Bristol East	8	6	2	0	31	3	14
Staple Hill	8	4	4	0	22	3	12
Fishponds	8	3	1	4	16	29	7
Weston (Bath)	8	1	1	6	7	19	3
Cotham	8	1	0	7	8	26	2
	15	8	17		84	80	38

Paulton Rovers joined while continuing in the Somerset Senior League. Weston Super Mare and Bedminster St. Francis also joined. The Division was increased to 8 clubs.

1900-01

Division One

	P	W	D	L	F	A	Pts
Portsmouth	16	11	2	3	36	23	24
Millwall	16	9	5	2	33	14	23
Tottenham Hotspur	16	8	5	3	37	19	21
Queens Park Rangers	16	7	4	5	39	24	18
Bristol City	16	6	4	6	27	24	16
Reading	16	5	5	6	23	31	15
Southampton	16	5	2	9	19	29	12
Bristol Rovers	16	4	1	11	18	42	9
Swindon Town	16	2	2	12	9	35	6

West Ham United replaced Bristol City.

Division Two

	P	W	D	L	F	A	Pts
Bristol East	12	11	0	1	41	8	22
Paulton Rovers	9	6	2	1	32	12	14
Staple Hill	10	6	1	3	34	17	13
Cotham	11	3	2	6	20	49	8
Bedminster St. Francis	6	3	1	2	16	13	7
Weston Super Mare	10	2	0	8	18	22	4
Fishponds	12	1	0	11	6	40	0
					167	161	

Fishponds had 2 points deducted for fielding an ineligible player. The unplayed games were ignored. Weston (Bath) resigned during the season before they had played a game.
Bedminster St. Francis and Fishponds left and Bristol Rovers Reserves, St. George, Swindon Town Reserves and Trowbridge Town joined. The Division was increased to 9 clubs. Cotham changed their name to Cotham Amateurs.

1901-02

Division One

	P	W	D	L	F	A	Pts
Portsmouth	16	13	1	2	53	16	27
Tottenham Hotspur	16	11	3	2	42	17	25
Reading	16	7	3	6	29	22	17
Millwall	16	8	1	7	25	29	17
Bristol Rovers	16	8	0	8	25	31	16
Southampton	16	7	1	8	30	28	15
West Ham United	16	6	2	8	30	20	14
Queens Park Rangers	16	5	1	10	17	43	11
Swindon Town	16	0	2	14	8	53	2

Brentford replaced Swindon Town.

Division Two

	P	W	D	L	F	A	Pts
Bristol East	16	13	1	2	55	11	27
Bristol Rovers Reserves	16	10	3	3	54	18	23
Paulton Rovers	16	9	3	4	51	29	21
Staple Hill	16	9	3	4	30	24	21
Swindon Town Reserves	16	7	2	7	44	35	16
Trowbridge Town	16	6	3	7	30	43	15
St. George	16	6	2	8	29	36	14
Weston Super Mare	16	1	2	13	19	68	4
Cotham Amateurs	16	1	1	14	23	71	3

Weston Super Mare left. The Division was reduced to 8 clubs.

1902-03

Division One

	P	W	D	L	F	A	Pts
Portsmouth	16	10	4	2	34	14	24
Bristol Rovers	16	9	2	5	36	22	20
Southampton	16	7	6	3	32	20	20
Tottenham Hotspur	16	6	7	3	20	14	19
Millwall	16	6	3	7	23	29	15
Reading	16	7	0	9	20	21	14
Queens Park Rangers	16	6	2	8	18	31	14
Brentford	16	3	4	9	16	34	10
West Ham United	16	2	4	10	15	29	8

Plymouth Argyle replaced Millwall.

Division Two

	P	W	D	L	F	A	Pts
Bristol Rovers Reserves	14	10	2	2	45	10	22
St. George	14	9	1	4	37	25	19
Swindon Town Reserves	14	8	0	6	59	24	16
Bristol East	14	6	3	5	23	27	15
Staple Hill	14	5	3	6	27	20	13
Paulton Rovers	14	6	1	7	27	27	13
Trowbridge Town	14	5	1	8	20	48	11
Cotham Amateurs	14	1	1	12	14	71	3

St. George and Cotham Amateurs left. Welton Rovers joined from the Somerset Senior League and Bristol City Reserves, Radstock Town and Warmley also joined. The Division was increased to 10 clubs.

1903-04

Division One

	P	W	D	L	F	A	Pts
Tottenham Hotspur	16	11	3	2	32	12	25
Southampton	16	9	3	4	30	18	21
Plymouth Argyle	16	8	4	4	23	19	20
Portsmouth	16	7	2	7	24	22	16
Brentford	16	6	4	6	19	23	16
Queens Park Rangers	16	5	5	6	15	21	15
Reading	16	4	4	8	16	26	12
Bristol Rovers	16	4	3	9	29	29	11
West Ham United	16	2	4	10	13	31	8

Fulham and Millwall joined. The Division was increased to 11 clubs.

Division Two

	P	W	D	L	F	A	Pts
Bristol City Reserves	18	15	2	1	64	17	32
Staple Hill	18	13	1	4	53	19	27
Swindon Town Reserves	18	10	3	5	50	30	23
Bristol Rovers Reserves	18	9	2	7	50	30	20
Bristol East	18	9	1	8	30	27	19
Paulton Rovers	18	9	1	8	37	46	19
Trowbridge Town	18	6	2	10	22	57	14
Warmley	18	3	3	12	32	52	9
Welton Rovers	18	3	3	12	32	67	9
Radstock Town	18	3	2	13	26	54	8
					396	399	

Paulton Rovers moved to the Somerset Senior League. Chippenham Town joined.

1904-05

Division One

Plymouth Argyle	20	13	4	3	52	18	30
Brentford	20	11	6	3	30	22	28
Southampton	20	11	2	7	45	22	24
Portsmouth	20	10	3	7	29	30	23
West Ham United	20	8	4	8	37	42	20
Fulham	20	7	3	10	29	32	17
Millwall	20	7	3	10	32	40	17
Tottenham Hotspur	20	5	6	9	20	28	16
Reading	20	6	3	11	27	37	15
Bristol Rovers	20	7	1	12	32	44	15
Queens Park Rangers	20	6	3	11	27	45	15

Division Two

Bristol Rovers Reserves	16	13	3	0	76	5	29
Bristol City Reserves	16	14	1	1	46	8	29
Swindon Town Reserves	16	11	2	3	53	21	24
Staple Hill	16	7	3	6	27	23	17
Bristol East	16	7	1	8	38	27	15
Welton Rovers	16	5	1	10	27	58	11
Radstock Town	16	4	1	11	21	57	9
Trowbridge Town	16	2	2	12	25	64	6
Chippenham Town	16	2	0	14	24	74	4

Warmley disbanded after playing 10 games and their record was expunged.
Swindon Town Reserves left but Paulton Rovers from the Somerset Senior League and Salisbury City from the Hampshire League, joined.

1905-06

Division One

Queens Park Rangers	20	11	4	5	33	27	26
Southampton	20	10	5	5	41	35	25
Plymouth Argyle	20	8	8	4	34	23	24
Tottenham Hotspur	20	7	7	6	28	17	21
Bristol Rovers	20	8	3	9	34	34	19
Millwall	20	7	5	8	28	29	19
Portsmouth	20	6	7	7	26	29	19
West Ham United	20	7	5	8	32	35	19
Reading	20	6	6	8	28	35	18
Fulham	20	5	5	10	23	32	15
Brentford	20	6	3	11	25	36	15

Chelsea joined, division split into two sections of 6 clubs each.

Division Two

Bristol Rovers Reserves	18	16	1	1	90	19	33
Bristol City Reserves	18	14	2	2	79	13	30
Welton Rovers	18	10	1	7	40	45	21
Radstock Town	18	8	2	8	37	31	18
Salisbury City	18	8	2	8	29	34	18
Staple Hill	18	8	1	9	32	38	17
Paulton Rovers	18	7	2	9	26	41	16
Chippenham Town	18	5	2	11	23	47	12
Bristol East	17	3	1	13	14	41	7
Trowbridge Town	17	2	2	13	13	73	6
					383	382	

Bristol East vs Trowbridge on 17th March 1906 was not played.
Salisbury City moved to the Southern League and Bristol East and Chippenham Town also left. Newport and Treharris joined from the South Wales League and 121st R.F.A. also joined.

1906-07

Division One – Section A

Fulham	10	7	1	2	16	9	15
Queens Park Rangers	10	5	1	4	17	11	11
Brentford	10	5	1	4	19	19	11
Reading	10	4	1	5	12	18	9
Bristol Rovers	10	3	1	6	17	17	7
Chelsea	10	2	3	5	7	14	7

Division One – Section B

West Ham United	10	7	1	2	25	14	15
Plymouth Argyle	10	5	3	2	16	10	13
Portsmouth	10	4	2	4	16	19	10
Tottenham Hotspur	10	3	3	4	13	15	9
Southampton	10	4	0	6	14	16	8
Millwall	10	1	3	6	5	15	5

Championship decider

West Ham United vs Fulham	1-0

(played at Stamford Bridge, 15th April 1907).

Chelsea and Fulham left and Brighton & Hove Albion, Crystal Palace, Leyton and Luton Town joined. Sections reorganised.

Division Two

Staple Hill	18	12	2	4	44	28	26
Newport	18	11	3	4	52	38	25
Bristol City Reserves	18	11	2	5	54	19	24
Treharris	18	12	0	6	62	24	24
Bristol Rovers Reserves	18	11	1	6	60	27	23
Radstock Town	18	7	3	8	37	41	17
Welton Rovers	18	7	1	10	33	54	15
Paulton Rovers	18	4	4	10	36	53	12
121st R.F.A.	18	5	2	11	27	53	12
Trowbridge Town	18	1	0	17	18	86	2

Newport disbanded, Trowbridge Town left and joined the Wiltshire County League and 121st R.F.A. also left. Kingswood Rovers and Weymouth joined. The Division was reduced to 9 clubs.

1907-08

Division One – Section A

Southampton	12	8	1	3	30	12	17
Portsmouth	12	7	1	4	25	18	15
Brighton & Hove Albion	12	6	2	4	19	19	14
Plymouth Argyle	12	5	2	5	14	12	12
Queens Park Rangers	12	5	1	6	20	23	11
Brentford	12	2	5	5	13	21	9
Leyton	12	2	2	8	11	27	6

Division One – Section B

Millwall	12	9	2	1	31	13	20
Tottenham Hotspur	12	7	0	5	26	15	14
Bristol Rovers	12	6	2	4	22	29	14
Luton Town	12	4	4	4	16	21	12
Reading	12	4	3	5	20	25	11
Crystal Palace	12	3	4	5	16	17	10
West Ham United	12	1	1	10	16	27	3

Championship decider

Millwall vs Southampton	1-0

(played at White Hart Lane, 13th April 1908).

Croydon Common replaced Tottenham Hotspur and the Sections were reorganised.

Division Two

Bristol City Reserves	16	12	1	3	55	13	25
Bristol Rovers Reserves	16	11	3	2	44	15	25
Treharris	16	11	1	4	53	19	23
Kingswood Rovers	16	7	1	8	27	33	15
Paulton Rovers	16	7	1	8	34	46	15
Welton Rovers	16	4	4	8	23	46	12
Weymouth	16	5	2	9	25	23	12
Radstock Town	16	4	3	9	25	39	11
Staple Hill	16	3	0	13	18	40	6
					304	274	

Barry District joined from the South Wales League and Aberdare and Bath City also joined. The Division was increased to 12 clubs.

1908-09

Division One – Section A

Brighton & Hove Albion	12	7	2	3	23	13	16
Queens Park Rangers	12	6	1	5	28	24	13
Crystal Palace	12	5	2	5	23	22	12
Luton Town	12	5	2	5	24	24	12
Croydon Common	12	5	2	5	16	24	12
Reading	12	4	2	6	19	21	10
Leyton	12	4	1	7	16	21	9

Division One – Section B

Millwall	12	8	2	2	24	11	18
Southampton	12	7	0	5	20	20	14
Plymouth Argyle	12	6	1	5	12	13	13
Portsmouth	12	5	2	5	21	21	12
West Ham United	12	5	0	7	21	23	10
Bristol Rovers	12	4	1	7	16	23	9
Brentford	12	3	2	7	10	13	8

Championship decider

Millwall vs Brighton & Hove Albion	1-1

(at The Boleyn Ground, Upton Park, 5th April 1909)

Championship decider replay

Millwall vs Brighton & Hove Albion	2-1

(at The Boleyn Ground, Upton Park, 22nd April 1909)

All 14 clubs resigned. Division One was scrapped.

Division Two

Bristol City Reserves	22	15	4	3	59	16	34
Bristol Rovers Reserves	22	16	0	6	81	29	32
Aberdare	22	12	5	5	56	30	29
Treharris	22	12	2	8	57	45	26
Staple Hill	22	9	4	9	41	60	22
Radstock Town	22	8	5	9	37	60	21
Weymouth	22	8	4	10	47	64	20
Bath City	22	6	7	9	39	45	19
Barry District	22	8	3	11	42	50	19
Welton Rovers	22	7	3	12	41	54	17
Kingswood Rovers	22	5	3	14	24	55	13
Paulton Rovers	22	5	2	15	39	55	12

Staple Hill disbanded. Merthyr Town and Ton Pentre joined. Aberdare changed their name to Aberdare Town. League became a single division of 13 clubs.

1909-10

Treharris	24	20	2	2	84	21	42
Bristol City Reserves	24	18	3	3	86	23	39
Bristol Rovers Reserves	24	15	3	6	79	25	33
Ton Pentre	24	14	4	6	68	26	32
Merthyr Town	24	14	3	7	57	24	31
Welton Rovers	24	13	5	6	51	46	31
Aberdare Town	23	13	2	8	57	30	28
Barry District	23	11	1	11	57	57	23
Bath City	24	5	6	13	31	66	15
Kingswood Rovers	23	4	2	17	28	80	10
Radstock Town	24	4	1	19	24	88	9
Weymouth	23	3	2	18	25	93	8
Paulton Rovers	24	2	2	20	28	96	6

Bath City had 1 point deducted for a breach of the rules.
Aberdare did not travel to Weymouth on 26th April 1910 and Kingswood Rovers did not travel to Barry on 27th April 1910.
Aberdare Town, Kingswood Rovers, Merthyr Town, Radstock Town, Ton Pentre and Treharris left. Camerton, Clevedon and Weston-super-Mare joined.

1910-11

Bristol City Reserves	18	15	3	0	58	14	33
Bristol Rovers Reserves	18	9	6	3	45	26	24
Bath City	18	9	4	5	38	30	22
Barry District	18	8	4	6	49	37	20
Welton Rovers	18	7	3	8	34	35	17
Weymouth	18	7	1	10	42	45	15
Weston super Mare	18	5	5	8	32	36	15
Camerton	18	3	7	8	31	42	13
Clevedon	18	4	3	11	22	54	11
Paulton Rovers	18	4	2	12	20	52	10

Bristol City Reserves left and Peasedown St. John and Street joined.

1911-12

Welton Rovers	20	15	2	3	52	19	32
Barry District	20	13	2	5	56	28	28
Weymouth	20	12	3	5	58	29	27
Bristol Rovers Reserves	20	12	1	7	53	39	25
Bath City	20	10	2	8	31	27	22
Camerton	20	8	1	11	30	35	17
Weston super Mare	20	7	3	10	24	30	17
Street	20	7	1	12	32	42	15
Peasedown St. John	20	6	2	12	22	37	14
Paulton Rovers	20	5	2	13	28	70	12
Clevedon	20	5	1	14	21	46	11
					407	402	

Cardiff City Reserves joined. League increased to 12 clubs.

1912-13

Bristol Rovers Reserves	22	17	3	2	85	23	37
Cardiff City Reserves	22	17	1	4	72	24	35
Welton Rovers	22	14	5	3	56	16	33
Bath City	22	13	1	8	52	35	27
Barry District	22	10	4	8	48	40	24
Peasedown St. John	22	9	3	10	33	35	21
Street	22	10	1	11	44	58	21
Weymouth	22	6	4	12	35	55	16
Weston super Mare	22	6	3	13	37	55	15
Camerton	22	6	3	13	27	48	15
Paulton Rovers	22	4	2	16	29	79	10
Clevedon	22	2	6	14	15	68	10
					533	536	

Barry District left and joined the Southern League. Trowbridge Town joined.

1913-14

Cardiff City Reserves	22	18	3	1	88	10	39
Bath City	22	17	2	3	67	34	36
Bristol Rovers Reserves	22	16	3	3	72	18	35
Weymouth	22	13	2	7	51	35	28
Peasedown St. John	22	12	4	6	33	35	28
Welton Rovers	22	12	2	8	55	33	26
Street	22	7	6	9	37	48	20
Trowbridge Town	22	7	2	13	33	43	16
Camerton	22	5	2	15	33	72	12
Paulton Rovers	22	4	2	16	24	73	10
Clevedon	22	3	3	16	19	60	9
Weston super Mare	22	2	1	19	21	72	5

1914-1919

No competition.

When the league resumed after the war, Camerton, Cardiff City Reserves, Clevedon, Weston super Mare and Weymouth did not rejoin. There were, however, 11 new members and the league was split into two divisions.

Douglas and Horfield United and the reserves of Barry, Bristol City, Newport County, Swansea Town and Swindon Town joined pre-war members Bath City, Bristol Rovers Reserves and Welton Rovers in a 10-club Division One. Frome Town, Glastonbury, Timsbury Athletic and Yeovil & Petters United joined pre-war members Paulton Rovers, Peasedown St. John, Street and Trowbridge Town in an 8-club Division Two.

1919-20

Division One

Douglas	18	12	4	2	58	18	28
Swansea Town Reserves	18	13	2	3	39	15	28
Bristol City Reserves	18	12	1	5	41	17	25
Swindon Town Reserves	18	11	3	4	30	21	25
Bath City	18	8	2	8	48	29	18
Welton Rovers	18	6	1	11	29	47	13
Barry Reserves	18	6	0	12	27	37	12
Bristol Rovers Reserves	18	4	4	10	28	51	12
Newport County Reserves	18	5	1	12	25	57	11
Horfield United	18	1	4	13	21	54	6

Horfield United and Newport County Reserves left the league. Abertillery Town joined while continuing in the Southern League and Mid-Rhondda, Pontypridd and Ton Pentre joined from the Welsh League (South). Cardiff City Reserves, Cardiff Corinthians and Exeter City Reserves also joined. Division One increased to 16 clubs. Yeovil & Petters United were promoted from Division Two.

Division Two

Frome Town	14	10	2	2	33	20	22
Trowbridge Town	14	8	2	4	36	18	18
Peasedown St. John	14	8	2	4	22	14	18
Paulton Rovers	14	6	4	4	26	21	16
Yeovil & Petters United	14	7	2	5	41	34	16
Timsbury Athletic	14	4	1	9	19	32	9
Street	14	2	3	9	18	29	7
Glastonbury	14	2	2	10	8	35	6

Yeovil & Petters United were promoted. Clandown, Radstock Town and Welton Amateurs joined, increasing the Division Two to 10 clubs.

1920-21

Division One

Bristol City Reserves	30	18	5	7	58	27	41
Cardiff City Reserves	30	20	1	9	64	42	41
Abertillery Town	30	16	7	7	61	35	39
Swansea Town Reserves	30	15	8	7	60	29	38
Douglas	30	15	8	7	52	32	38
Pontypridd	30	15	6	9	60	40	36
Yeovil & Petters United	30	13	6	11	52	46	32
Bath City	30	12	7	11	45	45	31
Swindon Town Reserves	30	12	6	12	62	50	30
Exeter City Reserves	30	10	9	11	48	53	29
Bristol Rovers Reserves	30	10	5	15	46	53	25
Ton Pentre	30	10	5	15	43	60	25
Welton Rovers	30	9	6	15	39	67	24
Mid Rhondda	30	8	6	16	23	57	22
Barry Reserves	30	6	5	19	33	72	17
Cardiff Corinthians	30	4	4	22	24	62	12

Bath City moved to the Southern League and Mid Rhondda moved to the Welsh League (South). Abertillery Town, Douglas, Pontypridd and Ton Pentre and the reserves of Barry, Bristol City, Bristol Rovers, Cardiff City, Exeter City, Swansea Town and Swindon Town also left. Torquay United joined from the Plymouth & District League, Weymouth joined from the Dorset League and Horfield United also joined. Peasedown St. John and Trowbridge Town were promoted from Division Two making an 8-club division.

Division Two

Peasedown St. John	18	13	3	2	34	12	29
Radstock Town	18	10	4	4	31	23	24
Trowbridge Town	18	10	3	5	36	18	23
Paulton Rovers	18	9	4	5	33	26	22
Timsbury Athletic	18	6	4	8	22	27	16
Street	18	7	2	9	21	35	16
Frome Town	18	5	3	10	26	30	13
Glastonbury	18	5	3	10	17	28	13
Clandown	18	5	3	10	13	24	13
Welton Amateurs	18	2	7	9	20	30	11

Peasedown St. John and Trowbridge Town were promoted. Coleford Athletic joined. The Division was reduced to 9 clubs.

1921-22

Division One

Yeovil & Petters United	14	10	2	2	26	9	22
Trowbridge Town	14	8	1	5	18	15	17
Welton Rovers	14	7	2	5	31	27	16
Cardiff Corinthians	14	7	1	6	30	22	15
Torquay United	14	6	2	6	25	17	14
Peasedown St. John	14	5	3	6	21	19	13
Weymouth	14	5	1	8	15	25	11
Horfield United	14	1	2	11	10	42	4

Division Two

Clandown	16	10	5	1	22	5	25
Coleford Athletic	16	11	1	4	35	19	23
Radstock Town	16	7	4	5	23	14	18
Timsbury Athletic	16	7	2	7	23	22	16
Welton Amateurs	16	8	0	8	22	22	16
Glastonbury	16	6	2	8	21	36	14
Paulton Rovers	16	4	5	7	26	22	13
Frome Town	16	5	2	9	21	29	12
Street	16	2	3	11	25	49	7

Torquay United moved to the Southern League and Clandown, Coleford Athletic, Frome Town, Glastonbury, Horfield United, Paulton Rovers, Street, Timsbury Athletic and Welton Amateurs also left. Bath City and Hanham Athletic joined. The League reverted to a single division of 9 clubs.

1922-23

Weymouth	16	10	2	4	35	14	22
Welton Rovers	16	9	2	5	27	14	20
Yeovil & Petters United	16	7	5	4	28	19	19
Trowbridge Town	16	6	6	4	14	22	18
Peasedown St. John	16	5	5	6	20	22	15
Radstock Town	16	4	7	5	14	19	15
Hanham Athletic	16	5	3	8	18	31	13
Bath City	16	4	3	9	15	19	11
Cardiff Corinthians	16	3	5	8	14	25	11

Welton Rovers moved to the Somerset Senior League and Hanham Athletic also left. Poole joined from the Hampshire League and Lovells Athletic, Minehead and Paulton Rovers also joined. League increased to 11 clubs.

1923-24

Lovells Athletic	20	16	3	1	43	10	35
Radstock Town	20	13	3	4	43	12	29
Weymouth	20	10	5	5	38	24	25
Cardiff Corinthians	20	11	3	6	32	26	25
Poole	20	8	6	6	37	35	22
Yeovil & Petters United	20	9	2	9	35	42	20
Trowbridge Town	20	6	2	12	29	42	14
Peasedown St. John	20	6	2	12	23	42	14
Minehead	20	5	3	12	32	44	13
Bath City	20	5	2	13	21	38	12
Paulton Rovers	20	3	5	12	20	38	11

Cardiff Corinthians left to join the Welsh League (South). Welton Rovers joined from the Somerset Senior League and Frome Town and Swindon Victoria also joined. The League increased to 13 clubs.

1924-25

Yeovil & Petters United	24	19	3	2	65	20	41
Weymouth	24	18	3	3	74	17	39
Swindon Victoria	24	14	3	7	51	48	31
Welton Rovers	24	9	10	5	50	28	28
Poole	24	11	6	7	50	38	28
Radstock Town	24	9	9	6	35	31	27
Frome Town	24	10	6	8	50	44	26
Trowbridge Town	24	9	6	9	46	37	24
Paulton Rovers	24	6	7	11	39	54	19
Minehead	24	7	1	16	47	74	15
Bath City	24	4	5	15	26	58	13
Peasedown St. John	24	4	5	15	19	65	13
Lovells Athletic	24	1	6	17	25	63	8

Peasedown St. John left the League but 10 additional clubs joined and the league which was split into two divisions. Taunton United and Torquay United and the reserves of Bristol City, Bristol Rovers, Exeter City, Plymouth Argyle, Swindon Town joined Bath City, Weymouth and Yeovil & Petters United in a 10-club Division One. Portland United and the reserves of Bath City, Weymouth and Yeovil & Petters United joined the nine other existing members in a 13-club Division Two.

1925-26

Division One

Bristol City Reserves	18	10	7	1	58	19	27
Bristol Rovers Reserves	18	11	2	5	53	36	24
Torquay United	18	9	4	5	28	22	22
Yeovil & Petters United	18	7	7	4	33	27	21
Swindon Town Reserves	18	6	8	4	32	33	20
Weymouth	18	7	4	7	37	45	18
Plymouth Argyle Reserves	18	6	5	7	31	25	17
Exeter City Reserves	18	6	4	8	33	41	16
Taunton United	18	3	3	12	18	45	9
Bath City	18	1	4	13	20	50	6

Poole and Lovells Athletic were promoted from Division Two, increasing the division to 12 clubs.

Division Two

Poole	24	17	3	4	76	30	37
Welton Rovers	24	16	4	4	62	37	36
Weymouth Reserves	24	12	4	8	69	47	28
Lovells Athletic	24	8	8	8	52	46	24
Radstock Town	24	9	6	9	31	28	24
Minehead	24	10	4	10	42	53	24
Portland United	24	8	7	9	49	56	23
Trowbridge Town	24	6	10	8	56	68	22
Swindon Victoria	24	9	3	12	55	71	21
Paulton Rovers	24	7	6	11	48	68	20
Bath City Reserves	24	7	5	12	50	53	19
Yeovil & Petters United Reserves	24	7	4	13	48	57	18
Frome Town	24	5	6	13	40	64	16

Poole and Lovells Athletic were promoted. Bath City Reserves, Paulton Rovers and Swindon Victoria left the League and Lovells Athletic Reserves and Poole Reserves joined. The Division was reduced to 10 clubs.

1926-27

Division One

Bristol City Reserves	22	16	2	4	59	32	34
Torquay United	22	14	4	4	47	27	32
Plymouth Argyle Reserves	22	13	1	8	63	37	27
Lovells Athletic	22	11	5	6	47	36	27
Bristol Rovers Reserves	22	12	3	7	49	41	27
Exeter City Reserves	22	10	3	9	61	53	23
Yeovil & Petters United	22	10	1	11	48	44	21
Swindon Town Reserves	22	9	2	11	41	47	20
Bath City	22	8	3	11	35	50	19
Poole	22	6	2	14	40	69	14
Taunton United	22	4	3	15	28	55	11
Weymouth	22	3	3	16	30	57	9

Poole left the League but continued in the Southern League and Swindon Town Reserves also left. Salisbury City joined from the Hampshire League and Torquay United were replaced by their reserves. The Division was reduced to 11 clubs.
Taunton United changed their name to Taunton Town.

Division Two

Poole Reserves	18	14	2	2	68	19	30
Radstock Town	18	12	1	5	43	29	25
Portland United	18	12	0	6	62	31	24
Welton Rovers	18	9	2	7	61	39	20
Yeovil & Petters United Reserves	18	8	3	7	44	40	19
Lovells Athletic Reserves	18	8	0	10	48	48	16
Trowbridge Town	18	5	2	11	44	52	12
Frome Town	18	5	2	11	28	62	12
Weymouth Reserves	18	4	4	10	25	60	12
Minehead	18	5	0	13	24	67	10

Frome Town left and joined the Somerset Senior League and Lovells Athletic Reserves also left. The Division was reduced to 8 clubs.

1927-28

Division One

Plymouth Argyle Reserves	20	13	5	2	76	32	31
Exeter City Reserves	20	13	4	3	50	24	30
Yeovil & Petters United	20	12	2	6	54	36	26
Bristol City Reserves	20	10	4	6	71	40	24
Bristol Rovers Reserves	20	11	2	7	61	39	24
Taunton Town	20	9	5	6	36	33	23
Lovells Athletic	20	7	2	11	40	49	16
Torquay United Reserves	20	5	6	9	34	52	16
Bath City	20	5	3	12	36	54	13
Weymouth	20	3	3	14	16	60	9
Salisbury City	20	3	2	15	23	72	8

Lovells Athletic left to join the Southern League.
Salisbury City and Weymouth were relegated.
The Division was reduced to 8 clubs.

Division Two

Trowbridge Town	14	12	0	2	43	16	24
Yeovil & Petters United Reserves	14	10	2	2	56	21	22
Portland United	14	7	1	6	35	30	15
Welton Rovers	14	7	0	7	44	26	14
Radstock Town	14	6	1	7	48	41	13
Weymouth Reserves	14	4	1	9	22	52	9
Poole Reserves	14	4	1	9	25	54	9
Minehead	14	3	0	11	17	50	6

Minehead, Poole Reserves and Weymouth Reserves left the League and Bristol St. George and Bath City Reserves joined.
Division Two was increased to 9 clubs.

1928-29

Division One

Bristol Rovers Reserves	14	10	0	4	39	21	20
Plymouth Argyle Reserves	14	6	4	4	31	19	16
Bath City	14	6	4	4	33	30	16
Taunton Town	14	7	2	5	32	30	16
Bristol City Reserves	14	7	1	6	34	31	15
Exeter City Reserves	14	4	4	6	36	42	12
Torquay United Reserves	14	3	3	8	21	30	9
Yeovil & Petters United	14	2	4	8	19	42	8

Division Two

Bath City Reserves	16	12	0	4	44	28	24
Portland United	16	10	3	3	44	26	23
Trowbridge Town	16	8	3	5	31	33	19
Yeovil & Petters United Reserves	16	8	1	7	51	33	17
Welton Rovers	16	5	5	6	30	32	15
Weymouth	16	4	6	6	35	41	14
Salisbury City	16	5	3	8	28	36	13
Bristol St. George	16	4	3	9	41	56	11
Radstock Town	16	3	2	11	27	46	8

Salisbury City left to join the Hampshire League and Yeovil & Petters United Reserves also left. Wells City joined from the Somerset Senior League and Bristol City "A" and Paulton Rovers also joined.
Division Two was increased to 10 clubs.

1929-30

Division One

Yeovil & Petters United	14	10	2	2	32	13	22
Exeter City Reserves	14	5	5	4	26	17	15
Bristol City Reserves	14	5	5	4	28	27	15
Plymouth Argyle Reserves	14	6	2	6	23	20	14
Taunton Town	14	6	2	6	17	30	14
Bath City	14	4	5	5	35	33	13
Torquay United Reserves	14	4	3	7	27	32	11
Bristol Rovers Reserves	14	3	2	9	18	34	8

Bath City left but continued in the Southern League.
Division One was reduced to 7 clubs.

Division Two

Trowbridge Town	18	12	2	4	50	28	26
Portland United	18	11	3	4	50	27	25
Wells City	18	10	3	5	52	31	23
Bristol City "A"	18	9	3	6	54	41	21
Welton Rovers	18	9	3	6	50	48	21
Bath City Reserves	18	6	6	6	43	39	18
Paulton Rovers	18	4	5	9	26	50	13
Bristol St. George	18	5	1	12	41	51	11
Radstock Town	18	5	1	12	32	57	11
Weymouth	18	4	3	11	26	52	11

Poole Town joined from the Southern League, Salisbury City joined from the Hampshire League and Chippenham Town, Coleford Athletic, Petters Westland, Street and Warminster Town also joined.
The Division was increased to 17 clubs.

1930-31

Division One

Exeter City Reserves	12	9	1	2	34	24	19
Yeovil & Petters United	12	7	2	3	43	27	16
Bristol Rovers Reserves	12	6	3	3	28	19	15
Bristol City Reserves	12	4	2	6	34	28	10
Taunton Town	12	5	0	7	20	34	10
Plymouth Argyle Reserves	12	3	1	8	23	33	7
Torquay United Reserves	12	1	5	6	18	35	7

Lovells Athletic joined from the London Combination.
The Division was increased to 8 clubs.

Division Two

Portland United	32	24	3	5	111	47	51
Salisbury City	32	22	4	6	93	50	48
Welton Rovers	32	20	6	6	106	64	46
Wells City	32	21	2	9	92	61	44
Bristol City "A"	32	19	5	8	111	72	43
Bath City Reserves	32	18	3	11	102	56	39
Warminster Town	32	15	5	12	94	77	35
Radstock Town	32	15	5	12	63	85	35
Poole Town	32	14	4	14	76	72	32
Chippenham Town	32	10	8	14	82	68	28
Trowbridge Town	32	9	9	14	58	60	27
Paulton Rovers	32	8	10	14	45	67	26
Petters Westland	32	10	2	20	76	101	22
Bristol St. George	32	10	1	21	80	135	21
Weymouth	32	9	1	22	81	128	19
Street	32	6	4	22	52	96	16
Coleford Athletic	32	6	0	26	60	143	12

Petters Westland left and Frome Town and Glastonbury joined.
The Division was increased to 18 clubs.

1931-32

Division One

Plymouth Argyle Reserves	14	10	1	3	41	15	21
Yeovil & Petters United	14	8	3	3	42	26	19
Lovells Athletic	14	7	3	4	33	25	17
Bristol Rovers Reserves	14	8	0	6	32	28	16
Torquay United Reserves	14	5	4	5	29	35	14
Bristol City Reserves	14	4	3	7	26	37	11
Exeter City Reserves	14	4	1	9	23	37	9
Taunton Town	14	2	1	11	18	41	5

Plymouth Argyle Reserves left the league and Bath City and Cardiff City Reserves joined. The Division was increased to 9 clubs.

Division Two

Portland United	34	27	1	6	122	55	55
Salisbury City	34	23	5	6	122	50	51
Bath City Reserves	34	23	4	7	104	53	50
Trowbridge Town	34	19	5	10	103	68	43
Bristol City "A"	34	19	2	13	124	89	40
Street	34	17	4	13	100	84	38
Paulton Rovers	34	17	3	14	78	59	37
Frome Town	34	18	1	15	86	105	37
Poole Town	34	16	4	14	81	82	36
Wells City	34	15	5	14	119	89	35
Weymouth	34	13	4	17	86	103	30
Chippenham Town	34	11	6	17	99	105	28
Bristol St. George	34	12	4	18	74	110	28
Welton Rovers	34	10	7	17	72	90	27
Glastonbury	34	12	2	20	86	113	26
Radstock Town	34	9	5	20	64	101	23
Warminster Town	34	8	6	20	68	119	22
Coleford Athletic	34	1	4	29	43	156	6

Swindon Town Reserves replaced Coleford Athletic.

1932-33

Division One

Exeter City Reserves	16	11	2	3	59	29	24
Torquay United Reserves	16	11	1	4	55	29	23
Yeovil & Petters United	16	10	0	6	51	31	20
Bath City	16	8	1	7	39	39	17
Bristol City Reserves	16	6	4	6	54	42	16
Bristol Rovers Reserves	16	7	2	7	34	34	16
Lovells Athletic	16	6	3	7	36	35	15
Cardiff City Reserves	16	3	1	12	31	66	7
Taunton Town	16	2	2	12	13	67	6

Bristol City Reserves and Cardiff City Reserves left the League.
The Division was reduced to 7 clubs.

Division Two

Swindon Town Reserves	34	28	1	5	124	51	57
Street	34	20	9	5	105	60	49
Bristol City "A"	34	18	6	10	91	64	42
Bath City Reserves	34	16	6	12	100	68	38
Bristol St. George	34	17	4	13	92	86	38
Salisbury City	34	16	4	14	92	70	36
Portland United	34	15	5	14	95	72	35
Radstock Town	34	15	5	14	71	65	35
Frome Town	34	16	2	16	92	112	34
Weymouth	34	15	3	16	109	92	33
Wells City	34	11	8	15	82	83	30
Glastonbury	34	13	4	17	67	92	30
Welton Rovers	34	13	3	18	72	91	29
Poole Town	34	13	3	18	75	97	29
Trowbridge Town	34	11	5	18	66	106	27
Warminster Town	34	10	4	20	68	125	24
Chippenham Town	34	9	5	20	71	99	23
Paulton Rovers	34	9	5	20	50	89	23

1933-34

Division One

Bath City	12	8	2	2	33	14	18
Torquay United Reserves	12	6	3	3	31	17	15
Bristol Rovers Reserves	12	7	1	4	40	22	15
Yeovil & Petters United	12	5	3	4	22	21	13
Lovells Athletic	12	5	2	5	21	20	12
Exeter City Reserves	12	5	1	6	25	31	11
Taunton Town	12	0	0	12	10	57	0

Taunton Town disbanded and were replaced by Cardiff City Reserves.

Division Two

Weymouth	34	20	7	7	101	54	47
Bath City Reserves	34	20	7	7	101	53	47
Swindon Town Reserves	34	20	6	8	99	61	46
Salisbury City	34	18	7	9	71	37	43
Portland United	34	17	6	11	99	73	40
Glastonbury	34	17	5	12	99	70	39
Street	34	16	5	13	98	89	37
Poole Town	34	14	8	12	83	66	36
Welton Rovers	34	15	5	14	77	82	35
Paulton Rovers	34	14	5	15	73	75	33
Radstock Town	34	13	5	16	67	70	32
Trowbridge Town	34	12	8	14	62	86	32
Wells City	34	11	9	14	69	85	31
Bristol City "A"	34	10	8	16	60	79	28
Frome Town	34	10	8	16	74	96	28
Chippenham Town	34	11	3	20	73	95	25
Warminster Town	34	6	5	23	43	95	17
Bristol St. George	34	7	2	25	62	145	16

Weymouth beat Bath City Reserves in a championship decider play-off.
Bristol Rovers "A" replaced Poole Town who left to join the Hampshire League.

1934-35

Division One

Yeovil & Petters United	12	9	1	2	38	21	19
Bath City	12	7	2	3	32	16	16
Bristol Rovers Reserves	12	6	3	3	34	21	15
Torquay United Reserves	12	4	2	6	25	25	10
Cardiff City Reserves	12	3	3	6	19	30	9
Exeter City Reserves	12	2	4	6	18	26	8
Lovells Athletic	12	3	1	8	15	42	7

Exeter City Reserves left the League. Division One was reduced to 6 clubs.

Division Two

Swindon Town Reserves	34	25	5	4	108	33	55
Salisbury City	34	21	6	7	86	41	48
Portland United	34	22	3	9	105	65	47
Weymouth	34	19	8	7	107	39	46
Frome Town	34	19	7	8	113	67	45
Bath City Reserves	34	18	5	11	85	52	41
Glastonbury	34	15	9	10	91	68	39
Street	34	14	8	12	83	65	36
Trowbridge Town	34	14	7	13	79	84	35
Bristol City "A"	34	15	4	15	87	69	34
Paulton Rovers	34	13	7	14	60	70	33
Bristol Rovers "A"	34	15	0	19	68	88	30
Welton Rovers	34	10	8	16	71	84	28
Warminster Town	34	11	4	19	63	112	26
Wells City	34	10	5	19	70	83	25
Radstock Town	34	6	7	21	48	101	19
Chippenham Town	34	7	3	24	53	126	17
Bristol St. George	34	2	4	28	43	173	8

Bristol St. George left and were replaced by Poole Town from the Hampshire League.

1935-36

Division One

Bristol Rovers Reserves	10	5	4	1	29	22	14
Lovells Athletic	10	4	4	2	17	18	12
Torquay United Reserves	10	4	3	3	28	20	11
Bath City	10	3	3	4	15	16	9
Cardiff City Reserves	10	3	3	4	13	18	9
Yeovil & Petters United	10	1	3	6	22	30	5

Bath City left but continued playing in the Southern League and Cardiff City Reserves also left. Bristol Rovers Reserves joined.
The Division was reduced to five clubs.

Division Two

Swindon Town Reserves	34	28	4	2	140	40	60
Weymouth	34	22	4	8	116	54	48
Street	34	21	5	8	106	54	47
Frome Town	34	17	5	12	92	86	39
Bath City Reserves	34	14	10	10	93	78	38
Portland United	34	16	6	12	95	82	38
Glastonbury	34	15	7	12	97	72	37
Poole Town	34	16	5	13	77	89	37
Paulton Rovers	34	14	8	12	69	77	36
Radstock Town	34	15	5	14	77	80	35
Salisbury City	34	13	8	13	60	65	34
Bristol City "A"	34	14	3	17	71	76	31
Wells City	34	12	7	15	61	72	31
Trowbridge Town	34	12	6	16	87	91	30
Warminster Town	34	9	4	21	58	103	22
Bristol Rovers "A"	34	8	5	21	57	78	21
Welton Rovers	34	5	5	24	49	125	15
Chippenham Town	34	6	1	27	64	147	13

Yeovil & Petters United Reserves replaced Bath City Reserves.

1936-37

Division One

	P	W	D	L	F	A	Pts
Bristol Rovers Reserves	8	6	0	2	26	15	12
Yeovil & Petters United	8	5	1	2	23	12	11
Bristol City Reserves	8	4	2	2	18	15	10
Torquay United Reserves	8	2	0	6	13	24	4
Lovells Athletic	8	1	1	6	11	25	3

Division Two

	P	W	D	L	F	A	Pts
Weymouth	34	27	4	3	144	38	58
Swindon Town Reserves	34	27	4	3	139	49	58
Salisbury City	34	20	9	5	97	45	49
Trowbridge Town	34	22	3	9	89	62	47
Portland United	34	21	3	10	115	60	45
Street	34	18	4	12	90	73	40
Wells City	34	14	9	11	65	60	37
Radstock Town	34	15	7	12	91	92	37
Warminster Town	34	14	7	13	64	69	35
Glastonbury	34	14	3	17	92	98	31
Frome Town	34	9	7	18	68	94	25
Chippenham Town	34	11	3	20	71	98	25
Bristol City "A"	34	11	2	21	62	90	24
Bristol Rovers "A"	34	8	7	19	84	112	23
Yeovil & Petters United Reserves	34	9	5	20	80	131	23
Welton Rovers	34	11	0	23	60	116	22
Poole Town	34	8	3	23	51	95	19
Paulton Rovers	34	5	4	25	46	126	14

Bath City Reserves replaced Swindon Town Reserves.

1937-38

Division One

	P	W	D	L	F	A	Pts
Bristol City Reserves	8	6	1	1	21	7	13
Yeovil & Petters United	8	5	1	2	20	16	11
Bristol Rovers Reserves	8	4	0	4	15	14	8
Torquay United Reserves	8	3	1	4	12	15	7
Lovells Athletic	8	0	1	7	9	25	1

Bath City joined while continuing to play in the Southern League.
Division One was increased to 6 clubs.

Division Two

	P	W	D	L	F	A	Pts
Weymouth	34	27	4	3	121	34	58
Street	34	21	4	9	113	53	46
Portland United	34	17	6	11	109	57	40
Yeovil & Petters United Reserves	34	15	10	9	99	61	40
Salisbury City	34	18	4	12	94	76	40
Chippenham Town	34	18	4	12	91	90	40
Radstock Town	34	18	4	12	79	80	40
Trowbridge Town	34	16	7	11	102	76	39
Glastonbury	34	18	2	14	85	67	38
Poole Town	34	14	7	13	79	67	35
Wells City	34	13	8	13	75	87	34
Bristol City "A"	34	15	1	18	86	100	31
Warminster Town	34	10	9	15	66	92	29
Frome Town	34	9	7	18	66	94	25
Bristol Rovers "A"	34	9	6	19	63	89	24
Paulton Rovers	34	9	6	19	61	124	24
Welton Rovers	34	5	7	22	52	142	17
Bath City Reserves	34	3	6	25	51	103	12

1938-39

Division One

	P	W	D	L	F	A	Pts
Lovells Athletic	10	7	2	1	27	14	16
Yeovil & Petters United	10	6	2	2	32	20	14
Bristol City Reserves	10	4	1	5	24	24	9
Bath City	10	2	5	3	16	22	9
Torquay United Reserves	10	2	4	4	14	17	8
Bristol Rovers Reserves	10	1	2	7	9	25	4

Division One was abandoned upon the outbreak of war but Division Two continued and Bristol City Reserves joined it.

Division Two

	P	W	D	L	F	A	Pts
Trowbridge Town	34	27	3	4	166	49	57
Yeovil & Petters United Reserves	34	22	4	8	112	66	48
Street	34	21	5	8	93	57	47
Poole Town	34	21	4	9	106	67	46
Weymouth	34	19	5	10	105	51	43
Radstock Town	34	19	5	10	97	64	43
Portland United	34	18	4	12	107	64	40
Bristol City "A"	34	17	6	11	87	58	40
Welton Rovers	34	14	4	16	64	118	32
Glastonbury	34	13	5	16	76	89	31
Frome Town	34	11	9	14	76	104	31
Bath City Reserves	34	8	8	18	64	100	24
Wells City	34	10	3	21	63	104	23
Warminster Town	34	8	7	19	49	105	23
Bristol Rovers "A"	34	9	4	21	58	92	22
Paulton Rovers	34	8	6	20	57	117	22
Salisbury City	34	7	7	20	50	93	21
Chippenham Town	34	8	3	23	56	87	19
					1486	1485	

Bristol City "A", Bristol Rovers "A", Frome Town, Poole Town, Portland United, Salisbury City, Street, Warminster Town, Weymouth and Yeovil & Petters United Reserves withdrew.
Bristol Aeroplane Company and Peasedown Miners Welfare joined to make a single division of 11 clubs.

1939-40

	P	W	D	L	F	A	Pts
Trowbridge Town	20	18	0	2	87	31	36
Bristol Aeroplane Company	20	13	4	3	78	33	30
Radstock Town	20	12	1	7	68	54	25
Peasedown Miners Welfare	20	9	5	6	45	36	23
Glastonbury	20	9	5	6	49	43	23
Bristol City Reserves	20	9	2	9	54	43	20
Chippenham Town	20	7	2	11	51	78	16
Welton Rovers	20	6	1	13	44	65	13
Wells City	20	6	1	13	37	66	13
Bath City Reserves	20	4	3	13	35	69	11
Paulton Rovers	20	3	4	13	34	64	10

1940-45

No competition.

The league restarted in 1945 with a single division of 14 clubs:
Bristol Aeroplane Company, Bristol City Reserves, Bristol Rovers Reserves, Chippenham Town, Clandown, Clevedon, Douglas, Paulton Rovers, Peasedown Miners Welfare, Radstock Town, Soundwell, Trowbridge Town, Welton Rovers, Yeovil Town Reserves.

1945-46

Bristol Rovers Reserves	26	17	6	3	120	46	40
Chippenham Town	26	15	4	7	84	41	34
Trowbridge Town	26	16	2	8	114	62	34
Peasedown Miners Welfare	26	13	8	5	75	44	34
Yeovil Town Reserves	26	12	5	9	66	58	29
Douglas	26	12	3	11	82	84	27
Bristol City Reserves	26	10	6	10	90	68	26
Clevedon	26	11	2	13	80	102	24
Bristol Aeroplane Company	26	10	4	12	62	81	24
Paulton Rovers	26	10	3	13	67	93	23
Clandown	26	10	2	14	58	66	22
Radstock Town	26	9	2	15	65	82	20
Soundwell	26	6	3	17	67	132	15
Welton Rovers	26	4	4	18	44	115	12

17 extra clubs joined the league which split into two divisions.
Clandown, Douglas and Soundwell were placed in a 13-club Division Two,
the other 11 existing members were placed in an 18-club Division One.
Of the 17 additional clubs, Bath City Reserves, Frome Town, Glastonbury,
Poole Town, Portland United, Street and Wells City joined Division One and
B.A.C. Reserves, Chippenham Town Reserves, Cinderford Town (from the
Gloucestershire Northern Senior League), Hoffman Athletic, RAF Colerne,
RAF Locking, RAF Melksham, Swindon Town Reserves, Thorney Pitts (Bath
& District League) and Trowbridge Town Reserves joined Division Two.

1946-47

Automatic promotion and relegation were introduced. Promoted clubs are
shown in bold type and relegated clubs are shown in bold italics.
Due to the severe winter, fixtures were not completed and the season was
eventually abandoned on 5th June 1947.

Division One

Trowbridge Town	31	27	1	3	123	43	55
Poole Town	29	20	5	4	86	26	45
Bristol Rovers Reserves	31	19	4	8	96	53	42
Chippenham Town	31	20	2	9	115	68	42
Yeovil Town Reserves	30	16	4	10	85	56	36
Clevedon	30	15	5	10	87	62	35
Portland United	31	14	4	13	92	69	32
Street	32	13	5	14	75	80	31
Paulton Rovers	31	13	3	15	79	110	29
Glastonbury	29	12	3	14	56	68	27
Bristol Aeroplane Company	29	12	3	14	72	87	27
Wells City	31	8	9	14	52	78	25
Radstock Town	29	9	3	17	66	92	21
Peasedown Miners Welfare	21	7	6	8	43	49	20
Bristol City Reserves	24	7	1	16	50	92	15
Bath City Reserves	26	5	4	17	34	72	14
Frome Town	*29*	*4*	*3*	*22*	*45*	*129*	*11*
Welton Rovers	*20*	*2*	*3*	*15*	*40*	*72*	*7*
					1296	1306	

Division Two

Clandown	23	20	2	1	130	33	42
Soundwell	24	17	3	4	111	44	37
Douglas	23	14	2	7	107	77	30
Trowbridge Town Reserves	22	13	3	6	82	50	29
Swindon Town Reserves	24	11	3	10	91	77	25
Hoffman Athletic	20	11	2	7	62	37	24
RAF Locking	21	11	1	9	83	69	23
RAF Melksham	23	7	4	12	56	83	18
Cinderford Town	21	7	3	11	58	60	17
B.A.C. Reserves	23	6	3	14	50	76	15
Chippenham Town Reserves	20	4	3	13	47	86	11
RAF Colerne	20	2	5	13	48	99	9
Thorney Pitts	18	1	0	17	24	158	2

Thorney Pitts disbanded but Cheltenham Town Reserves, Dorchester Town
(from the Dorset Combination), National Smelting Company, Salisbury (a
new club), Stonehouse and Weymouth joined.

Division Two increased to 18 clubs.

1947-48

Division One

Trowbridge Town	34	29	3	2	131	33	61
Glastonbury	34	26	3	5	119	40	55
Street	34	23	7	4	98	40	53
Bristol Rovers Reserves	34	21	6	7	121	60	48
Clevedon	34	20	4	10	117	66	44
Clandown	34	16	5	13	84	80	37
Poole Town	33	14	6	13	73	72	34
Yeovil Town Reserves	34	14	4	16	70	79	32
Paulton Rovers	34	13	5	16	78	93	31
Portland United	34	11	7	16	64	72	29
Bristol City Reserves	34	11	7	16	69	104	29
Bath City Reserves	34	10	8	16	56	82	28
Wells City	34	11	5	18	58	71	27
Peasedown Miners Welfare	34	11	5	18	74	96	27
Soundwell	32	8	7	17	64	103	23
Chippenham Town	33	8	6	19	65	97	22
Radstock Town	*34*	*8*	*3*	*23*	*64*	*108*	*19*
Bristol Aeroplane Company	*34*	*4*	*1*	*29*	*56*	*165*	*9*

Division Two

Salisbury	34	29	1	4	145	33	59
Weymouth	34	26	4	4	148	37	56
Cheltenham Town Reserves	34	25	3	6	142	42	53
Welton Rovers	34	21	3	10	85	49	45
Frome Town	33	22	0	11	114	76	44
Hoffman Athletic	34	19	5	10	79	50	43
Trowbridge Town Reserves	33	17	5	11	92	59	39
Swindon Town Reserves	34	17	4	13	95	76	38
Douglas	34	18	2	14	104	88	38
Dorchester Town	34	13	6	15	64	79	32
Cinderford Town	34	12	7	15	87	103	31
National Smelting Company	34	13	5	16	80	102	31
Stonehouse	34	7	7	20	64	113	21
Chippenham Town Reserves	34	8	4	22	63	117	20
RAF Locking	33	9	1	23	52	126	19
RAF Melksham	34	7	4	23	63	136	18
RAF Colerne	33	6	4	23	64	146	16
B.A.C. Reserves	34	2	1	31	48	157	5

The 2 unplayed games in each division were ignored.
The reserves of Bristol City and Bristol Rovers were replaced by their Colts.
BAC Reserves, RAF Colerne and RAF Locking left and were replaced by
Chippenham United (a new club), Barnstaple Town who joined from the
Exeter & East Devon League, and Weston-super-Mare

1948-49

Division One

Glastonbury	34	24	6	4	93	50	54
Trowbridge Town	34	22	6	6	109	44	50
Weymouth	34	22	4	8	100	44	48
Chippenham Town	34	19	5	10	94	50	43
Street	34	18	4	12	90	58	40
Salisbury	34	17	5	12	78	51	39
Bristol Rovers Colts	34	12	12	10	65	63	36
Paulton Rovers	34	13	6	15	57	64	32
Wells City	34	14	4	16	51	67	32
Bath City Reserves	34	14	4	16	63	92	32
Poole Town	34	13	5	16	59	65	31
Soundwell	34	13	5	16	76	100	31
Peasedown Miners Welfare	34	12	3	19	54	81	27
Clandown	34	12	3	19	55	102	27
Portland United	34	11	4	19	51	70	26
Yeovil Town Reserves	34	7	12	15	61	81	26
Clevedon	*34*	*5*	*10*	*19*	*48*	*74*	*20*
Bristol City Colts	*34*	*7*	*4*	*23*	*57*	*105*	*18*

Division Two

	P	W	D	L	F	A	Pts
Chippenham United	34	29	3	2	145	35	61
Cheltenham Town Reserves	34	26	3	5	133	48	55
Welton Rovers	34	23	4	7	139	68	50
Radstock Town	34	21	5	8	107	64	47
Weston-super-Mare	34	21	5	8	101	63	47
Hoffman Athletic	34	20	2	12	88	41	42
Trowbridge Town Reserves	34	17	5	12	124	75	39
Frome Town	34	16	4	14	85	73	36
Cinderford Town	34	13	6	15	82	103	32
Dorchester Town	34	13	5	16	78	96	31
Barnstaple Town	34	13	3	18	94	88	29
Douglas	34	14	1	19	77	112	29
Chippenham Town Reserves	34	11	4	19	81	89	26
Swindon Town Reserves	34	10	6	18	78	107	26
Stonehouse	34	11	2	21	71	102	24
Bristol Aeroplane Company	34	9	5	20	74	109	23
RAF Melksham	34	5	0	29	50	167	10
National Smelting Company	34	2	1	31	42	209	5

Weymouth joined the Southern League and were replaced by their Reserves. Swindon Town replaced their Reserves with their Colts. RAF Melksham left and Bridgwater Town replaced them in Division Two. An 11-club Third Division was formed by the reserves of Barnstaple Town, Bridgwater Town, Chippenham United, Clevedon, Stonehouse, Welton Rovers and Weston-super-Mare, plus Bristol Rovers "A" and the first XI's of Bideford Town, Ilfracombe Town (from the Exeter & District League) and Minehead.

Division Three

	P	W	D	L	F	A	Pts
Bideford Town	20	19	1	0	103	20	39
Ilfracombe Town	20	16	0	4	74	37	32
Minehead	20	11	5	4	49	30	27
Clevedon Reserves	20	9	7	4	50	41	25
Chippenham United Reserves	20	8	2	10	45	48	18
Weston-super-Mare Reserves	20	7	3	10	44	64	17
Bristol Rovers "A"	20	5	6	9	36	43	16
Barnstaple Town Reserves	20	5	5	10	31	45	15
Welton Rovers Reserves	20	5	2	13	36	64	12
Bridgwater Town Reserves	20	5	1	14	38	62	11
Stonehouse Reserves	20	2	4	14	19	69	8
					525	523	

Division Three was disbanded and all but the 3 promoted clubs left the league. Bristol Aeroplane Company and Douglas also left. Chipping Sodbury joined, increasing Division Two to 20 clubs.

1949-50

Division One

	P	W	D	L	F	A	Pts
Wells City	34	22	7	5	87	43	51
Poole Town	34	22	7	5	88	45	51
Glastonbury	34	23	4	7	78	38	50
Trowbridge Town	34	22	5	7	104	40	49
Cheltenham Town Reserves	34	21	4	9	91	58	46
Chippenham United	34	16	8	10	57	49	40
Bristol Rovers Colts	34	15	7	12	54	50	37
Chippenham Town	34	13	7	14	77	70	33
Street	34	12	9	13	71	75	33
Weymouth Reserves	34	13	5	16	67	49	31
Salisbury	34	14	3	17	64	66	31
Yeovil Town Reserves	34	13	5	16	55	102	31
Paulton Rovers	34	12	3	19	60	76	27
Peasedown Miners Welfare	34	8	9	17	56	82	25
Portland United	34	8	6	20	44	74	22
Clandown	34	8	5	21	46	80	21
Soundwell	*34*	*6*	*6*	*22*	*61*	*116*	*18*
Bath City Reserves	*34*	*5*	*6*	*23*	*45*	*103*	*16*
					1205	*1216*	

Division Two

	P	W	D	L	F	A	Pts
Barnstaple Town	34	23	7	4	102	41	53
Dorchester Town	34	21	8	5	96	51	50
Welton Rovers	34	20	7	7	87	63	47
Stonehouse	34	19	6	9	83	63	44
Bridgwater Town	34	17	8	9	86	49	42
Trowbridge Town Reserves	34	17	8	9	81	53	42
Clevedon	34	18	6	10	92	61	42
Weston-super-Mare	34	16	9	9	86	73	41
Bristol City Colts	34	14	8	12	89	60	36
Cinderford Town	34	13	9	12	82	80	35
Chippenham Town Reserves	34	14	4	16	74	73	32
Frome Town	34	12	7	15	72	74	31
Radstock Town	34	10	7	17	72	98	27
National Smelting Company	34	8	9	17	69	99	25
Swindon Town Colts	34	9	3	22	58	89	21
Hoffman Athletic	34	4	13	17	33	69	21
Bristol Aeroplane Company	34	3	6	25	43	138	12
Douglas	34	3	5	26	49	114	11
					1354	*1348*	

1950-51

Division One

	P	W	D	L	F	A	Pts
Glastonbury	34	26	6	2	102	27	58
Wells City	34	22	9	3	83	39	53
Chippenham Town	34	18	8	8	86	48	44
Chippenham United	34	18	6	10	72	44	42
Trowbridge Town	34	17	7	10	83	49	41
Barnstaple Town	34	18	4	12	71	62	40
Poole Town	34	18	3	13	71	71	39
Salisbury	34	14	7	13	65	55	35
Dorchester Town	34	13	8	13	64	58	34
Street	34	13	8	13	74	69	34
Weymouth Reserves	34	13	6	15	54	56	32
Cheltenham Town Reserves	34	12	7	15	56	46	31
Bristol Rovers Colts	34	11	8	15	60	85	30
Clandown	34	10	9	15	49	58	29
Paulton Rovers	34	9	9	16	62	75	27
Portland United	34	6	7	21	56	112	19
Yeovil Town Reserves	*34*	*8*	*3*	*23*	*38*	*79*	*19*
Peasedown Miners Welfare	*34*	*1*	*3*	*30*	*25*	*123*	*5*
					1171	*1156*	

Division Two

	P	W	D	L	F	A	Pts
Stonehouse	38	29	7	2	133	36	65
Bath City Reserves	38	28	5	5	114	44	61
Bideford Town	38	27	6	5	158	54	60
Cinderford Town	38	21	12	5	112	51	54
Bridgwater Town	38	24	5	9	124	50	53
Ilfracombe Town	38	23	5	10	105	68	51
Clevedon	38	18	6	14	95	81	42
Welton Rovers	38	18	5	15	103	95	41
Minehead	38	16	8	14	73	74	40
Hoffman Athletic	38	16	4	18	74	66	36
Frome Town	38	12	10	16	81	102	34
Bristol City Colts	38	14	5	19	75	84	33
Radstock Town	38	11	9	18	85	112	31
Chippenham Town Reserves	38	12	6	20	83	115	30
Swindon Town Colts	38	10	9	19	88	95	29
Trowbridge Town Reserves	38	11	6	21	69	100	28
Chipping Sodbury	38	10	3	25	75	113	23
Weston-super-Mare	38	8	7	23	46	100	23
Soundwell	38	6	3	29	46	164	15
National Smelting Company	38	3	2	33	50	184	8
	760	*317*	*123*	*320*	*1789*	*1788*	*757*

National Smelting Company and Soundwell left the League. Gloucester City Reserves joined. The Division was reduced to 19 clubs.

1951-52

Division One

Chippenham Town	34	23	4	7	103	41	50
Glastonbury	34	20	6	8	87	64	46
Barnstaple Town	34	18	6	10	87	62	42
Weymouth Reserves	34	18	5	11	84	54	41
Trowbridge Town	34	19	3	12	85	58	41
Stonehouse	34	15	7	12	82	61	37
Wells City	34	12	13	9	65	60	37
Bath City Reserves	34	14	8	12	53	51	36
Cheltenham Town Reserves	34	13	8	13	58	55	34
Street	34	14	6	14	65	71	34
Clandown	34	11	10	13	63	75	32
Salisbury	34	10	9	15	62	68	29
Dorchester Town	34	11	7	16	61	81	29
Chippenham United	34	10	8	16	59	70	28
Portland United	34	9	8	17	49	73	26
Paulton Rovers	34	10	5	19	64	96	25
Bristol Rovers Colts	*34*	*6*	*11*	*17*	*46*	*75*	*23*
Poole Town	*34*	*8*	*6*	*20*	*50*	*106*	*22*
					1223	*1221*	

Division Two

Bideford Town	36	29	3	4	179	55	61
Bridgwater Town	36	28	1	7	126	38	57
Ilfracombe Town	36	25	4	7	106	50	54
Minehead	36	24	2	10	80	60	50
Gloucester City Reserves	36	19	5	12	107	73	43
Cinderford Town	36	18	6	12	95	69	42
Peasedown Miners Welfare	36	17	8	11	80	72	42
Bristol City Colts	36	17	7	12	87	58	41
Yeovil Town Reserves	36	18	4	14	94	102	40
Frome Town	36	15	7	14	89	76	37
Clevedon	36	16	5	15	98	89	37
Radstock Town	36	17	2	17	108	103	36
Chippenham Town Reserves	36	12	5	19	63	89	29
Hoffman Athletic	36	13	3	20	66	101	29
Welton Rovers	36	11	2	23	73	116	24
Weston-super-Mare	36	7	5	24	42	115	19
Swindon Town Colts	36	7	4	25	54	120	18
Trowbridge Town Reserves	36	5	4	27	56	117	14
Chipping Sodbury	36	3	5	28	43	143	11

Cheltenham Town Reserves, Chipping Sodbury and Swindon Town Colts left the League and Stonehouse Reserves joined. Division One was reduced to 17 clubs and Division Two was reduced to 18 clubs.

1952-53

Division One

Barnstaple Town	32	18	8	6	77	37	44
Street	32	19	6	7	89	43	44
Trowbridge Town	32	17	7	8	76	48	41
Bideford Town	32	13	13	6	79	52	39
Chippenham Town	32	17	3	12	84	58	37
Weymouth Reserves	32	16	5	11	75	58	37
Chippenham United	32	15	5	12	62	62	35
Salisbury	32	11	10	11	60	65	32
Glastonbury	32	15	1	16	61	49	31
Bath City Reserves	32	10	11	11	64	63	31
Stonehouse	32	11	8	13	57	58	30
Portland United	32	11	8	13	66	77	30
Bridgwater Town	32	12	4	16	58	73	28
Wells City	32	9	6	17	52	71	24
Clandown	32	7	9	16	40	74	23
Dorchester Town	32	8	5	19	46	74	21
Paulton Rovers	*32*	*6*	*5*	*21*	*42*	*125*	*17*
					1088	*1087*	

Division Two

Chippenham Town Reserves	34	24	4	6	99	51	52
Ilfracombe Town	**34**	**20**	**11**	**3**	**67**	**28**	**51**
Poole Town	**34**	**21**	**7**	**6**	**97**	**42**	**49**
Peasedown Miners Welfare	34	19	3	12	76	63	41
Minehead	34	15	8	11	81	53	38
Clevedon	34	17	3	14	82	92	37
Cinderford Town	34	15	6	13	77	50	36
Bristol City Colts	34	14	6	14	75	56	34
Bristol Rovers Colts	34	12	9	13	74	54	33
Frome Town	34	13	6	15	66	66	32
Yeovil Town Reserves	34	13	5	16	83	78	31
Gloucester City Reserves	34	11	6	17	81	97	28
Radstock Town	34	11	6	17	74	102	28
Trowbridge Town Reserves	34	11	4	19	70	89	26
Stonehouse Reserves	34	10	6	18	68	107	26
Welton Rovers	34	10	6	18	53	98	26
Weston-super-Mare	34	10	4	20	66	113	24
Hoffman Athletic	34	8	4	22	60	109	20
					1349	*1348*	

Chippenham Town Reserves could not be promoted to join their first XI in Division One so Poole Town were promoted instead and Poole Town Reserves joined Division Two. Division One was increased to 18 clubs.

1953-54

Division One

Weymouth Reserves	34	21	4	9	102	53	46
Poole Town	34	18	8	8	73	49	44
Trowbridge Town	34	19	5	10	78	62	43
Barnstaple Town	34	17	7	10	74	42	41
Chippenham Town	34	18	5	11	79	49	41
Salisbury	34	17	6	11	74	60	40
Portland United	34	18	3	13	71	63	39
Wells City	34	15	7	12	63	68	37
Bridgwater Town	34	15	6	13	72	76	36
Bideford Town	34	13	8	13	70	66	34
Dorchester Town	34	14	5	15	79	69	33
Chippenham United	34	13	6	15	60	63	32
Glastonbury	34	12	8	14	59	70	32
Street	34	12	8	14	55	69	32
Bath City Reserves	34	10	6	18	40	66	26
Ilfracombe Town	34	9	5	20	40	77	23
Stonehouse	*34*	*7*	*6*	*21*	*51*	*80*	*20*
Clandown	*34*	*4*	*5*	*25*	*29*	*87*	*13*

Division Two

Bristol Rovers Colts	**34**	**24**	**6**	**4**	**89**	**43**	**54**
Bristol City Colts	**34**	**22**	**6**	**6**	**87**	**39**	**50**
Frome Town	34	21	7	6	99	50	49
Chippenham Town Reserves	34	18	9	7	87	58	45
Welton Rovers	34	16	6	12	54	53	38
Cinderford Town	34	15	7	12	82	72	37
Poole Town Reserves	34	15	5	14	79	61	35
Weston-super-Mare	34	14	7	13	89	70	35
Trowbridge Town Reserves	34	12	9	13	90	88	33
Gloucester City Reserves	34	13	7	14	89	96	33
Hoffman Athletic	34	13	5	16	74	61	31
Yeovil Town Reserves	34	12	7	15	90	89	31
Paulton Rovers	34	12	7	15	69	84	31
Minehead	34	11	6	17	62	78	28
Clevedon	34	11	4	19	77	101	26
Radstock Town	34	10	4	20	71	107	24
Peasedown Miners Welfare	34	8	5	21	56	133	21
Stonehouse Reserves	34	4	3	27	45	102	11
					1389	*1385*	

Stonehouse Reserves left the League and Taunton Town joined from the Somerset Senior League.

1954-55

Division One

Dorchester Town	34	23	5	6	103	46	51
Chippenham Town	34	21	7	6	83	39	49
Bath City Reserves	34	22	4	8	87	52	48
Salisbury	34	17	8	9	71	50	42
Portland United	34	18	6	10	89	70	42
Bideford Town	34	18	6	10	69	56	42
Bridgwater Town	34	18	5	11	91	69	41
Poole Town	34	13	12	9	80	62	38
Bristol Rovers Colts	34	16	5	13	73	55	37
Barnstaple Town	34	13	8	13	69	66	34
Trowbridge Town	34	14	5	15	65	55	33
Bristol City Colts	34	11	4	19	53	62	26
Weymouth Reserves	34	10	6	18	49	67	26
Chippenham United	34	10	5	19	57	97	25
Glastonbury	34	8	9	17	51	89	25
Wells City	34	5	9	20	49	90	19
Street	*34*	*7*	*4*	*23*	*51*	*100*	*18*
Ilfracombe Town	*34*	*5*	*6*	*23*	*35*	*100*	*16*

Division Two

Yeovil Town Reserves	**34**	**23**	**5**	**6**	**115**	**49**	**51**
Frome Town	**34**	**24**	**3**	**7**	**106**	**49**	**51**
Weston-super-Mare	34	22	4	8	122	58	48
Chippenham Town Reserves	34	18	8	8	102	60	44
Taunton Town	34	20	3	11	95	57	43
Gloucester City Reserves	34	16	8	10	80	61	40
Minehead	34	15	6	13	104	65	36
Cinderford Town	34	12	12	10	85	79	36
Stonehouse	34	15	5	14	87	83	35
Poole Town Reserves	34	15	4	15	82	71	34
Welton Rovers	34	13	6	15	70	77	32
Peasedown Miners Welfare	34	12	6	16	79	102	30
Clandown	34	12	6	16	45	75	30
Clevedon	34	12	4	18	82	90	28
Hoffman Athletic	34	11	3	20	53	97	25
Trowbridge Town Reserves	34	10	3	21	43	86	23
Radstock Town	34	5	6	23	54	135	16
Paulton Rovers	34	5	0	29	47	157	10

Bath City Reserves left Division One which was reduced to 17 clubs while Frome Town Reserves and Torquay United Reserves joined Division Two which increased to 20 clubs.

1955-56

Division One

Trowbridge Town	32	24	2	6	100	36	50
Poole Town	32	20	7	5	79	33	47
Dorchester Town	32	21	4	7	106	57	46
Chippenham Town	32	20	4	8	70	50	44
Salisbury	32	17	7	8	64	31	41
Bideford Town	32	14	10	8	58	50	38
Portland United	32	16	3	13	87	76	35
Barnstaple Town	32	15	4	13	61	66	34
Weymouth Reserves	32	10	12	10	63	70	32
Frome Town	32	10	7	15	69	64	27
Yeovil Town Reserves	32	11	5	16	57	86	27
Bristol Rovers Colts	32	10	4	18	49	65	24
Bristol City Colts	32	8	7	17	43	63	23
Wells City	32	8	7	17	53	92	23
Bridgwater Town	32	7	5	20	59	98	19
Chippenham United	32	7	5	20	54	90	19
Glastonbury	32	3	9	20	47	92	15

Division Two

Torquay United Reserves	38	27	6	5	135	38	60
Taunton Town	38	26	3	9	115	46	55
Gloucester City Reserves	38	24	5	9	104	56	53
Weston-super-Mare	38	21	9	8	126	59	51
Stonehouse	38	21	7	10	92	55	49
Trowbridge Town Reserves	38	20	7	11	98	74	47
Minehead	38	20	6	12	104	69	46
Clevedon	38	19	8	11	99	71	46
Frome Town Reserves	38	20	6	12	101	76	46
Ilfracombe Town	38	18	5	15	82	70	41
Poole Town Reserves	38	14	8	16	86	71	36
Chippenham Town Reserves	38	13	7	18	80	97	33
Clandown	38	13	6	19	87	105	32
Cinderford Town	38	13	5	20	85	82	31
Welton Rovers	38	12	6	20	73	95	30
Street	38	11	4	23	70	112	26
Peasedown Miners Welfare	38	8	9	21	57	141	25
Hoffman Athletic	38	7	6	25	46	109	20
Radstock Town	38	7	3	28	52	165	17
Paulton Rovers	38	6	4	28	56	157	16

Chippenham Town Reserves and Frome Town Reserves left Division Two and were replaced by Bath City Reserves and Dorchester Town Reserves. As no clubs were relegated, Division One was increased to 19 clubs and Division Two reduced to 18 clubs.

1956-57

Division One

Poole Town	36	26	4	6	115	48	56
Trowbridge Town	36	21	5	10	83	55	47
Salisbury	36	20	5	11	98	60	45
Torquay United Reserves	36	18	8	10	91	55	44
Portland United	36	18	8	10	84	64	44
Bridgwater Town	36	17	7	12	58	54	41
Dorchester Town	36	16	7	13	83	70	39
Chippenham Town	36	16	7	13	77	67	39
Yeovil Town Reserves	36	18	2	16	79	73	38
Glastonbury	36	16	3	17	82	102	35
Bristol Rovers Colts	36	14	6	16	67	90	34
Weymouth Reserves	36	16	1	19	87	94	33
Barnstaple Town	36	14	4	18	76	70	32
Bideford Town	36	12	8	16	70	71	32
Taunton Town	36	11	9	16	59	71	31
Chippenham United	36	12	6	18	80	97	30
Bristol City Colts	36	13	4	19	58	74	30
Frome Town	36	10	2	24	46	91	22
Wells City	*36*	*4*	*4*	*28*	*46*	*133*	*12*

Division Two

Cinderford Town	**34**	**28**	**2**	**4**	**114**	**31**	**58**
Trowbridge Town Reserves	34	25	4	5	112	35	54
Poole Town Reserves	34	23	6	5	87	39	52
Minehead	**34**	**20**	**5**	**9**	**83**	**52**	**45**
Dorchester Town Reserves	34	18	6	10	113	69	42
Gloucester City Reserves	34	17	7	10	81	50	41
Welton Rovers	34	18	3	13	87	74	39
Stonehouse	34	14	10	10	98	70	38
Bath City Reserves	34	16	6	12	91	82	38
Weston-super-Mare	34	11	7	16	68	80	29
Peasedown Miners Welfare	34	10	6	18	69	99	26
Hoffman Athletic	34	8	10	16	52	92	26
Street	34	9	7	18	48	68	25
Clevedon	34	10	4	20	64	85	24
Ilfracombe Town	34	7	8	19	43	82	22
Radstock Town	34	9	3	22	65	141	21
Paulton Rovers	34	7	3	24	50	111	17
Clandown	34	6	3	25	49	114	15

Poole Town left to join the Southern League. Taunton Town Reserves joined.

1957-58

Division One

Salisbury	36	18	11	7	55	30	47
Bridgwater Town	36	20	5	11	78	53	45
Dorchester Town	36	19	6	11	87	57	44
Barnstaple Town	36	17	7	12	83	48	41
Trowbridge Town	36	15	11	10	80	61	41
Bristol Rovers Colts	36	16	8	12	80	74	40
Torquay United Reserves	36	15	9	12	70	56	39
Bristol City Colts	36	16	7	13	70	59	39
Minehead	36	16	5	15	68	76	37
Frome Town	36	16	5	15	66	77	37
Cinderford Town	36	17	2	17	72	70	36
Taunton Town	36	11	13	12	48	55	35
Bideford Town	36	14	5	17	62	55	33
Weymouth Reserves	36	13	7	16	89	85	33
Chippenham Town	36	13	7	16	71	74	33
Glastonbury	36	12	7	17	50	79	31
Yeovil Town Reserves	36	13	4	19	66	92	30
Portland United	36	12	3	21	58	80	27
Chippenham United	*36*	*5*	*6*	*25*	*51*	*123*	*16*

Division Two

Poole Town Reserves	34	26	3	5	141	48	55
Gloucester City Reserves	34	24	5	5	109	40	53
Weston-super-Mare	34	22	9	3	102	46	53
Dorchester Town Reserves	34	19	6	9	73	41	44
Welton Rovers	34	18	6	10	87	64	42
Trowbridge Town Reserves	34	19	3	12	88	69	41
Wells City	34	16	6	12	82	68	38
Street	34	13	7	14	60	73	33
Bath City Reserves	34	12	8	14	76	64	32
Peasedown Miners Welfare	34	13	6	15	75	98	32
Ilfracombe Town	34	13	3	18	84	99	29
Radstock Town	34	11	5	18	78	114	27
Clandown	34	10	7	17	52	78	27
Hoffman Athletic	34	9	5	20	55	85	23
Taunton Town Reserves	34	9	4	21	51	89	22
Paulton Rovers	34	7	7	20	59	98	21
Clevedon	34	9	2	23	67	112	20
Stonehouse	34	8	4	22	62	115	20

Trowbridge Town left to join the Southern League. Clevedon also left the League and Bridgwater Town Reserves joined. Division Two was reduced to 17 clubs.

1958-59

Division One

Yeovil Town Reserves	36	26	3	7	115	54	55
Salisbury	36	24	3	9	91	53	51
Dorchester Town	36	23	2	11	110	61	48
Bridgwater Town	36	21	6	9	81	57	48
Barnstaple Town	36	20	5	11	85	68	45
Chippenham Town	36	20	3	13	104	66	43
Bideford Town	36	15	11	10	83	60	41
Torquay United Reserves	36	18	3	15	70	70	39
Weymouth Reserves	36	18	2	16	84	63	38
Cinderford Town	36	15	4	17	60	63	34
Bristol Rovers Colts	36	14	6	16	73	77	34
Glastonbury	36	15	3	18	63	81	33
Taunton Town	36	15	2	19	53	68	32
Bristol City Colts	36	12	7	17	75	88	31
Portland United	36	13	5	18	68	82	31
Poole Town Reserves	36	10	7	19	63	91	27
Gloucester City Reserves	36	9	5	22	64	91	23
Minehead	36	6	7	23	50	111	19
Frome Town	*36*	*4*	*4*	*28*	*52*	*140*	*12*

Division Two

Bath City Reserves	32	20	7	5	95	39	47
Trowbridge Town Reserves	32	20	5	7	88	56	45
Street	32	18	5	9	73	56	41
Bridgwater Town Reserves	32	16	8	8	81	55	40
Welton Rovers	32	18	3	11	80	53	39
Dorchester Town Reserves	32	16	6	10	73	52	38
Weston-super-Mare	32	16	5	11	80	59	37
Paulton Rovers	32	16	5	11	87	71	37
Stonehouse	32	16	4	12	85	47	36
Chippenham United	32	14	7	11	65	54	35
Taunton Town Reserves	32	11	6	15	58	81	28
Peasedown Miners Welfare	32	9	9	14	64	89	27
Clandown	32	10	6	16	58	74	26
Radstock Town	32	10	5	17	61	76	25
Ilfracombe Town	32	7	5	20	48	108	19
Hoffman Athletic	32	4	4	24	49	107	12
Wells City	32	5	2	25	44	112	12

Cinderford Town, Hoffman Athletic and Ilfracombe Town all left the League. Division Two was reduced to 14 clubs.

1959-60

Division One

Torquay United Reserves	36	29	5	2	132	40	63
Salisbury	36	20	7	9	85	43	47
Chippenham Town	36	18	6	12	70	56	42
Bridgwater Town	36	18	5	13	79	62	41
Weymouth Reserves	36	18	4	14	72	58	40
Portland United	36	17	6	13	61	68	40
Bideford Town	36	15	8	13	61	62	38
Bath City Reserves	36	15	7	14	63	61	37
Yeovil Town Reserves	36	17	3	16	74	77	37
Poole Town Reserves	36	15	6	15	73	66	36
Dorchester Town	36	17	2	17	87	88	36
Minehead	36	12	11	13	68	72	35
Bristol Rovers Colts	36	13	8	15	79	80	34
Glastonbury	36	11	10	15	66	78	32
Barnstaple Town	36	13	5	18	50	65	31
Taunton Town	36	11	7	18	67	96	29
Bristol City Colts	36	12	4	20	65	82	28
Gloucester City Reserves	36	9	4	23	49	92	22
Trowbridge Town Reserves	36	5	6	25	36	91	16

Division Two

Welton Rovers	26	20	2	4	95	40	42
Stonehouse	26	17	4	5	78	43	38
Weston-super-Mare	26	15	6	5	100	42	36
Frome Town	26	14	5	7	63	38	33
Chippenham United	26	14	2	10	64	52	30
Clandown	26	9	9	8	48	43	27
Paulton Rovers	26	11	5	10	58	64	27
Radstock Town	26	12	3	11	48	62	27
Street	26	10	5	11	48	53	25
Wells City	26	8	5	13	46	73	21
Bridgwater Town Reserves	26	8	4	14	58	64	20
Taunton Town Reserves	26	5	7	14	43	59	17
Dorchester Town Reserves	26	5	5	16	43	82	15
Peasedown Miners Welfare	26	1	4	21	38	114	6
					830	829	

Chippenham United disbanded and Frome Town and Clandown left to join the Wiltshire Premier League. Bridgwater Town Reserves, Dorchester Town Reserves, Gloucester City Reserves, Paulton Rovers, Peasedown Miners Welfare, Radstock Town, Stonehouse, Street, Taunton Town Reserves and Wells City also all left. Exeter City Reserves joined from the South-Western League and Welton Rovers and Weston-super-Mare were promoted to form a single division of 21 clubs.

1960-61

Salisbury	40	31	4	5	135	42	66
Dorchester Town	40	26	6	8	115	63	58
Minehead	40	24	8	8	100	62	56
Torquay United Reserves	40	23	6	11	122	70	52
Bridgwater Town	40	18	12	10	88	71	48
Exeter City Reserves	40	18	11	14	99	68	47
Weymouth Reserves	40	19	9	12	91	79	47
Bristol City Colts	40	18	10	12	94	70	46
Welton Rovers	40	18	9	15	119	110	45
Portland United	40	16	10	14	93	87	42
Yeovil Town Reserves	40	18	5	17	73	73	41
Chippenham Town	40	18	5	17	79	81	41
Bristol Rovers Colts	40	12	12	16	80	74	36
Bath City Reserves	40	11	11	18	75	79	33
Weston-super-Mare	40	13	7	20	76	98	33
Bideford Town	40	12	9	19	76	99	33
Glastonbury	40	13	4	23	66	114	30
Poole Town Reserves	40	8	9	23	57	87	25
Trowbridge Town Reserves	40	9	7	24	62	122	25
Barnstaple Town	40	8	4	28	55	111	20
Taunton Town	40	5	6	29	59	153	16
					1814	*1813*	

Exeter City Reserves and Trowbridge Town Reserves left the League and Bristol City Colts were replaced by Bristol City Reserves. Bridport joined the League which was reduced to 20 clubs.

1962-63

Bristol City Reserves	42	31	5	6	120	56	67
Bideford Town	42	29	7	6	115	51	65
Minehead	42	25	6	11	102	62	56
Andover	42	25	5	12	106	59	55
Bridgwater Town	42	23	8	11	77	48	54
Salisbury	42	21	9	12	89	56	51
Portland United	42	23	5	14	80	66	51
Weymouth Reserves	42	20	5	17	104	78	45
Yeovil Town Reserves	42	18	9	15	67	72	45
Barnstaple Town	42	19	6	17	81	75	44
Dorchester Town	42	17	9	16	92	79	43
Chippenham Town	42	15	12	15	92	60	42
Poole Town Reserves	42	17	7	18	82	77	41
Exeter City Reserves	42	15	10	17	55	74	40
Bath City Reserves	42	14	6	22	82	96	34
Weston-super-Mare	42	11	9	22	72	108	31
Welton Rovers	42	11	8	23	71	107	30
Glastonbury	42	13	4	25	56	114	30
Torquay United Reserves	42	10	8	24	48	78	28
Bridport	42	9	8	25	66	111	26
Taunton Town	42	11	4	27	56	112	26
Bristol Rovers Colts	42	6	8	28	56	120	20
					1769	*1759*	

Bristol Rovers Colts left and were replaced by Frome Town.

1961-62

Bristol City Reserves	38	28	7	3	132	36	63
Salisbury	38	27	2	9	105	41	56
Bideford Town	38	21	11	6	84	49	53
Torquay United Reserves	38	20	5	13	95	78	45
Poole Town Reserves	38	19	5	14	115	85	43
Dorchester Town	38	19	5	14	102	85	43
Bridgwater Town	38	17	8	13	89	69	42
Minehead	38	17	8	13	80	68	42
Chippenham Town	38	17	6	15	79	71	40
Portland United	38	16	8	14	92	85	40
Weston-super-Mare	38	14	11	13	63	68	39
Weymouth Reserves	38	16	6	16	85	71	38
Bath City Reserves	38	13	9	16	74	80	35
Bridport	38	11	8	19	72	93	30
Yeovil Town Reserves	38	13	3	22	74	99	29
Welton Rovers	38	11	7	20	61	104	29
Taunton Town	38	11	4	23	59	114	26
Bristol Rovers Colts	38	6	13	19	59	93	25
Barnstaple Town	38	8	7	23	52	120	23
Glastonbury	38	7	5	26	44	107	19

Andover (from the Hampshire League) and Exeter City Reserves joined the League which increased to 22 clubs.

1963-64

Bideford	42	30	6	6	113	36	66
Bristol City Reserves	42	24	15	3	122	43	63
Bridgwater Town	42	25	10	7	82	32	60
Welton Rovers	42	24	6	12	84	54	54
Dorchester Town	42	19	14	9	94	56	52
Salisbury	42	21	8	13	80	61	50
Barnstaple Town	42	20	9	13	92	69	49
Minehead	42	20	8	14	96	85	48
Weymouth Reserves	42	16	12	14	94	74	44
Andover	42	17	10	15	89	78	44
Torquay United Reserves	42	18	7	17	81	73	43
Yeovil Town Reserves	42	17	9	16	73	99	43
Chippenham Town	42	15	8	19	75	62	38
Bath City Reserves	42	12	12	18	77	92	36
Frome Town	42	11	11	20	69	97	33
Weston-super-Mare	42	11	11	20	58	86	33
Glastonbury	42	11	9	22	70	91	31
Exeter City Reserves	42	8	15	19	73	100	31
Poole Town Reserves	42	11	6	25	56	98	28
Bridport	42	7	14	21	40	100	28
Portland United	42	10	5	27	63	127	25
Taunton Town	42	8	9	25	37	105	25

1964-65

Welton Rovers	42	35	3	4	148	36	73
Bideford	42	32	6	4	120	29	70
Minehead	42	27	7	8	88	42	61
Dorchester Town	42	26	4	12	89	53	56
Weston-super-Mare	42	22	9	11	89	58	53
Weymouth Reserves	42	24	4	14	96	46	52
Bridgwater Town	42	20	9	13	74	59	49
Torquay United Reserves	42	21	5	16	74	59	47
Bristol City Reserves	42	21	4	17	96	82	46
Salisbury	42	17	9	16	80	67	43
Frome Town	42	17	8	17	66	71	42
Exeter City Reserves	42	18	5	19	92	84	41
Chippenham Town	42	16	8	18	75	82	40
Glastonbury	42	15	6	21	69	109	36
Yeovil Town Reserves	42	15	5	22	65	99	35
Andover	42	13	8	21	74	66	34
Bath City Reserves	42	12	6	24	54	98	30
Bridport	42	11	7	24	60	99	29
Taunton Town	42	10	8	24	54	104	28
Barnstaple Town	42	11	5	26	51	89	27
Portland United	42	6	8	28	40	122	20
Poole Town Reserves	42	5	2	35	49	149	12

Bath City Reserves, Chippenham Town, Poole Town Reserves and Yeovil Town Reserves left the League. Bristol City Colts replaced Bristol City Reserves and the League was reduced to 18 clubs.

1965-66

Welton Rovers	34	25	9	0	105	28	59
Portland United	34	23	2	9	75	50	48
Bideford	34	19	8	7	90	49	46
Andover	34	16	8	10	74	57	40
Minehead	34	13	12	9	46	44	38
Frome Town	34	14	9	11	53	53	37
Glastonbury	34	12	11	11	61	46	35
Taunton Town	34	15	5	14	73	69	35
Bridgwater Town	34	12	10	12	63	62	34
Salisbury	34	12	8	14	62	57	32
Torquay United Reserves	34	11	10	13	56	56	32
Exeter City Reserves	34	13	4	17	63	70	30
Weymouth Reserves	34	11	8	15	65	76	30
Weston-super-Mare	34	12	5	17	48	61	29
Bridport	34	12	5	17	57	90	29
Dorchester Town	34	9	5	20	41	79	23
Barnstaple Town	34	7	8	19	35	59	22
Bristol City Colts	34	4	5	25	33	94	13

Plymouth Argyle Colts, St. Luke's College (from the South-Western League) and Yeovil Town Reserves joined the League which increased to 21 clubs.

1966-67

Welton Rovers	40	29	7	4	102	37	65
Minehead	40	25	10	5	98	42	60
Bridgwater Town	40	25	7	8	93	47	57
Salisbury	40	22	9	9	83	54	53
Dorchester Town	40	22	8	10	89	48	52
Bideford	40	23	6	11	76	47	52
Glastonbury	40	20	9	11	71	54	49
Exeter City Reserves	40	17	7	16	54	63	41
Torquay United Reserves	40	15	9	16	66	56	39
Andover	40	13	13	14	69	60	39
Portland United	40	15	7	18	61	76	37
Frome Town	40	17	1	22	60	82	35
Bristol City Colts	40	13	8	19	63	64	34
Weston-super-Mare	40	12	9	19	52	69	33
Taunton Town	40	11	10	19	67	77	32
Plymouth Argyle Colts	40	12	8	20	66	97	32
Bridport	40	11	8	21	50	80	30
Weymouth Reserves	40	12	4	24	39	75	28
St. Luke's College	40	10	7	23	61	90	27
Barnstaple Town	40	8	8	24	50	92	24
Yeovil Town Reserves	40	8	5	27	52	111	21
					1422	*1421*	

Exeter City Reserves and Weymouth Reserves left the League and were replaced by Bath City Reserves and Devizes Town.

1967-68

Bridgwater Town	40	27	8	5	92	41	62
Salisbury	40	28	3	9	105	35	59
Glastonbury	40	24	7	9	103	64	55
Bath City Reserves	40	21	9	10	81	63	51
Frome Town	40	22	6	12	98	72	50
Minehead	40	18	13	9	72	49	49
Dorchester Town	40	17	14	9	81	50	48
Welton Rovers	40	20	6	14	74	55	46
Plymouth Argyle Colts	40	18	7	15	76	72	43
Bridport	40	18	5	17	68	58	41
Torquay United Reserves	40	17	7	16	58	55	41
Andover	40	17	5	18	61	66	39
Taunton Town	40	11	15	14	76	68	37
Bideford	40	13	9	18	52	63	35
St. Luke's College	40	12	9	19	60	78	33
Portland United	40	10	12	18	39	80	32
Bristol City Colts	40	9	10	21	33	59	28
Weston-super-Mare	40	9	10	21	40	79	28
Barnstaple Town	40	8	6	26	48	91	22
Devizes Town	40	7	7	26	56	113	21
Yeovil Town Reserves	40	5	10	25	36	98	20

Salisbury left to join the Southern League and Plymouth Argyle Colts also left. The League was reduced to 19 clubs.

1968-69

Taunton Town	36	24	5	7	96	53	53
Bideford	36	21	7	8	77	44	49
Bridgwater Town	36	18	12	6	72	30	48
Glastonbury	36	22	4	10	85	49	48
Frome Town	36	18	11	7	57	38	47
Andover	36	16	9	11	63	43	41
Minehead	36	16	9	11	57	43	41
Welton Rovers	36	14	9	13	51	51	37
Dorchester Town	36	15	6	15	53	53	36
Bath City Reserves	36	15	6	15	58	49	36
Barnstaple Town	36	14	7	15	58	67	35
Devizes Town	36	14	7	15	56	77	35
Torquay United Reserves	36	15	3	18	51	60	33
Bristol City Colts	36	13	6	17	64	68	32
Bridport	36	8	11	17	34	54	27
Weston-super-Mare	36	7	11	18	29	54	25
St. Luke's College	36	9	5	22	44	74	23
Portland United	36	7	8	21	36	80	22
Yeovil Town Reserves	36	4	8	24	41	105	16

Weymouth Reserves joined the League which increased to 20 clubs.

1969-70

Glastonbury	38	29	5	4	100	37	63
Andover	38	26	6	6	76	20	58
Bridgwater Town	38	23	7	8	97	41	53
Minehead	38	21	10	7	70	37	52
Taunton Town	38	21	8	9	84	56	50
Bideford	38	20	7	11	84	58	47
Dorchester Town	38	18	8	12	78	69	44
Torquay United Reserves	38	15	10	13	70	54	40
Bath City Reserves	38	16	7	15	71	67	39
Welton Rovers	38	17	3	18	72	62	37
Weston-super-Mare	38	14	8	16	53	72	36
Frome Town	38	12	10	16	62	73	34
Portland United	38	14	6	18	63	94	34
Bristol City Colts	38	13	7	18	58	76	33
Devizes Town	38	10	9	19	44	60	29
Barnstaple Town	38	11	6	21	58	73	28
Yeovil Town Reserves	38	9	6	23	38	78	24
Weymouth Reserves	38	10	4	24	34	74	24
Bridport	38	6	9	23	43	86	21
St. Luke's College	38	4	6	28	35	93	14

Portland United, Weymouth Reserves and Yeovil Town Reserves left the League and Plymouth City joined. The League was reduced to 18 clubs.

1970-71

	P	W	D	L	F	A	Pts
Bideford	34	26	4	4	96	39	56
Andover	34	21	8	5	65	24	50
Bridgwater Town	34	20	9	5	63	38	49
Glastonbury	34	18	8	8	78	52	44
Minehead	34	18	5	11	66	40	41
Taunton Town	34	17	7	10	66	42	41
Plymouth City	34	17	6	11	67	41	40
Welton Rovers	34	17	6	11	60	56	40
Dorchester Town	34	16	6	12	58	50	38
Devizes Town	34	12	11	11	53	50	35
Barnstaple Town	34	13	7	14	60	61	33
Bridport	34	11	8	15	43	49	30
Weston-super-Mare	34	9	6	19	36	73	24
Torquay United Reserves	34	8	6	20	43	54	22
Bristol City Colts	34	7	8	19	40	78	22
Frome Town	34	8	3	23	50	91	19
Bath City Reserves	34	7	5	22	33	77	19
St. Luke's College	34	2	5	27	21	83	9

Andover left to join the Southern League and Bath City Reserves, Bristol City Colts and Plymouth City also left. The League was reduced to 14 clubs.

1971-72

	P	W	D	L	F	A	Pts
Bideford	26	19	4	3	63	21	42
Minehead	26	18	5	3	59	22	41
Glastonbury	26	16	5	5	58	26	37
Devizes Town	26	11	9	6	44	33	31
Welton Rovers	26	10	7	9	38	37	27
Frome Town	26	9	7	10	33	45	25
Dorchester Town	26	9	6	11	39	38	24
Weston-super-Mare	26	9	5	12	39	45	23
Bridport	26	9	5	12	32	47	23
Bridgwater Town	26	7	9	10	28	42	23
Taunton Town	26	7	7	12	50	54	21
Torquay United Reserves	26	5	9	12	29	55	19
Barnstaple Town	26	6	6	14	40	46	18
St. Luke's College	26	3	4	19	25	66	10

Bideford, Dorchester Town and Minehead all left to join the Southern League. Avon (Bradford), Ashtonians United, Bristol City Colts, Exeter City Reserves and Mangotsfield United (from the Avon Premier Combination) all joined. The League was increased to 16 clubs.

1972-73

	P	W	D	L	F	A	Pts
Devizes Town	30	21	5	4	68	27	47
Taunton Town	30	19	7	4	69	26	45
Mangotsfield United	30	21	3	6	69	35	45
Bridgwater Town	30	17	7	6	65	24	41
Weston-super-Mare	30	13	9	8	42	36	35
Glastonbury	30	14	6	10	45	44	34
Barnstaple Town	30	13	7	10	57	52	33
Bridport	30	10	10	10	40	30	30
Torquay United Reserves	30	11	6	13	53	47	28
Frome Town	30	9	9	12	30	44	27
Welton Rovers	30	9	8	13	35	41	26
Exeter City Reserves	30	7	11	12	39	47	25
St. Luke's College	30	9	3	18	33	73	21
Avon (Bradford)	30	6	3	21	27	68	15
Bristol City Colts	30	5	4	21	35	76	14
Ashtonians United	30	4	6	20	26	63	14

Bristol City Colts and Torquay United Reserves left the League. Dawlish, Exmouth Town and Tiverton Town joined from the Devon & Exeter League, Chippenham Town joined from the Hellenic League and Keynsham Town also joined. The League was increased to 19 clubs.

1973-74

	P	W	D	L	F	A	Pts
Welton Rovers	36	27	5	4	80	32	59
Taunton Town	36	25	8	3	86	19	58
Bridgwater Town	36	23	6	7	71	34	52
Exeter City Reserves	36	21	7	8	61	33	49
Devizes Town	36	18	9	9	73	44	45
Glastonbury	36	18	7	11	69	46	43
Frome Town	36	16	9	11	64	43	41
Barnstaple Town	36	17	7	12	76	60	41
Mangotsfield United	36	17	7	12	57	52	41
Dawlish	36	17	6	13	53	67	40
St. Luke's College	36	14	5	17	48	48	33
Weston-super-Mare	36	13	7	16	44	50	33
Keynsham Town	36	11	5	20	39	65	27
Tiverton Town	36	7	11	18	42	67	25
Bridport	36	10	5	21	41	67	25
Exmouth Town	36	6	11	19	31	70	23
Ashtonians United	36	8	5	23	43	75	21
Avon (Bradford)	36	5	6	25	36	85	16
Chippenham Town	36	3	6	27	25	82	12

Ashtonians United merged with Clevedon who took over Ashtonians' place in the league. Avon (Bradford) leftto join the Wiltshire County League and Exeter City Reserves also left. Falmouth Town joined from the South-Western League, Paulton Rovers joined from the Somerset Senior League and Melksham Town and Westland Yeovil also joined.
The League was increased to 21 clubs.

Three points were awarded for a win from the next season onwards.

1974-75

	P	W	D	L	F	A	Pts
Falmouth Town	40	31	9	0	122	26	102
Taunton Town	40	30	9	1	136	24	99
Bridgwater Town	40	27	8	5	92	38	89
Mangotsfield United	40	24	6	10	88	44	78
Barnstaple Town	40	17	11	12	79	66	62
Frome Town	40	17	10	13	65	59	61
Glastonbury	40	17	10	13	62	57	61
Westland Yeovil	40	17	7	16	66	60	58
Welton Rovers	40	15	11	14	63	59	56
Dawlish	40	16	7	17	69	72	55
Keynsham Town	40	15	10	15	63	67	55
Paulton Rovers	40	13	11	16	63	59	50
Devizes Town	40	11	11	18	39	59	44
Weston-super-Mare	40	11	10	19	39	52	43
Chippenham Town	40	10	12	18	55	85	42
St. Luke's College	40	11	7	22	44	83	40
Tiverton Town	40	9	12	19	45	79	39
Bridport	40	9	7	24	71	110	34
Melksham Town	40	7	12	21	39	82	33
Clevedon	40	8	8	24	52	94	32
Exmouth Town	40	8	6	26	39	96	30
					1391	*1371*	

Bideford joined from the Southern League and Exeter City Reserves also joined. The League was increased to 23 clubs.

1975-76

Falmouth Town	44	35	5	4	134	43	110
Taunton Town	44	27	8	9	86	43	89
Clevedon	44	27	6	11	77	51	87
Bridgwater Town	44	25	10	9	81	44	85
Glastonbury	44	23	10	11	84	49	79
Barnstaple Town	44	21	9	14	95	66	72
Tiverton Town	44	20	12	12	73	70	72
Paulton Rovers	44	19	12	13	60	58	69
Mangotsfield United	44	18	10	16	63	63	64
Bideford	44	17	12	15	60	56	63
Frome Town	44	17	10	17	76	61	61
Exeter City Reserves	44	16	10	18	64	69	57
St. Luke's College	44	16	7	21	60	70	55
Weston-super-Mare	44	13	15	16	52	57	54
Westland Yeovil	44	14	11	19	66	82	53
Welton Rovers	44	14	9	21	57	71	51
Bridport	44	13	11	20	49	72	50
Dawlish	44	13	10	21	51	69	49
Devizes Town	*44*	*10*	*15*	*19*	*45*	*59*	*45*
Chippenham Town	*44*	*12*	*7*	*25*	*66*	*94*	*43*
Melksham Town	*44*	*12*	*7*	*25*	*66*	*106*	*43*
Keynsham Town	*44*	*8*	*6*	*30*	*50*	*86*	*30*
Exmouth Town	*44*	*5*	*10*	*29*	*38*	*114*	*25*

Exeter City Reserves had 1 point deducted for fielding an ineligible player.

The League was split into two divisions. The top 18 clubs formed the new Premier Division while the bottom 5 club plus Brixham United (from the Plymouth & District League), Chard Town and Shepton Mallet Town (both from the Somerset Senior League), Clandown, Heavitree United, Ilminster Town, Larkhall Athletic, Ottery St. Mary and Saltash United (both from the South-Western League), Portway-Bristol, Swanage Town & Herston, Torquay United Reserves and Yeovil Town Reserves formed a new 18-club First Division.

1976-77

Premier Division

Falmouth Town	34	26	2	6	69	24	80
Weston-super-Mare	34	18	12	4	57	31	66
Clevedon	34	18	10	6	58	31	64
Bridgwater Town	34	17	10	7	51	36	61
Barnstaple Town	34	16	9	9	64	48	57
Bideford	34	15	11	8	70	38	56
Bridport	34	16	8	10	53	35	56
Paulton Rovers	34	13	10	11	52	46	49
Taunton Town	34	14	6	14	49	46	48
Dawlish	34	11	10	13	36	41	43
Glastonbury	34	11	8	15	56	58	41
Frome Town	34	10	11	13	45	52	41
Tiverton Town	34	11	7	16	35	61	40
Welton Rovers	34	9	9	16	35	46	36
Mangotsfield United	34	10	4	20	36	66	34
St. Luke's College	34	7	6	21	32	61	27
Exeter City Reserves	34	7	3	24	36	76	23
Westland Yeovil	*34*	*4*	*10*	*20*	*31*	*69*	*22*

Exeter City Reserves had 1 point deducted.

First Division

Saltash United	34	24	6	4	81	29	78
Shepton Mallet Town	34	23	7	4	84	39	76
Keynsham Town	34	23	2	9	87	38	71
Melksham Town	34	20	7	7	69	36	67
Chippenham Town	34	17	6	11	53	43	57
Devizes Town	34	15	8	11	58	44	52
Torquay United Reserves	34	15	3	16	61	59	48
Portway-Bristol	34	13	9	12	57	58	48
Larkhall Athletic	34	13	7	14	59	69	46
Clandown	34	10	12	12	54	58	42
Yeovil Town Reserves	34	11	7	16	52	55	40
Brixham United	34	9	8	17	45	77	35
Ottery St. Mary	34	8	10	16	41	61	34
Exmouth Town	34	9	7	18	40	68	34
Chard Town	34	8	9	17	43	63	33
Swanage Town & Herston	34	8	9	17	48	72	33
Ilminster Town	34	8	9	17	39	69	33
Heavitree United	34	4	10	20	23	56	22

Devizes Town had 1 point deducted for fielding an ineligible player.

Taunton Town moved to the Southern League. Bristol Manor Farm (from the Somerset Senior League) and Odd Down joined Division One which increased to 19 clubs. Clevedon changed their name to Clevedon Town.

Goal difference replaced goal average to decided places for teams with equal points from the next season.

1977-78

Premier Division

Falmouth Town	34	26	5	3	98	30	83
Bideford	34	25	8	1	86	25	83
Barnstaple Town	34	18	10	6	75	37	64
Saltash United	34	17	7	10	66	53	58
Bridport	34	14	13	7	44	21	55
Clevedon Town	34	16	9	9	62	41	55
Frome Town	34	14	8	12	43	39	50
Paulton Rovers	34	15	5	14	55	52	50
Weston-super-Mare	34	14	8	12	44	48	50
Exeter City Reserves	34	11	13	10	48	41	46
Bridgwater Town	34	12	9	13	52	56	45
Tiverton Town	34	8	10	16	47	61	34
Shepton Mallet Town	34	9	6	19	52	93	33
Glastonbury	34	9	5	20	46	77	32
Mangotsfield United	34	7	10	17	50	75	31
Welton Rovers	34	8	6	20	34	68	30
Dawlish	34	6	10	18	39	67	28
St. Luke's College	34	1	10	23	20	78	13
					961	962	

Clevedon Town had 2 points deducted for fielding ineligible players.

First Division

Keynsham Town	36	23	10	3	77	22	79
Clandown	36	22	4	10	77	36	70
Ilminster Town	36	21	6	9	69	47	69
Bristol Manor Farm	36	20	5	11	67	38	65
Devizes Town	36	20	5	11	73	52	65
Torquay United Reserves	36	18	5	13	69	53	59
Portway-Bristol	36	17	8	11	57	42	59
Melksham Town	36	17	7	12	76	60	58
Ottery St. Mary	36	16	7	13	55	55	55
Larkhall Athletic	36	15	8	13	58	66	53
Exmouth Town	36	13	7	16	41	55	46
Brixham United	36	11	9	16	61	79	41
Chard Town	36	12	5	19	56	81	41
Westland Yeovil	36	8	12	16	40	52	36
Odd Down	36	9	9	18	52	75	36
Yeovil Town Reserves	36	9	8	19	52	65	35
Heavitree United	36	9	5	22	32	64	32
Swanage Town & Herston	36	6	11	19	48	85	29
Chippenham Town	36	8	4	24	40	74	28
	274	*135*	*275*	*1100*	*1101*	*956*	

Brixham United had 1 point deducted for fielding an ineligible player.
St. Luke's College disbanded. AFC Bournemouth Reserves, Elmore (from the
South-Western League) and Wellington joined the League.
The Premier Division was increased to 20 clubs.

1978-79

Premier Division

	P	W	D	L	F	A	Pts
Frome Town	38	21	12	5	60	29	75
Bideford	38	22	8	8	76	39	74
Saltash United	38	19	10	9	65	39	67
Barnstaple Town	38	18	10	10	65	35	64
Tiverton Town	38	17	9	12	71	60	60
Clandown	38	16	11	11	58	49	59
Weston-super-Mare	38	14	15	9	65	48	57
Falmouth Town	38	15	9	14	51	47	54
Paulton Rovers	38	15	9	14	40	48	54
Bridport	38	13	13	12	54	50	52
Bridgwater Town	38	14	9	15	57	53	51
Keynsham Town	38	13	12	13	47	57	51
Mangotsfield United	38	15	2	21	53	64	47
Ilminster Town	38	11	12	15	45	55	45
Welton Rovers	38	11	8	19	44	59	41
Exeter City Reserves	38	12	5	21	48	75	41
Clevedon Town	38	11	7	20	50	64	40
Dawlish	38	10	10	18	43	61	40
Shepton Mallet Town	*38*	*10*	*10*	*18*	*48*	*74*	*40*
Glastonbury	*38*	*8*	*9*	*21*	*42*	*76*	*33*

First Division

	P	W	D	L	F	A	Pts
AFC Bournemouth Reserves	**36**	**25**	**6**	**5**	**101**	**41**	**81**
Portway-Bristol	**36**	**23**	**5**	**8**	**81**	**43**	**74**
Bristol Manor Farm	36	20	5	11	59	47	65
Chippenham Town	36	19	7	10	56	43	64
Torquay United Reserves	36	20	4	12	82	47	62
Melksham Town	36	18	4	14	58	57	58
Devizes Town	36	16	9	11	71	54	57
Wellington	36	18	3	15	48	46	57
Chard Town	36	15	6	15	57	58	51
Brixham United	36	15	5	16	55	61	50
Elmore	36	15	3	18	48	65	48
Ottery St. Mary	36	13	5	18	51	60	43
Larkhall Athletic	36	12	6	18	52	56	42
Westland Yeovil	36	11	9	16	43	53	42
Heavitree United	36	12	5	19	39	61	41
Swanage Town & Herston	36	11	6	19	51	60	39
Odd Down	36	10	5	21	38	71	35
Exmouth Town	36	8	9	19	41	72	33
Yeovil Town Reserves	36	5	10	21	30	65	24
						1061	1060

Torquay United Reserves had 2 points deducted for fielding ineligible
players. Ottery St. Mary and Yeovil Town Reserves each had 1 point
deducted for fielding an ineligible player.
Bath City Reserves, Liskeard Athletic (from the South-Western League) and
Radstock Town (from the Somerset Senior League) all joined the League.
Division One was increased to 22 clubs.

**Two points were awarded for a win from the next
season onwards.**

1979-80

Premier Division

	P	W	D	L	F	A	Pts
Barnstaple Town	38	23	10	5	67	31	56
AFC Bournemouth Reserves	38	24	7	7	100	26	55
Weston-super-Mare	38	22	11	5	81	45	55
Frome Town	38	19	10	9	57	38	48
Bridgwater Town	38	17	12	9	64	43	46
Exeter City Reserves	38	16	11	11	71	59	43
Clevedon Town	38	16	10	12	74	58	42
Portway-Bristol	38	16	10	12	66	53	42
Saltash United	38	14	14	10	64	51	42
Bideford	38	16	10	12	61	51	42
Keynsham Town	38	16	10	12	56	53	42
Falmouth Town	38	14	10	14	58	53	38
Dawlish	38	10	11	17	39	67	31
Clandown	38	12	6	20	53	76	30
Tiverton Town	38	8	14	16	36	65	30
Welton Rovers	38	10	9	19	59	84	29
Paulton Rovers	38	11	6	21	50	68	28
Mangotsfield United	38	7	10	21	37	80	24
Bridport	38	4	14	20	31	67	21
Ilminster Town	*38*	*2*	*11*	*25*	*31*	*87*	*15*

Bridport had 1 point deducted for fielding an ineligible player.

First Division

	P	W	D	L	F	A	Pts
Melksham Town	**42**	**27**	**8**	**7**	**78**	**27**	**62**
Devizes Town	**42**	**25**	**9**	**8**	**91**	**42**	**59**
Liskeard Athletic	**42**	**23**	**10**	**9**	**70**	**31**	**56**
Bath City Reserves	42	22	8	12	89	62	52
Exmouth Town	42	22	8	12	67	43	52
Torquay United Reserves	42	21	10	11	84	61	52
Elmore	42	20	9	13	63	45	49
Bristol Manor Farm	42	20	9	13	70	58	49
Ottery St. Mary	42	16	12	14	64	52	44
Glastonbury	42	16	11	15	60	68	43
Chippenham Town	42	16	10	16	58	62	42
Radstock Town	42	15	10	17	63	75	40
Shepton Mallet Town	42	15	9	18	75	78	39
Chard Town	42	14	11	17	51	59	39
Yeovil Town Reserves	42	14	10	18	71	85	38
Brixham United	42	14	9	19	60	70	37
Heavitree United	42	11	14	17	57	69	36
Larkhall Athletic	42	11	10	21	48	85	32
Odd Down	42	9	12	21	46	76	30
Wellington	42	8	13	21	38	59	29
Swanage Town & Herston	42	6	13	23	45	91	24
Westland Yeovil	42	5	9	28	31	81	19

Swanage Town & Herston had 1 point deducted for fielding an ineligible
player.

Westland Yeovil left to join the Dorset Combination and AFC Bournemouth
Reserves and Exeter City Reserves also left.
The First Division was reduced to 19 clubs.

1980-81

Premier Division

	P	W	D	L	F	A	Pts
Bridgwater Town	38	25	6	7	54	25	56
Barnstaple Town	38	22	6	10	58	40	50
Frome Town	38	21	6	11	74	51	48
Falmouth Town	38	18	9	11	71	53	45
Bideford	38	18	8	12	58	42	44
Saltash United	38	17	9	12	73	47	43
Portway-Bristol	38	16	11	11	55	45	43
Clevedon Town	38	15	11	12	65	52	41
Clandown	38	16	9	13	60	53	41
Devizes Town	38	14	13	11	61	56	41
Bridport	38	12	15	11	56	52	39
Keynsham Town	38	12	15	11	33	34	39
Melksham Town	38	13	11	14	45	49	37
Liskeard Athletic	38	11	11	16	58	70	33
Mangotsfield United	38	8	15	15	43	66	31
Dawlish Town	38	7	16	15	40	50	30
Welton Rovers	38	9	11	18	50	69	29
Weston-super-Mare	38	11	7	20	42	61	29
Paulton Rovers	*38*	*9*	*11*	*18*	*45*	*72*	*29*
Tiverton Town	*38*	*1*	*10*	*27*	*23*	*77*	*12*

First Division

	P	W	D	L	F	A	Pts
Chippenham Town	**36**	**25**	**8**	**3**	**76**	**24**	**58**
Wellington	**36**	**22**	**8**	**6**	**80**	**36**	**52**
Exmouth Town	36	22	7	7	74	37	51
Bath City Reserves	36	19	11	6	79	44	49
Odd Down	36	20	8	8	59	41	47
Yeovil Town Reserves	36	18	9	9	58	38	45
Torquay United Reserves	36	16	11	9	60	35	43
Swanage Town & Herston	36	13	11	12	58	55	37
Chard Town	36	11	14	11	42	38	36
Bristol Manor Farm	36	14	8	14	53	57	36
Shepton Mallet Town	36	13	8	15	68	75	34
Elmore	36	12	10	14	44	53	34
Glastonbury	36	9	10	17	44	60	28
Brixham United	36	11	5	20	50	70	27
Larkhall Athletic	36	5	12	19	44	76	22
Ottery St. Mary	36	7	8	21	37	77	22
Heavitree United	36	7	8	21	40	86	22
Ilminster Town	36	7	6	23	39	70	20
Radstock Town	36	8	4	24	47	80	20

Odd Down had 1 point deducted for fielding an ineligible player.
Brixham United moved to the South Devon League and were replaced by Wimborne Town from the Dorset County League.

1981-82

Premier Division

	P	W	D	L	F	A	Pts
Bideford	38	26	10	2	88	20	62
Barnstaple Town	38	26	8	4	78	31	59
Bridgwater Town	38	16	16	6	70	46	48
Clandown	38	17	12	9	49	37	46
Melksham Town	38	17	11	10	58	50	45
Frome Town	38	16	9	13	67	58	41
Weston-super-Mare	38	15	11	12	47	42	41
Saltash United	38	15	7	16	47	53	37
Devizes Town	38	14	7	17	53	60	35
Dawlish Town	38	11	13	14	45	53	35
Liskeard Athletic	38	11	12	15	39	48	34
Bridport	38	12	10	16	43	54	34
Clevedon Town	38	11	12	15	58	60	33
Chippenham Town	38	12	9	17	33	39	33
Falmouth Town	38	12	9	17	46	55	33
Portway-Bristol	38	9	13	16	40	47	31
Wellington	38	10	11	17	50	62	31
Keynsham Town	38	9	13	16	39	55	31
Mangotsfield United	*38*	*11*	*6*	*21*	*30*	*59*	*28*
Welton Rovers	*38*	*7*	*7*	*24*	*37*	*88*	*21*

Barnstaple Town and Clevedon Town each had 1 point deducted for fielding ineligible players.

First Division

	P	W	D	L	F	A	Pts
Shepton Mallet Town	**36**	**25**	**8**	**3**	**88**	**30**	**58**
Exmouth Town	**36**	**24**	**8**	**4**	**74**	**31**	**56**
Swanage Town & Herston	36	21	5	10	90	47	47
Wimborne Town	36	19	9	8	67	35	47
Bath City Reserves	36	19	6	11	72	46	44
Elmore	36	19	6	11	58	45	44
Paulton Rovers	36	17	6	13	54	48	40
Bristol Manor Farm	36	15	9	12	58	50	39
Torquay United Reserves	36	15	9	12	50	44	39
Tiverton Town	36	13	8	15	62	63	34
Chard Town	36	12	10	14	43	55	34
Odd Down	36	14	5	17	51	57	33
Radstock Town	36	10	11	15	44	67	31
Glastonbury	36	12	6	18	63	69	30
Heavitree United	36	11	7	18	39	69	29
Yeovil Town Reserves	36	10	8	18	40	53	28
Larkhall Athletic	36	10	5	21	42	85	25
Ottery St. Mary	36	6	3	27	28	79	15
Ilminster Town	36	3	5	28	20	70	11

Bridgwater Town left to join the Southern League and were replaced in the Premier Division by Plymouth Argyle Reserves from the Football Combination.
Ilminster Town left to join the Somerset Senior League and Torquay United Reserves also left. They were replaced by Bristol City Reserves and Weymouth Reserves.

1982-83

Premier Division

	P	W	D	L	F	A	Pts
Bideford	38	26	9	3	67	32	61
Frome Town	38	23	10	5	75	34	56
Dawlish Town	38	20	8	10	68	47	48
Clandown	38	19	9	10	54	39	47
Saltash United	38	14	18	6	50	39	46
Falmouth Town	38	16	13	9	63	57	45
Plymouth Argyle Reserves	38	15	14	9	67	41	44
Barnstaple Town	38	18	6	14	67	57	42
Liskeard Athletic	38	16	9	13	69	47	41
Weston-super-Mare	38	15	11	12	57	46	41
Shepton Mallet Town	38	15	4	19	50	55	34
Devizes Town	38	12	9	17	50	58	33
Chippenham Town	38	12	8	18	40	54	32
Clevedon Town	38	9	12	17	36	56	30
Bridport	38	8	13	17	49	60	29
Exmouth Town	38	10	9	19	40	59	29
Melksham Town	38	8	13	17	43	63	29
Wellington	38	8	12	18	46	74	28
Keynsham Town	*38*	*7*	*11*	*20*	*32*	*68*	*25*
Portway-Bristol	*38*	*8*	*4*	*26*	*35*	*72*	*20*

First Division

	P	W	D	L	F	A	Pts
Bristol Manor Farm	**36**	**26**	**7**	**3**	**85**	**31**	**59**
Mangotsfield United	**36**	**24**	**8**	**4**	**75**	**32**	**56**
Paulton Rovers	36	20	12	4	75	37	52
Odd Down	36	19	9	8	56	41	47
Glastonbury	36	15	15	6	69	47	45
Swanage Town & Herston	36	21	1	14	83	54	43
Wimborne Town	36	17	9	10	74	51	43
Bath City Reserves	36	14	9	13	64	49	37
Chard Town	36	15	5	16	54	50	35
Weymouth Reserves	36	12	8	16	43	56	32
Welton Rovers	36	12	8	16	46	61	32
Yeovil Town Reserves	36	14	3	19	49	55	31
Bristol City Reserves	36	9	11	16	57	77	29
Elmore	36	12	4	20	48	65	28
Heavitree United	36	11	5	20	40	66	27
Larkhall Athletic	36	9	8	19	46	64	26
Radstock Town	36	9	6	21	50	79	24
Tiverton Town	36	8	5	23	42	85	21
Ottery St. Mary	36	8	1	27	35	85	17

Bridport left to join the Dorset Combination and Falmouth Town left and joined the Cornwall Combination. They were replaced in the Premier Division by Minehead and Taunton Town, both from the Southern League. Backwell United (from the Somerset Senior League) and Warminster Town (from the Wiltshire County League) joined the First Division which increased to 21 clubs.

1983-84

Premier Division

Exmouth Town	38	21	11	6	59	35	53
Saltash United	38	22	7	9	72	39	51
Barnstaple Town	38	21	9	8	68	40	51
Frome Town	38	20	10	8	78	35	50
Liskeard Athletic	38	18	9	11	64	38	45
Bideford	38	16	10	12	71	49	42
Clevedon Town	38	16	8	14	55	56	40
Bristol Manor Farm	38	14	11	13	54	42	39
Plymouth Argyle Reserves	38	16	8	14	68	58	38
Minehead	38	15	7	16	55	68	37
Shepton Mallet Town	38	14	9	15	55	74	37
Taunton Town	38	10	15	13	46	52	35
Mangotsfield United	38	12	10	16	47	48	34
Dawlish Town	38	13	8	17	38	43	34
Weston-super-Mare	38	13	8	17	46	54	34
Chippenham Town	38	13	8	17	44	56	34
Clandown	38	12	10	16	34	51	34
Melksham Town	38	9	11	18	49	66	29
Devizes Town	38	7	11	20	41	74	25
Wellington	*38*	*4*	*8*	*26*	*29*	*95*	*16*

Plymouth Argyle Reserves had 2 points deducted for fielding ineligible players.

First Division

Bristol City Reserves	**40**	**26**	**8**	**6**	**96**	**36**	**60**
Chard Town	**40**	**22**	**8**	**10**	**82**	**44**	**52**
Paulton Rovers	**40**	**20**	**12**	**8**	**74**	**46**	**52**
Swanage Town & Herston	40	19	12	9	89	61	50
Keynsham Town	40	19	11	10	50	36	49
Backwell United	40	18	13	9	47	42	49
Glastonbury	40	15	9	16	68	61	39
Welton Rovers	40	13	13	14	49	56	39
Portway-Bristol	40	13	12	15	57	49	38
Wimborne Town	40	14	10	16	51	60	38
Bath City Reserves	40	13	11	16	61	57	37
Warminster Town	40	15	7	18	61	67	37
Odd Down	40	12	13	15	60	66	37
Larkhall Athletic	40	12	12	16	50	55	36
Radstock Town	40	13	10	17	51	63	36
Heavitree United	40	14	8	18	66	80	36
Yeovil Town Reserves	40	11	13	16	65	72	35
Ottery St. Mary	40	14	7	19	42	58	35
Elmore	40	11	12	17	47	78	34
Weymouth Reserves	40	12	7	21	43	64	31
Tiverton Town	40	5	10	25	37	95	20

Ilfracombe Town (from the North Devon League), Torrington (South-Western League) and Westbury United (Wiltshire County League) joined the League. Both divisions were increased to 22 clubs.

1984-85

Premier Division

Saltash United	42	26	12	4	88	43	64
Bideford	42	26	8	8	78	29	60
Bristol City Reserves	42	21	14	7	69	49	56
Exmouth Town	42	22	8	12	83	51	52
Paulton Rovers	42	20	11	11	61	45	51
Bristol Manor Farm	42	21	7	14	70	55	49
Chippenham Town	42	16	14	12	62	49	46
Mangotsfield United	42	17	11	14	63	56	45
Melksham Town	42	17	11	14	57	59	45
Liskeard Athletic	42	17	10	15	69	54	44
Chard Town	42	15	13	14	58	57	43
Minehead	42	16	9	17	55	54	41
Barnstaple Town	42	18	5	19	65	65	41
Clandown	42	14	12	16	51	52	40
Plymouth Argyle Reserves	42	12	14	16	58	62	38
Dawlish Town	42	12	13	17	44	54	37
Clevedon Town	42	12	12	18	45	56	35
Frome Town	42	10	14	18	56	63	34
Weston-super-Mare	42	11	11	20	58	78	33
Taunton Town	42	11	11	20	53	74	33
Shepton Mallet Town	42	4	15	23	35	86	22
Devizes Town	*42*	*2*	*9*	*31*	*34*	*121*	*13*

Clevedon Town and Shepton Mallet Town each had 1 point deducted for fielding an ineligible player.

First Division

Portway-Bristol	42	30	3	9	97	42	63
Torrington	**42**	**27**	**8**	**7**	**83**	**35**	**62**
Wimborne Town	42	26	7	9	81	37	59
Swanage Town & Herston	42	23	13	6	86	50	59
Wellington	42	20	12	10	78	57	52
Radstock Town	42	23	5	14	79	47	51
Backwell United	42	21	9	12	62	42	51
Keynsham Town	42	20	9	13	70	54	49
Ottery St. Mary	42	17	14	11	58	51	48
Larkhall Athletic	42	18	7	17	51	46	43
Heavitree United	42	14	11	17	81	84	39
Glastonbury	42	14	11	17	55	63	39
Bath City Reserves	42	16	7	19	60	69	39
Elmore	42	16	6	20	69	95	38
Yeovil Town Reserves	42	14	10	18	53	63	37
Welton Rovers	42	14	9	19	61	72	37
Tiverton Town	42	11	12	19	61	66	34
Weymouth Reserves	42	14	3	25	67	96	31
Warminster Town	42	8	13	21	54	93	29
Westbury United	42	10	7	25	57	99	27
Ilfracombe Town	42	6	7	29	47	101	19
Odd Down	42	5	7	30	38	83	17

Yeovil Town Reserves had 1 point deducted for fielding an ineligible player.

1985-86

Premier Division

Exmouth Town	42	30	9	3	95	31	69
Liskeard Athletic	42	31	6	5	103	34	68
Bideford	42	27	8	7	97	27	62
Saltash United	42	21	13	8	78	46	55
Chippenham Town	42	21	10	11	60	45	52
Mangotsfield United	42	18	13	11	87	58	49
Taunton Town	42	19	9	14	59	54	47
Dawlish Town	42	19	8	15	53	49	45
Bristol City Reserves	42	18	6	18	74	61	42
Clevedon Town	42	12	18	12	55	47	42
Bristol Manor Farm	42	16	9	17	71	73	41
Minehead	42	16	9	17	55	70	41
Frome Town	42	14	12	16	49	62	39
Clandown	42	15	8	19	46	57	38
Torrington	42	13	11	18	51	62	37
Melksham Town	42	11	13	18	50	77	35
Barnstaple Town	42	13	7	22	46	68	33
Weston-super-Mare	42	12	8	22	69	90	32
Paulton Rovers	42	9	12	21	50	82	30
Plymouth Argyle Reserves	42	9	11	22	60	67	29
Chard Town	42	8	4	30	35	109	20
Shepton Mallet Town	42	4	8	30	36	110	15

Dawlish Town, Frome Town and Shepton Mallet Town all had 1 point deducted for fielding ineligible players.

First Division

Portway-Bristol	42	27	9	6	100	42	63
Radstock Town	42	26	9	7	116	54	61
Yeovil Town Reserves	42	25	7	10	79	36	56
Wimborne Town	42	18	13	11	77	51	49
Larkhall Athletic	42	18	11	13	72	56	47
Backwell United	42	19	9	14	63	47	47
Ottery St. Mary	42	18	11	13	61	60	47
Swanage Town & Herston	42	18	9	15	91	79	45
Weymouth Reserves	42	18	8	16	84	78	44
Heavitree United	42	17	10	15	60	69	44
Bath City Reserves	42	16	10	16	74	69	42
Wellington	42	14	12	16	70	70	40
Tiverton Town	42	16	7	19	68	74	39
Devizes Town	42	10	18	14	43	58	38
Elmore	42	12	13	17	56	78	37
Keynsham Town	42	9	18	15	37	53	36
Welton Rovers	42	13	9	20	61	84	35
Glastonbury	42	12	11	19	52	79	35
Ilfracombe Town	42	10	14	18	55	69	34
Westbury United	42	10	10	22	55	82	30
Odd Down	42	9	12	21	57	90	30
Warminster Town	42	9	6	27	40	93	24

Yeovil Town Reserves had 1 deducted for fielding an ineligible player.
Shepton Mallet Town moved to the Somerset Premier League.
Calne Town joined from the Wiltshire County League.

1986-87

Premier Division

Saltash United	42	31	8	3	101	40	70
Exmouth Town	42	22	10	10	82	62	54
Bristol City Reserves	42	23	5	14	94	57	51
Liskeard Athletic	42	20	9	13	69	45	49
Bristol Manor Farm	42	19	10	13	58	46	48
Bideford	42	21	4	17	58	57	46
Plymouth Argyle Reserves	42	21	4	17	92	55	45
Taunton Town	42	17	9	16	61	64	43
Chippenham Town	42	14	14	14	53	50	42
Mangotsfield United	42	17	8	17	69	71	42
Barnstaple Town	42	15	12	15	55	66	42
Clevedon Town	42	14	13	15	58	60	41
Weston-super-Mare	42	13	13	16	66	70	39
Dawlish Town	42	14	10	18	63	62	38
Torrington	42	14	10	18	61	71	38
Paulton Rovers	42	14	8	20	55	72	36
Radstock Town	42	11	13	18	55	73	35
Melksham Town	42	10	15	17	39	64	35
Frome Town	42	12	10	20	50	65	34
Clandown	42	12	10	20	40	59	34
Minehead	42	10	12	20	53	86	32
Chard Town	*42*	*11*	*7*	*24*	*52*	*89*	*29*

Plymouth Argyle Reserves had 1 point deducted for fielding an ineligible player.

First Division

Swanage Town & Herston	42	25	12	5	93	52	62
Portway-Bristol	42	25	8	9	103	51	58
Bath City Reserves	42	25	6	11	85	58	56
Yeovil Town Reserves	42	21	10	11	85	53	52
Wimborne Town	42	23	6	13	96	58	51
Devizes Town	42	21	10	11	62	43	51
Larkhall Athletic	42	21	8	13	71	53	50
Welton Rovers	42	20	6	16	66	53	46
Backwell United	42	15	15	12	55	53	45
Warminster Town	42	18	10	14	72	71	45
Ottery St. Mary	42	17	6	19	66	68	40
Odd Down	42	13	13	16	57	65	39
Keynsham Town	42	16	7	19	57	69	39
Elmore	42	14	10	18	60	69	38
Tiverton Town	42	12	12	18	66	79	36
Weymouth Reserves	42	12	12	18	75	87	35
Wellington	42	14	7	21	55	67	35
Westbury United	42	12	10	20	78	87	34
Calne Town	42	11	12	19	54	73	34
Ilfracombe Town	42	11	8	23	40	68	30
Heavitree United	42	9	9	24	48	96	26
Glastonbury	42	5	7	30	38	109	17

Wimborne Town, Devizes Town, Warminster Town, Weymouth Reserves and Heavitree United each had 1 point deducted for fielding ineligible players

Portway-Bristol disbanded, Wimborne Town left to join the Wessex League and Weymouth Reserves also left the league.
The First Division was reduced to 19 clubs.

1987-88

Premier Division

	P	W	D	L	F	A	Pts
Liskeard Athletic	42	29	10	3	98	33	68
Saltash United	42	27	6	9	116	41	60
Mangotsfield United	42	25	10	7	99	38	60
Plymouth Argyle Reserves	42	26	8	8	105	46	60
Weston-super-Mare	42	21	8	13	81	62	50
Exmouth Town	42	19	10	13	61	55	48
Bristol City Reserves	42	16	15	11	76	53	47
Bristol Manor Farm	42	17	14	11	66	52	47
Taunton Town	42	15	15	12	49	48	45
Bideford	42	17	9	16	60	61	43
Swanage Town & Herston	42	16	10	16	73	63	42
Barnstaple Town	42	17	6	19	62	72	40
Clevedon Town	42	13	12	17	42	56	38
Paulton Rovers	42	13	10	19	46	72	36
Dawlish Town	42	14	6	22	49	77	34
Radstock Town	42	13	9	20	44	57	33
Torrington	42	12	7	23	49	83	31
Frome Town	42	9	13	20	36	69	30
Minehead	42	10	10	22	47	87	30
Chippenham Town	42	10	8	24	35	62	28
Melksham Town	*42*	*7*	*14*	*21*	*45*	*84*	*28*
Clandown	*42*	*5*	*12*	*25*	*33*	*102*	*22*
					1372	*1373*	

Radstock Town had 2 points deducted for fielding ineligible players.
Bristol Manor Farm and Frome Town each had 1 point deducted for fielding an ineligible player.

First Division

	P	W	D	L	F	A	Pts
Welton Rovers	**36**	**21**	**12**	**3**	**74**	**36**	**54**
Chard Town	**36**	**21**	**11**	**4**	**75**	**41**	**53**
Tiverton Town	36	21	7	8	82	46	49
Bath City Reserves	36	18	11	7	61	46	47
Larkhall Athletic	36	17	8	11	72	49	42
Devizes Town	36	15	9	12	44	38	39
Keynsham Town	36	16	7	13	53	54	39
Westbury United	36	15	7	14	61	56	37
Ottery St. Mary	36	16	5	15	43	41	37
Backwell United	36	11	13	12	49	52	35
Warminster Town	36	15	5	16	46	55	35
Wellington	36	14	6	16	60	67	34
Calne Town	36	11	10	15	45	59	32
Odd Down	36	10	11	15	51	62	31
Ilfracombe Town	36	11	7	18	45	59	29
Heavitree United	36	11	6	19	49	62	28
Yeovil Town Reserves	36	7	11	18	39	57	25
Elmore	36	7	6	23	46	81	20
Glastonbury	36	5	8	23	39	73	18

Bristol City Reserves left the League and Bridport joined from the Dorset Combination.
The Premier Division was reduced to 21 clubs and the First Division increased to 20 clubs.

1988-89

Premier Division

	P	W	D	L	F	A	Pts
Saltash United	40	26	10	4	90	35	62
Exmouth Town	40	29	4	7	79	43	62
Taunton Town	40	23	10	7	95	41	56
Liskeard Athletic	40	20	12	8	46	25	52
Plymouth Argyle Reserves	40	19	13	8	84	39	51
Bristol Manor Farm	40	20	7	13	72	49	47
Weston-super-Mare	40	17	8	15	73	52	42
Paulton Rovers	40	14	14	12	60	53	42
Barnstaple Town	40	17	7	16	61	54	41
Swanage Town & Herston	40	15	10	15	71	73	40
Clevedon Town	40	16	7	17	63	70	39
Chippenham Town	40	11	14	15	48	52	36
Welton Rovers	40	13	10	17	50	57	36
Radstock Town	40	9	18	13	38	65	36
Chard Town	40	12	11	17	49	78	35
Bideford	40	12	9	19	49	72	33
Frome Town	40	11	10	19	54	80	32
Mangotsfield United	40	10	9	21	53	74	29
Dawlish Town	40	11	7	22	48	69	29
Torrington	40	7	12	21	46	84	26
Minehead	*40*	*5*	*4*	*31*	*30*	*94*	*14*

First Division

	P	W	D	L	F	A	Pts
Larkhall Athletic	38	25	11	2	88	40	61
Tiverton Town	**38**	**27**	**6**	**5**	**108**	**33**	**60**
Bridport	38	24	7	7	90	35	55
Calne Town	38	17	14	7	58	34	48
Devizes Town	38	19	9	10	55	39	47
Odd Down	38	17	12	9	57	45	46
Wellington	38	17	11	10	72	56	45
Ilfracombe Town	38	16	13	9	59	47	45
Backwell United	38	15	8	15	49	46	38
Keynsham Town	38	11	13	14	55	55	35
Heavitree United	38	13	9	16	54	58	35
Melksham Town	38	11	13	14	43	49	35
Ottery St. Mary	38	12	8	18	46	71	32
Clandown	38	10	11	17	47	63	31
Bath City Reserves	38	11	7	20	60	67	29
Westbury United	38	10	9	19	59	66	29
Yeovil Town Reserves	38	10	9	19	42	49	29
Warminster Town	38	5	11	22	34	84	21
Glastonbury	38	6	9	23	38	97	21
Elmore	38	8	2	28	38	118	18

Three points were awarded for a win from the next season onwards.

1989-90

Premier Division

	P	W	D	L	F	A	Pts
Taunton Town	40	28	8	4	80	41	92
Liskeard Athletic	40	28	7	5	91	30	91
Mangotsfield United	40	27	7	6	96	42	88
Tiverton Town	40	26	6	8	92	51	84
Exmouth Town	40	24	5	11	74	37	77
Weston-super-Mare	40	20	8	12	86	56	68
Plymouth Argyle Reserves	40	19	10	11	75	47	67
Saltash United	40	19	9	12	62	41	66
Swanage Town & Herston	40	18	7	15	77	67	61
Clevedon Town	40	16	8	16	58	60	56
Paulton Rovers	40	16	7	17	51	52	55
Bristol Manor Farm	40	13	12	15	49	59	51
Chippenham Town	40	14	7	19	36	46	49
Dawlish Town	40	12	7	21	55	78	43
Chard Town	40	8	14	18	50	74	38
Bideford	40	8	14	18	37	76	38
Torrington	40	8	11	21	48	74	35
Barnstaple Town	40	8	10	22	38	75	34
Radstock Town	40	7	12	21	43	82	33
Frome Town	40	4	14	22	43	77	26
Welton Rovers	40	3	5	32	30	106	14

First Division

	P	W	D	L	F	A	Pts
Ottery St. Mary	38	27	4	7	72	36	85
Backwell United	38	21	10	7	63	32	73
Ilfracombe Town	38	20	11	7	67	38	71
Bridport	38	20	8	10	69	46	68
Odd Down	38	20	6	12	53	44	66
Larkhall Athletic	38	19	8	11	73	57	65
Westbury United	38	17	8	13	66	55	59
Keynsham Town	38	15	11	12	57	46	56
Melksham Town	38	16	7	15	46	41	55
Devizes Town	38	14	12	12	38	44	54
Heavitree United	38	15	8	15	53	44	53
Calne Town	38	14	11	13	52	45	53
Clandown	38	14	8	16	45	45	50
Elmore	38	14	5	19	46	60	47
Warminster Town	38	10	12	16	43	54	42
Yeovil Town Reserves	39	9	9	20	46	67	36
Wellington	38	7	13	18	40	60	34
Bath City Reserves	38	9	4	25	37	82	31
Glastonbury	38	7	7	24	35	72	28
Minehead	38	5	12	21	29	62	27

Swanage Town & Herston left to join the Wessex League. Crediton United joined from the Devon & Exeter League and Torquay United Reserves also joined. The First Division was increased to 21 clubs.

1990-91

Premier Division

	P	W	D	L	F	A	Pts
Mangotsfield United	40	28	8	4	113	39	92
Torrington	40	25	7	8	91	41	82
Plymouth Argyle Reserves	40	25	8	7	100	28	81
Tiverton Town	40	22	11	7	85	45	77
Weston-super-Mare	40	20	10	10	74	57	70
Saltash United	40	20	6	14	67	46	66
Taunton Town	40	18	9	13	62	49	63
Liskeard Athletic	40	18	7	15	85	69	61
Dawlish Town	40	15	16	9	58	49	61
Paulton Rovers	40	16	11	13	74	60	59
Clevedon Town	40	16	10	14	52	55	58
Bideford	40	13	10	17	61	76	49
Frome Town	40	14	6	20	56	78	48
Bristol Manor Farm	40	12	9	19	52	66	45
Welton Rovers	40	11	11	18	40	61	44
Chard Town	40	11	10	19	48	86	43
Chippenham Town	40	10	12	18	42	64	42
Ottery St. Mary	40	11	4	25	43	88	37
Exmouth Town	40	9	8	23	59	93	35
Barnstaple Town	*40*	*8*	*10*	*22*	*44*	*86*	*34*
Radstock Town	*40*	*4*	*5*	*31*	*46*	*116*	*17*

Plymouth Argyle Reserves had 2 points deducted for fielding ineligible players.

First Division

	P	W	D	L	F	A	Pts
Minehead	40	28	9	3	102	42	93
Elmore	40	24	6	10	89	47	78
Calne Town	40	25	2	13	85	55	77
Odd Down	40	22	10	8	59	36	76
Westbury United	40	21	9	10	60	44	72
Bridport	40	18	11	11	65	48	65
Torquay United Reserves	40	17	10	13	62	52	61
Devizes Town	40	17	10	13	68	66	61
Ilfracombe Town	40	15	12	13	62	54	57
Crediton United	40	14	13	13	55	48	55
Wellington	40	15	10	15	58	55	55
Bath City Reserves	40	14	11	15	67	64	53
Keynsham Town	40	14	9	17	59	58	51
Clandown	40	14	8	18	43	71	50
Melksham Town	40	13	10	17	54	60	49
Backwell United	40	11	9	20	56	70	42
Yeovil Town Reserves	40	10	6	24	59	91	36
Warminster Town	40	9	9	22	39	74	36
Larkhall Athletic	40	9	8	23	38	70	35
Heavitree United	40	6	12	22	32	81	30
Glastonbury	40	5	14	21	39	65	29

Yeovil Town Reserves left the League and Bishop Sutton and Brislington both joined from the Somerset Senior League. The First Division was increased to 22 clubs.

1991-92

Premier Division

Weston-super-Mare	40	32	2	6	110	44	98
Clevedon Town	40	28	5	7	90	28	89
Tiverton Town	40	27	5	8	106	47	85
Bideford	40	25	9	6	102	49	84
Saltash United	40	24	5	11	89	51	77
Plymouth Argyle Reserves	40	24	4	12	89	52	76
Taunton Town	40	17	11	12	88	56	62
Mangotsfield United	40	16	13	11	53	39	61
Elmore	40	17	10	13	76	72	61
Paulton Rovers	40	16	11	13	71	60	59
Minehead	40	16	10	14	65	74	58
Liskeard Athletic	40	14	10	16	68	69	52
Dawlish Town	40	15	5	20	77	76	50
Chippenham Town	40	13	7	20	58	95	46
Torrington	40	11	10	19	48	62	43
Bristol Manor Farm	40	10	10	20	42	66	40
Exmouth Town	40	10	8	22	56	97	38
Chard Town	40	8	8	24	48	76	32
Frome Town	40	9	5	26	44	91	32
Welton Rovers	*40*	*8*	*6*	*26*	*32*	*78*	*30*
Ottery St. Mary	*40*	*2*	*2*	*36*	*26*	*156*	*8*

Tiverton Town had 1 point deducted for fielding an ineligible player.

First Division

Westbury United	**42**	**27**	**10**	**5**	**80**	**39**	**91**
Torquay United Reserves	**42**	**26**	**11**	**5**	**96**	**32**	**89**
Crediton United	42	20	12	10	57	32	72
Bath City Reserves	42	22	6	14	91	68	72
Warminster Town	42	19	13	10	80	49	70
Keynsham Town	42	19	13	10	80	69	70
Calne Town	42	20	9	13	73	49	69
Brislington	42	21	6	15	70	51	69
Bridport	42	17	16	9	61	50	67
Ilfracombe Town	42	17	14	11	76	44	65
Odd Down	42	20	5	17	58	46	65
Backwell United	42	17	10	15	64	49	61
Bishop Sutton	42	17	10	15	58	50	61
Glastonbury	42	14	8	20	52	61	50
Larkhall Athletic	42	12	12	18	58	65	48
Radstock Town	42	11	14	17	65	68	47
Barnstaple Town	42	12	8	22	42	55	44
Clandown	42	10	13	19	56	72	43
Wellington	42	9	11	22	42	70	38
Devizes Town	42	8	13	21	57	84	37
Melksham Town	42	8	12	22	44	77	36
Heavitree United	42	2	2	38	26	206	8

Weston-super-Mare were promoted to the Southern League, Clandown left to join the Somerset Senior League and Bath City Reserves also left. Clyst Rovers joined from the South-Western League. The Premier Division was reduced to 20 clubs and the First Division was reduced to 21 clubs.

1992-93

Premier Division

Clevedon Town	38	34	4	0	137	23	106
Tiverton Town	38	28	8	2	134	30	92
Saltash United	38	22	8	8	98	51	74
Taunton Town	38	22	8	8	62	37	74
Mangotsfield United	38	20	8	10	89	47	68
Torrington	38	17	10	11	69	44	61
Westbury United	38	18	7	13	50	45	61
Paulton Rovers	38	15	10	13	76	51	55
Torquay United Reserves	38	16	7	15	58	62	55
Plymouth Argyle Reserves	38	15	9	14	72	64	54
Exmouth Town	38	14	9	15	47	59	51
Elmore	38	14	5	19	54	71	47
Bristol Manor Farm	38	10	13	15	49	59	43
Bideford	38	11	8	19	59	66	41
Frome Town	38	9	12	17	57	75	39
Chippenham Town	38	8	14	16	65	86	38
Minehead	38	10	8	20	59	88	38
Liskeard Athletic	38	8	9	21	61	87	33
Chard Town	*38*	*6*	*3*	*29*	*37*	*119*	*21*
Dawlish Town	*38*	*2*	*2*	*34*	*17*	*186*	*8*

First Division

Odd Down	**40**	**27**	**10**	**3**	**87**	**26**	**91**
Calne Town	**40**	**23**	**12**	**5**	**97**	**47**	**81**
Crediton United	**40**	**23**	**11**	**6**	**79**	**43**	**80**
Brislington	40	22	8	10	77	41	74
Warminster Town	40	22	7	11	70	50	73
Clyst Rovers	40	18	13	9	75	48	67
Keynsham Town	40	19	10	11	66	50	67
Backwell United	40	16	14	10	68	52	62
Barnstaple Town	40	15	10	15	62	58	55
Bridport	40	14	13	13	67	66	55
Heavitree United	40	14	9	17	64	69	51
Devizes Town	40	15	6	19	61	84	51
Bishop Sutton	40	14	8	18	55	55	50
Welton Rovers	40	12	11	17	69	65	47
Wellington	40	11	14	15	53	65	47
Glastonbury	40	13	5	22	52	70	44
Larkhall Athletic	40	11	5	24	59	81	38
Ilfracombe Town	40	8	9	23	47	94	33
Ottery St. Mary	40	9	5	26	53	116	32
Radstock Town	40	7	10	23	38	60	31
Melksham Town	40	6	12	22	39	98	30

Clevedon Town were promoted to the Southern League, Melksham Town left to join the Wiltshire County League and Plymouth Argyle Reserves and Torquay United Reserves also left. Pewsey Vale joined from the Wiltshire County League. The Premier Division was reduced to 18 clubs and the First Division was reduced to 20 clubs.

1993-94

Premier Division

Tiverton Town	34	31	3	0	125	22	96
Taunton Town	34	26	2	6	98	38	80
Mangotsfield United	34	19	6	9	75	40	63
Paulton Rovers	34	18	7	9	55	42	61
Saltash United	34	18	6	10	67	36	60
Torrington	34	16	10	8	66	46	58
Liskeard Athletic	34	16	5	13	66	50	53
Chippenham Town	34	14	7	13	58	51	49
Bideford	34	13	8	13	58	69	44
Odd Down Athletic	34	10	12	12	59	58	42
Crediton United	34	10	8	16	42	65	38
Westbury United	34	9	9	16	40	61	36
Bristol Manor Farm	34	11	3	20	51	71	36
Calne Town	34	8	9	17	50	76	33
Frome Town	34	9	6	19	33	61	33
Elmore	34	8	8	18	51	83	32
Exmouth Town	*34*	*6*	*4*	*24*	*35*	*93*	*22*
Minehead	*34*	*6*	*3*	*25*	*38*	*105*	*15*

Minehead had 6 points deducted for fielding ineligible players.
Bideford had 3 points deducted for fielding ineligible players.

First Division

Barnstaple Town	**38**	**27**	**8**	**3**	**107**	**39**	**89**
Bridport	**38**	**24**	**7**	**7**	**90**	**46**	**79**
Brislington	38	23	8	7	73	35	77
Pewsey Vale	38	20	11	7	84	47	71
Keynsham Town	38	21	7	10	80	50	70
Clyst Rovers	38	16	15	7	68	50	63
Backwell United	38	18	8	12	64	45	62
Welton Rovers	38	16	10	12	73	53	58
Devizes Town	38	16	10	12	64	61	58
Chard Town	38	16	9	13	48	51	57
Ilfracombe Town	38	16	8	14	70	42	56
Bishop Sutton	38	12	14	12	58	48	50
Glastonbury	38	14	8	16	68	66	50
Larkhall Athletic	38	12	7	19	52	69	43
Warminster Town	38	8	11	19	47	57	35
Wellington	38	9	6	23	51	92	33
Dawlish Town	38	9	5	24	46	125	32
Heavitree United	38	8	7	23	47	90	31
Radstock Town	38	8	6	24	44	73	30
Ottery St. Mary	38	2	5	31	37	132	11

Ottery St. Mary left to join the Devon County League and Radstock Town left to join the Somerset Senior League. Amesbury Town and Melksham Town joined from the Wiltshire League and Bridgwater Town joined from the Somerset Senior League. The First Division was increased to 21 clubs.

1994-95

Premier Division

Tiverton Town	34	28	3	3	128	23	87
Elmore	34	27	5	2	94	39	86
Taunton Town	34	15	12	7	59	28	57
Barnstaple Town	34	16	8	10	58	48	56
Westbury United	34	16	6	12	71	53	54
Mangotsfield United	34	16	6	12	51	50	54
Paulton Rovers	34	15	7	12	62	71	52
Chippenham Town	34	14	9	11	54	54	51
Bristol Manor Farm	34	14	6	14	51	48	48
Liskeard Athletic	34	12	9	13	59	55	45
Saltash United	34	12	9	13	38	43	45
Odd Down Athletic	34	11	9	14	47	53	42
Bridport	34	11	6	17	44	59	39
Calne Town	34	11	3	20	36	68	36
Bideford	34	10	5	19	48	69	35
Crediton United	34	8	6	20	43	77	30
Torrington	34	6	10	18	49	89	28
Frome Town	34	3	3	28	36	101	12

First Division

Brislington	40	30	7	3	113	25	97
Glastonbury	40	26	8	6	91	35	86
Backwell United	**40**	**26**	**8**	**6**	**75**	**33**	**86**
Warminster Town	40	26	7	7	93	42	85
Chard Town	40	25	10	5	74	35	85
Bridgwater Town	40	18	13	9	62	47	67
Keynsham Town	40	17	11	12	73	62	62
Bishop Sutton	40	17	7	16	61	61	58
Exmouth Town	40	16	6	18	55	63	54
Melksham Town	40	14	10	16	62	61	52
Clyst Rovers	40	15	5	20	60	84	50
Amesbury Town	40	14	7	19	67	61	49
Wellington	40	14	7	19	55	59	49
Ilfracombe Town	40	13	8	19	64	58	47
Heavitree United	40	12	7	21	52	94	43
Welton Rovers	40	11	9	20	50	62	42
Devizes Town	40	11	7	22	57	82	40
Pewsey Vale	40	10	8	22	52	77	38
Larkhall Athletic	40	8	8	24	39	89	32
Dawlish Town	40	8	8	24	43	92	32
Minehead	40	5	7	28	24	98	22

Liskeard Athletic and Saltash United both left to join the South-Western League. The First Division was reduced to 19 clubs.

1995-96

Premier Division

Taunton Town	34	25	7	2	84	20	82
Tiverton Town	34	25	4	5	101	34	79
Mangotsfield United	34	22	7	5	88	23	73
Torrington	34	23	4	7	64	37	73
Brislington	34	16	6	12	60	41	54
Bideford	34	16	7	11	63	47	55
Backwell United	34	15	7	12	54	46	52
Paulton Rovers	34	14	10	10	59	53	52
Calne Town	34	14	9	11	41	40	51
Chippenham Town	34	11	12	11	53	41	45
Bridport	34	13	5	16	51	60	44
Bristol Manor Farm	34	11	6	17	55	69	39
Westbury United	34	9	9	16	39	53	36
Barnstaple Town	34	10	6	18	61	61	36
Odd Down Athletic	34	6	6	22	39	77	24
Elmore	34	6	6	22	30	91	24
Frome Town	*34*	*5*	*7*	*22*	*30*	*84*	*22*
Crediton United	*34*	*3*	*6*	*25*	*18*	*96*	*15*

First Division

Bridgwater Town	**36**	**29**	**3**	**4**	**93**	**29**	**90**
Chard Town	**36**	**28**	**6**	**2**	**65**	**17**	**90**
Keynsham Town	36	22	7	7	69	35	73
Bishop Sutton	36	18	9	9	48	36	63
Clyst Rovers	36	18	7	11	74	52	61
Welton Rovers	36	15	11	10	52	43	56
Devizes Town	36	15	10	11	61	50	55
Dawlish Town	36	14	9	13	56	53	51
Melksham Town	36	13	11	12	59	54	50
Warminster Town	36	14	6	16	51	57	48
Glastonbury	36	12	10	14	45	54	46
Wellington	36	12	8	16	47	52	44
Pewsey Vale	36	10	6	20	34	71	36
Heavitree United	36	9	8	19	64	81	35
Larkhall Athletic	36	10	4	22	50	78	34
Amesbury Town	36	7	10	19	37	67	31
Minehead	36	8	7	21	41	73	31
Exmouth Town	36	9	3	24	44	67	30
Ilfracombe Town	36	6	11	19	43	64	29

Yeovil Town Reserves joined the League.
The First Division was increased to 20 clubs.

1996-97

Premier Division

Tiverton Town	34	31	1	2	103	20	94
Taunton Town	34	24	6	4	99	28	78
Mangotsfield United	34	19	8	7	75	44	65
Paulton Rovers	34	17	10	7	86	42	61
Chippenham Town	34	12	12	10	58	52	48
Brislington	34	12	9	13	53	48	45
Calne Town	34	13	6	15	55	52	45
Torrington	34	11	11	12	54	54	44
Bridgwater Town	34	12	8	14	53	55	44
Bridport	34	11	10	13	41	50	43
Odd Down	34	11	15	8	42	46	39
Bideford	34	11	6	17	51	84	39
Barnstaple Town	34	10	8	16	54	62	38
Bristol Manor Farm	34	9	10	15	40	60	37
Backwell United	34	9	9	16	42	55	36
Chard Town	34	9	7	18	45	67	34
Westbury United	34	8	6	20	40	70	30
Elmore	34	4	4	26	30	132	16

Odd Down had 9 points deducted for fielding ineligible players.

First Division

Melksham Town	**38**	**27**	**8**	**3**	**82**	**20**	**89**
Keynsham Town	**38**	**27**	**7**	**4**	**77**	**21**	**88**
Exmouth Town	38	23	7	8	77	42	76
Clyst Rovers	38	23	6	9	92	48	75
Bishop Sutton	38	21	7	10	96	52	70
Wellington	38	21	5	12	82	62	68
Devizes Town	38	18	11	9	75	39	65
Dawlish Town	38	18	9	11	66	36	63
Ilfracombe Town	38	15	12	11	62	44	57
Welton Rovers	38	15	7	16	68	59	52
Minehead	38	16	4	18	61	56	52
Frome Town	38	12	11	15	45	60	47
Yeovil Town Reserves	38	12	8	18	66	77	44
Glastonbury	38	12	7	19	54	72	43
Crediton United	38	12	4	22	58	91	40
Warminster Town	38	9	8	21	44	75	35
Larkhall Athletic	38	7	13	18	51	92	34
Heavitree United	38	7	11	20	44	95	32
Pewsey Vale	38	5	4	29	26	105	19
Amesbury Town	38	1	9	28	27	107	12

Amesbury Town left the League. Bitton joined from the Gloucestershire County League and Street joined from the Somerset Senior League. The Premier Division was increased to 20 clubs and the First Division was reduced to 19 clubs.

1997-98

Premier Division

Tiverton Town	38	36	2	0	154	20	110
Taunton Town	38	31	3	4	107	28	96
Melksham Town	38	22	7	9	75	37	73
Bridgwater Town	38	22	6	10	73	43	72
Paulton Rovers	38	19	6	13	76	69	63
Mangotsfield United	38	18	8	12	76	50	62
Barnstaple Town	38	18	5	15	79	64	59
Brislington	38	17	8	13	62	55	59
Calne Town	38	16	9	13	68	67	57
Backwell United	38	15	7	16	70	68	52
Bridport	38	16	4	18	62	72	52
Chippenham Town	38	13	11	14	53	57	50
Bideford	38	14	6	18	68	90	48
Elmore	38	10	8	20	54	100	38
Westbury United	38	9	8	21	39	65	35
Bristol Manor Farm	38	8	10	20	37	73	34
Keynsham Town	38	10	4	24	46	94	34
Odd Down	38	9	6	23	33	80	33
Chard Town	**38**	**8**	**8**	**22**	**44**	**77**	**32**
Torrington	**38**	**2**	**8**	**28**	**21**	**88**	**14**

First Division

Bishop Sutton	**36**	**26**	**8**	**2**	**86**	**25**	**86**
Yeovil Town Reserves	**36**	**24**	**6**	**6**	**95**	**47**	**78**
Devizes Town	36	22	7	7	83	38	73
Street	36	21	7	8	61	32	70
Clyst Rovers	36	20	10	6	89	39	67
Minehead	36	16	14	6	60	39	62
Dawlish Town	36	17	10	9	78	48	58
Crediton United	36	15	8	13	65	67	53
Exmouth Town	36	15	6	15	68	60	51
Bitton	36	14	8	14	55	53	50
Wellington	36	13	10	13	72	54	49
Ilfracombe Town	36	14	7	15	75	67	49
Larkhall Athletic	36	12	7	17	45	58	43
Welton Rovers	36	9	6	21	51	78	33
Warminster Town	36	9	5	22	40	83	32
Glastonbury	36	9	4	23	41	86	31
Frome Town	36	8	6	22	47	74	30
Heavitree United	36	3	7	26	34	135	16
Pewsey Vale	36	3	8	25	40	102	14

Clyst Rovers, Dawlish Town and Pewsey Vale each had 3 points deducted. Crediton United left to join the Devon County League. They were replaced by Corsham Town from the Wiltshire League.

1998-99

Premier Division

Taunton Town	38	33	3	2	134	33	102
Tiverton Town	38	29	4	5	118	27	91
Chippenham Town	38	25	7	6	93	41	82
Melksham Town	38	20	10	8	73	44	70
Paulton Rovers	38	18	12	8	70	42	66
Brislington	38	18	10	10	74	44	64
Yeovil Town Reserves	38	18	4	16	70	66	58
Bridport	38	16	7	15	61	68	55
Bridgwater Town	38	15	9	14	68	51	54
Backwell United	38	15	7	16	56	48	52
Mangotsfield United	38	14	9	15	60	58	51
Barnstaple Town	38	14	8	16	72	55	50
Bristol Manor Farm	38	15	4	19	61	57	49
Elmore	38	14	6	18	68	82	48
Bishop Sutton	38	12	7	19	65	81	43
Westbury United	38	9	8	21	42	103	35
Bideford	38	10	1	27	40	108	31
Odd Down	38	5	15	18	44	86	30
Keynsham Town	**38**	**6**	**7**	**25**	**33**	**99**	**25**
Calne Town	**38**	**3**	**4**	**31**	**34**	**143**	**13**

First Division

Minehead	**36**	**31**	**4**	**1**	**124**	**25**	**97**
Dawlish Town	**36**	**27**	**6**	**3**	**83**	**28**	**87**
Street	36	27	4	5	85	36	85
Devizes Town	36	20	7	9	79	43	67
Clyst Rovers	36	21	4	11	76	51	67
Wellington	36	20	6	10	71	42	66
Exmouth Town	36	20	4	12	80	49	64
Pewsey Vale	36	18	4	14	72	46	58
Corsham	36	15	10	11	47	58	55
Welton Rovers	36	13	7	16	61	58	46
Bitton	36	12	9	15	67	59	45
Larkhall Athletic	36	13	5	18	51	65	44
Ilfracombe Town	36	12	7	17	61	71	43
Torrington	36	13	0	23	56	79	39
Warminster Town	36	9	3	24	40	79	30
Chard Town	36	9	2	25	49	102	29
Frome Town	36	7	5	24	44	102	26
Glastonbury	36	3	6	27	47	111	15
Heavitree United	36	4	3	29	31	120	15

Tiverton Town were promoted to the Southern League, Glastonbury moved down to the Somerset Senior League and Heavitree United moved down to the Devon County League. The Premier Division was reduced to 19 clubs and the First Division was reduced to 17 clubs.

1999-2000

Premier Division

Taunton Town	36	30	4	2	116	37	94
Mangotsfield United	36	23	9	4	95	31	78
Brislington	36	20	5	11	64	43	65
Chippenham Town	36	18	9	9	69	41	63
Paulton Rovers	36	16	11	9	53	34	59
Melksham Town	36	15	11	10	50	46	56
Backwell United	36	15	9	12	50	44	54
Bridport	36	12	13	11	56	56	49
Dawlish Town	36	12	11	13	51	45	47
Yeovil Town Reserves	36	11	14	11	64	63	47
Elmore	36	13	8	15	51	63	47
Bishop Sutton	36	13	4	19	51	73	43
Bideford	36	10	10	16	46	68	40
Bridgwater Town	36	10	8	18	42	53	38
Barnstaple Town	36	9	7	20	35	51	34
Westbury United	36	9	7	20	39	67	34
Bristol Manor Farm	36	8	9	19	48	78	33
Odd Down	36	9	6	21	36	82	33
Minehead	36	9	5	22	60	101	32

First Division

Devizes Town	**32**	**23**	**9**	**0**	**88**	**30**	**78**
Welton Rovers	**32**	**22**	**4**	**6**	**74**	**19**	**70**
Clyst Rovers	32	19	5	8	83	39	62
Exmouth Town	32	16	9	7	67	43	57
Keynsham Town	32	16	9	7	48	34	57
Bitton	32	16	6	10	60	47	54
Torrington	32	16	6	10	62	50	54
Street	32	13	10	9	56	40	49
Larkhall Athletic	32	11	8	13	45	55	41
Wellington	32	11	7	14	46	44	40
Ilfracombe Town	32	12	2	18	59	65	38
Warminster Town	32	10	6	16	40	77	36
Calne Town	32	10	5	17	48	71	35
Pewsey Vale	32	10	2	20	51	88	32
Chard Town	32	8	7	17	31	52	31
Corsham Town	32	5	5	22	36	86	20
Frome Town	32	3	2	27	30	84	11

Mangotsfield United were promoted to the Southern League. Cadbury Heath joined from the Gloucestershire County League, Hallen joined from the Hellenic League and Worle St. Johns (an amalgamation of Worle from the Somerset Senior League and Weston St. Johns), Team Bath and Bath City Reserves (both newly formed) also joined. Both divisions were increased to 20 clubs.

2000-01

Premier Division

Taunton Town	38	31	4	3	133	41	97
Chippenham Town	38	30	5	3	109	27	95
Paulton Rovers	38	23	10	5	92	44	79
Yeovil Town Reserves	38	21	8	9	84	46	71
Bideford	38	19	10	9	71	45	67
Backwell United	38	19	7	12	59	37	64
Devizes Town	38	19	5	14	88	62	62
Brislington	38	17	10	11	67	48	61
Melksham Town	38	17	6	15	58	54	57
Welton Rovers	38	15	8	15	63	53	53
Dawlish Town	38	14	6	18	50	68	48
Elmore	38	14	4	20	67	80	46
Bridport	38	10	13	15	51	63	43
Barnstaple Town	38	12	7	19	45	79	43
Bridgwater Town	38	11	11	16	45	58	41
Odd Down	38	10	8	20	34	57	38
Bishop Sutton	38	9	11	18	57	86	38
Bristol Manor Farm	38	8	8	22	37	66	32
Westbury United	38	3	5	30	27	101	14
Minehead	*38*	*5*	*0*	*33*	*34*	*156*	*15*

Bridgwater Town had 3 points deducted.

First Division

Team Bath	**36**	**26**	**6**	**4**	**108**	**22**	**84**
Keynsham Town	**36**	**25**	**7**	**4**	**79**	**35**	**82**
Frome Town	36	21	4	11	77	45	67
Hallen	36	20	6	10	81	52	66
Bitton	36	19	7	10	66	49	64
Bath City Reserves	36	17	6	13	74	70	57
Exmouth Town	36	15	7	14	76	54	52
Warminster Town	36	14	10	12	48	53	52
Corsham Town	36	16	4	16	60	67	52
Torrington	36	14	8	14	69	72	50
Chard Town	36	11	9	16	52	75	42
Pewsey Vale	36	12	6	18	48	79	42
Street	36	10	9	17	40	63	39
Wellington	36	11	5	20	40	63	38
Larkhall Athletic	36	11	5	20	46	73	38
Ilfracombe Town	36	9	10	17	48	64	37
Cadbury Heath	36	10	5	21	48	68	35
Worle St. Johns	36	10	5	21	64	87	35
Calne Town	36	8	7	21	35	68	31

Clyst Rovers failed to complete the season due to issues caused by the outbreak of Foot and Mouth Disease. Their record was expunged but they rejoined the league for the 2001-02 season.

Chippenham Town were promoted to the Southern League and Pewsey Vale moved to the Hellenic League. Shepton Mallet joined from the Somerset Senior League and Willand Rovers joined from the Devon County League. Worle St. Johns changed their name to Weston St. Johns.

2001-02

Premier Division

Bideford	38	28	7	3	105	37	91
Taunton Town	38	26	5	7	104	43	83
Brislington	38	24	11	3	72	32	83
Team Bath	38	22	7	9	74	36	73
Devizes Town	38	22	4	12	72	51	70
Dawlish Town	38	21	6	11	86	56	69
Paulton Rovers	38	18	11	9	77	54	65
Bridgwater Town	38	17	9	12	53	45	60
Backwell United	38	16	9	13	56	41	57
Melksham Town	38	15	9	14	47	46	54
Odd Down	38	13	11	14	49	45	50
Barnstaple Town	38	12	8	18	57	66	44
Keynsham Town	38	11	9	18	47	71	42
Elmore	38	10	7	21	47	96	37
Bishop Sutton	38	9	8	21	53	89	35
Yeovil Town Reserves	38	10	4	24	57	86	34
Bridport	38	9	6	23	51	86	33
Welton Rovers	38	7	9	22	46	67	30
Bristol Manor Farm	*38*	*7*	*8*	*23*	*30*	*80*	*29*
Westbury United	*38*	*7*	*4*	*27*	*35*	*91*	*25*

First Division

Frome Town	**38**	**29**	**5**	**4**	**104**	**22**	**92**
Bath City Reserves	**38**	**24**	**12**	**2**	**79**	**22**	**81**
Exmouth Town	38	23	11	4	84	39	80
Torrington	38	23	5	10	87	49	74
Clyst Rovers	38	18	11	9	73	53	65
Bitton	38	18	9	11	66	55	63
Shepton Mallet	38	18	8	12	59	47	62
Street	38	17	10	11	76	58	61
Corsham Town	38	14	13	11	55	48	55
Hallen	38	16	6	16	69	60	54
Chard Town	38	14	8	16	66	59	50
Larkhall Athletic	38	13	8	17	55	71	47
Weston St. Johns	38	13	7	18	71	78	46
Ilfracombe Town	38	14	4	20	59	84	46
Willand Rovers	38	9	15	14	59	58	42
Cadbury Heath	38	10	7	21	55	84	37
Wellington	38	9	8	21	48	89	35
Minehead Town	38	9	5	24	52	90	32
Calne Town	38	6	7	25	40	86	25
Warminster Town	38	2	3	33	35	140	9

Bath City Reserves had 3 points deducted.
Taunton Town were promoted to the Southern League and Yeovil Town Reserves left the league. Warminster Town moved down to the Wiltshire League. The Premier Division was reduced to 18 clubs and the First Division was reduced to 19 clubs.

2002-03

Premier Division

Team Bath	34	27	3	4	109	28	84
Brislington	34	22	7	5	71	28	73
Bideford	34	21	7	6	105	35	70
Backwell United	34	21	4	9	70	33	67
Paulton Rovers	34	18	9	7	68	35	63
Bridgwater Town	34	17	8	9	71	43	59
Bath City Reserves	34	14	5	15	66	57	47
Melksham Town	34	12	7	15	65	68	43
Odd Down	34	12	6	16	49	67	42
Keynsham Town	34	11	7	16	55	65	40
Frome Town	34	11	7	16	49	62	40
Bishop Sutton	34	11	5	18	57	83	38
Dawlish Town	34	11	5	18	47	107	38
Bridport	34	9	8	17	40	54	35
Barnstaple Town	34	8	8	18	41	68	32
Welton Rovers	34	9	5	20	40	99	32
Elmore	34	8	7	19	45	81	31
Devizes Town	34	6	8	20	40	75	26

First Division

Torrington	**36**	**27**	**5**	**4**	**113**	**47**	**86**
Exmouth Town	**36**	**26**	**7**	**3**	**83**	**29**	**85**
Westbury United	36	20	8	8	92	65	68
Hallen	36	19	6	11	70	56	63
Calne Town	36	16	9	11	62	43	57
Clyst Rovers	36	17	5	14	67	55	56
Willand Rovers	36	16	6	14	63	53	54
Bitton	36	13	10	13	50	48	49
Shepton Mallet	36	13	10	13	53	55	49
Chard Town	36	12	10	14	59	60	46
Bristol Manor Farm	36	14	4	18	56	71	46
Wellington	36	12	8	16	49	57	44
Larkhall Athletic	36	13	4	19	48	73	43
Cadbury Heath	36	10	11	15	49	61	41
Street	36	13	7	16	59	81	40
Corsham Town	36	8	12	16	44	51	36
Weston St. Johns	36	9	4	23	54	76	31
Ilfracombe Town	36	7	9	20	47	85	30
Minehead Town	36	7	5	24	34	86	26

Street had 6 points deducted.
Team Bath were promoted to the Southern League and Bath City Reserves left to join the Severnside Reserve League. Clevedon United joined from the Somerset County League and Shrewton United joined from the Wiltshire League.

2003-04

Premier Division

Bideford	34	25	7	2	110	30	82
Paulton Rovers	34	25	2	7	85	28	77
Frome Town	34	21	5	8	84	43	68
Backwell United	34	20	5	9	67	35	65
Exmouth Town	34	19	7	8	70	34	64
Bridgwater Town	34	19	3	12	67	47	60
Brislington	34	18	4	12	57	40	58
Welton Rovers	34	14	7	13	62	54	49
Odd Down	34	13	10	11	48	44	49
Barnstaple Town	34	12	11	11	47	42	47
Torrington	34	12	10	12	69	74	46
Bridport	34	12	6	16	52	52	42
Devizes Town	34	11	2	21	55	69	35
Melksham Town	34	9	6	19	38	61	33
Keynsham Town	34	8	5	21	45	84	29
Bishop Sutton	34	8	4	22	42	77	28
Dawlish Town	*34*	*6*	*5*	*23*	*30*	*103*	*23*
Elmore	*34*	*4*	*1*	*29*	*26*	*137*	*13*

First Division

Hallen	**36**	**24**	**7**	**5**	**75**	**26**	**79**
Bitton	**36**	**23**	**7**	**6**	**84**	**37**	**76**
Bristol Manor Farm	**36**	**20**	**14**	**2**	**74**	**38**	**74**
Clyst Rovers	**36**	**21**	**9**	**6**	**74**	**41**	**72**
Corsham Town	**36**	**19**	**9**	**8**	**70**	**41**	**66**
Willand Rovers	36	17	8	11	72	50	59
Shrewton United	36	17	4	15	86	70	55
Larkhall Athletic	36	15	10	11	65	54	55
Calne Town	36	13	10	13	49	45	49
Wellington	36	14	7	15	54	55	49
Westbury United	36	14	6	16	52	56	48
Street	36	11	10	15	54	51	43
Clevedon United	36	11	9	16	60	75	42
Weston St. Johns	36	11	9	16	72	95	42
Cadbury Heath	36	9	10	17	50	64	37
Ilfracombe Town	36	7	6	23	43	106	27
Chard Town	36	7	5	24	48	87	26
Shepton Mallet	36	5	9	22	49	82	24
Minehead Town	36	5	9	22	35	93	24

Paulton Rovers were promoted to the Southern League. Almondsbury joined from the Gloucestershire County League, Biddestone joined from the Wiltshire League, Radstock Town joined from the Somerset County League and Saltash United joined from the South-Western League. Both divisions were increased to 20 clubs.

2004-05

Premier Division

Bideford	38	28	4	6	105	26	88
Corsham Town	38	25	8	5	79	33	83
Frome Town	38	23	7	8	78	35	76
Hallen	38	23	6	9	81	38	75
Exmouth Town	38	21	8	9	64	39	71
Bridgwater Town	38	22	4	12	66	46	70
Bristol Manor Farm	38	17	7	14	56	59	58
Bitton	38	15	12	11	64	66	57
Backwell United	38	14	13	11	58	46	55
Brislington	38	14	8	16	50	51	50
Keynsham Town	38	14	7	17	39	62	49
Barnstaple Town	38	15	3	20	51	68	48
Odd Down	38	12	9	17	47	57	45
Melksham Town	38	10	9	19	57	70	39
Devizes Town	38	10	8	20	37	63	38
Torrington	38	11	5	22	50	83	38
Welton Rovers	38	8	12	18	59	80	36
Bishop Sutton	38	9	9	20	44	71	36
Bridport	*38*	*10*	*4*	*24*	*52*	*75*	*34*
Clyst Rovers	*38*	*3*	*9*	*26*	*44*	*113*	*18*

First Division

Team	P	W	D	L	F	A	Pts
Willand Rovers	38	27	7	4	88	31	88
Calne Town	38	23	10	5	91	30	79
Radstock Town	38	24	7	7	67	38	79
Dawlish Town	38	20	12	6	81	42	72
Larkhall Athletic	38	21	8	9	65	35	71
Shrewton United	38	22	3	13	83	56	69
Street	38	17	12	9	68	46	63
Ilfracombe Town	38	16	11	11	72	76	59
Clevedon United	38	15	7	16	61	64	52
Elmore	38	14	7	17	59	67	49
Weston St. Johns	38	14	7	17	62	88	49
Almondsbury	38	11	10	17	55	79	43
Cadbury Heath	38	10	12	16	46	58	42
Wellington	38	11	9	18	58	76	42
Chard Town	38	11	8	19	43	63	41
Westbury United	38	8	14	16	57	75	38
Saltash United	38	8	11	19	61	77	35
Minehead Town	38	8	10	20	41	64	34
Biddestone	38	3	14	21	40	81	23
Shepton Mallet	38	3	9	26	38	90	18

Bradford Town joined from the Wiltshire League, Portishead joined from the Somerset County League and Longwell Green Sports joined from the Gloucestershire County League.
The Premier Division was increased to 21 clubs and the First Division was increased to 22 clubs.

First Division

Team	P	W	D	L	F	A	Pts
Dawlish Town	42	33	6	3	115	33	105
Chard Town	42	29	10	3	87	27	97
Street	42	24	11	7	80	39	83
Ilfracombe Town	42	23	9	10	82	50	78
Westbury United	42	22	10	10	95	50	76
Bridport	42	22	6	14	81	60	72
Larkhall Athletic	42	19	11	12	93	56	68
Portishead	42	18	12	12	59	49	66
Shrewton United	42	18	7	17	88	79	61
Bradford Town	42	15	13	14	71	81	58
Clevedon United	42	15	12	15	62	67	57
Weston St. Johns	42	18	3	21	63	81	57
Longwell Green Sports	42	15	9	18	49	52	51
Cadbury Heath	42	15	8	19	70	62	53
Saltash United	42	15	7	20	71	84	52
Biddestone	42	13	11	18	54	59	50
Wellington	42	14	8	20	69	81	50
Almondsbury	42	10	11	21	46	70	41
Minehead Town	42	9	9	24	47	100	36
Shepton Mallet	42	10	4	28	34	85	34
Clyst Rovers	42	7	7	28	47	92	28
Elmore	42	4	4	34	42	148	16

Longwell Green Sports had 3 points deducted.
Truro City joined from the South-Western League, Sherborne Town joined from the Dorset Premier League and Hengrove Athletic joined from the Somerset County League. Saltash United moved to the South-Western League.

2005-06

Premier Division

Team	P	W	D	L	F	A	Pts
Bideford	38	29	7	2	93	25	94
Corsham Town	38	24	10	4	78	30	82
Bristol Manor Farm	38	24	4	10	86	43	76
Welton Rovers	38	19	12	7	61	39	69
Calne Town	38	19	10	9	70	41	67
Willand Rovers	38	18	11	9	63	42	65
Frome Town	38	18	10	10	61	45	64
Bitton	38	18	9	11	63	41	63
Hallen	38	15	12	11	71	54	57
Brislington	38	15	8	15	55	53	53
Bridgwater Town	38	15	7	16	66	54	52
Radstock Town	38	14	5	19	62	73	47
Barnstaple Town	38	12	9	17	54	62	45
Melksham Town	38	12	8	18	43	68	44
Odd Down	38	11	10	17	34	44	43
Bishop Sutton	38	7	13	18	36	52	34
Keynsham Town	38	5	11	22	34	78	26
Devizes Town	38	7	5	26	27	94	26
Torrington	38	6	7	25	33	89	25
Backwell United	38	3	10	25	30	93	19

Exmouth Town resigned from the league during January 2006 and their record was expunged: 17 3 2 12 19 42 11

2006-07

Premier Division

Team	P	W	D	L	F	A	Pts
Corsham Town	42	29	9	4	81	30	96
Bridgwater Town	42	29	7	6	91	34	94
Frome Town	42	28	7	7	86	41	91
Bideford	42	23	8	11	88	48	77
Melksham Town	42	21	10	11	84	48	73
Willand Rovers	42	21	10	11	69	46	73
Barnstaple Town	42	21	9	12	72	71	72
Bitton	42	19	10	13	66	49	67
Hallen	42	20	7	15	72	60	67
Dawlish Town	42	17	8	17	73	66	59
Odd Down	42	17	7	18	50	53	58
Bristol Manor Farm	42	14	12	16	50	51	54
Calne Town	42	15	7	20	57	58	52
Devizes Town	42	14	10	18	58	70	52
Welton Rovers	42	12	15	15	54	47	51
Radstock Town	42	14	5	23	58	78	47
Brislington	42	11	13	18	44	61	46
Chard Town	42	9	11	22	51	78	38
Street	42	9	11	22	50	83	38
Torrington	42	9	6	27	46	105	33
Bishop Sutton	42	9	4	29	38	89	31
Keynsham Town	42	4	8	30	35	107	20

First Division

Truro City	42	37	4	1	185	23	115
Portishead	42	29	6	7	88	33	93
Ilfracombe Town	42	29	5	8	98	51	92
Sherborne Town	42	25	8	9	87	44	83
Larkhall Athletic	42	24	8	10	88	41	80
Westbury United	42	19	10	13	71	57	67
Wellington	42	18	9	15	63	60	63
Longwell Green Sports	42	17	11	14	51	44	62
Cadbury Heath	42	17	9	16	78	69	60
Hengrove Athletic	42	17	7	18	58	64	58
Bridport	42	17	6	19	84	81	57
Shrewton United	42	15	11	16	65	71	56
Biddestone	42	15	9	18	69	73	54
Clevedon United	42	14	12	16	54	69	54
Almondsbury	42	11	11	20	47	73	44
Elmore	42	10	14	18	62	94	44
Bradford Town	42	12	4	26	42	86	40
Backwell United	42	10	8	24	48	105	38
Weston St. Johns	42	8	10	24	47	93	34
Shepton Mallet	42	8	10	24	34	83	34
Clyst Rovers	42	8	9	25	61	108	33
Minehead Town	42	7	9	26	42	100	30

Bridgwater Town were promoted to the Southern League and Torrington moved to the North Devon League. Roman Glass St. George joined from the Gloucestershire County League and Oldland Abbotonians joined from the Somerset County League. Clyst Rovers moved to the South West Peninsula League and Biddestone withdrew from senior football.

First Division

Wellington	40	27	8	5	124	45	89
Sherborne Town	40	26	7	7	111	41	85
Larkhall Athletic	40	26	7	7	87	43	85
Shrewton United	40	23	5	12	82	71	74
Cadbury Heath	40	22	7	11	82	59	73
Hengrove Athletic	40	20	9	11	83	61	69
Westbury United	40	20	8	12	92	62	68
Longwell Green Sports	40	19	11	10	71	47	68
Portishead	40	17	12	11	81	59	63
Roman Glass St. George	40	15	10	15	70	55	55
Shepton Mallet	40	16	5	19	71	79	53
Oldland Abbotonians	40	13	11	16	80	77	50
Bradford Town	40	14	8	18	62	84	50
Keynsham Town	40	14	7	19	51	67	49
Clevedon United	40	12	8	20	50	75	44
Elmore	40	11	7	22	73	106	40
Minehead Town	40	10	10	20	55	96	40
Bridport	40	10	6	24	64	77	36
Backwell United	40	7	10	23	48	101	31
Almondsbury	40	6	12	22	44	82	30
Weston St. Johns	40	5	6	29	54	148	21

Truro City were promoted to the Southern League. Wells City joined from the Somerset County League and Gillingham Town joined from the Dorset Premier League. Backwell United moved to the Somerset County League and Weston St. Johns also left. Portishead changed their name to Portishead Town.

2007-08

Premier Division

Truro City	40	33	4	3	132	39	103
Dawlish Town	40	25	11	4	103	45	86
Willand Rovers	40	22	10	8	78	48	76
Frome Town	40	21	11	8	86	41	74
Corsham Town	40	20	11	9	71	63	71
Bideford	40	17	17	6	85	46	68
Bitton	40	19	7	14	71	46	64
Ilfracombe Town	40	19	7	14	76	69	64
Welton Rovers	40	17	10	13	44	35	61
Devizes Town	40	16	12	12	68	70	60
Melksham Town	40	13	12	15	51	57	51
Barnstaple Town	40	14	8	18	71	67	50
Brislington	40	12	13	15	55	61	49
Calne Town	40	15	4	21	57	70	49
Hallen	40	13	10	17	64	81	49
Bristol Manor Farm	40	10	9	21	64	84	39
Radstock Town	40	10	8	22	60	83	38
Street	40	8	9	23	36	80	33
Bishop Sutton	40	7	8	25	41	99	29
Chard Town	40	8	4	28	53	104	28
Odd Down	*40*	*5*	*7*	*28*	*30*	*108*	*22*

2008-09

Premier Division

Bitton	40	26	6	8	85	32	84
Frome Town	40	23	7	10	74	44	76
Willand Rovers	40	20	13	7	72	49	73
Dawlish Town	40	23	3	14	93	52	72
Bristol Manor Farm	40	22	6	12	75	53	72
Bideford	40	20	9	11	68	43	69
Wellington	40	20	7	13	87	53	67
Welton Rovers	40	19	9	12	64	52	66
Hallen	40	19	8	13	57	40	65
Brislington	40	18	6	16	62	54	60
Melksham Town	40	15	14	11	59	53	59
Sherborne Town	40	17	8	15	55	59	59
Street	40	13	7	20	55	65	46
Ilfracombe Town	40	11	11	18	48	70	44
Bishop Sutton	40	9	16	15	48	48	43
Calne Town	40	11	10	19	70	78	43
Radstock Town	40	12	6	22	56	95	42
Barnstaple Town	40	10	9	21	49	82	39
Corsham Town	40	10	8	22	37	80	38
Chard Town	*40*	*9*	*5*	*26*	*30*	*77*	*32*
Devizes Town	*40*	*5*	*8*	*27*	*41*	*106*	*23*

First Division

Larkhall Athletic	38	30	5	3	127	27	95
Longwell Green Sports	38	27	4	7	78	40	85
Bradford Town	38	22	6	10	106	55	72
Cadbury Heath	38	21	8	9	84	54	68
Keynsham Town	38	19	9	10	62	46	66
Hengrove Athletic	38	19	4	15	57	52	61
Oldland Abbotonians	38	17	8	13	65	60	59
Shrewton United	38	18	4	16	73	66	57
Westbury United	38	16	8	14	71	50	55
Wells City	38	14	10	14	54	70	52
Portishead Town	38	14	9	15	56	59	51
Gillingham Town	38	14	8	16	71	72	50
Bridport	38	14	7	17	51	65	49
Elmore	38	12	7	19	72	104	43
Clevedon United	38	11	7	20	60	78	40
Roman Glass St. George	38	8	15	15	58	77	39
Shepton Mallet	38	10	6	22	51	88	36
Almondsbury	38	8	11	19	70	91	35
Odd Down	38	7	9	22	51	80	30
Minehead Town	38	5	3	30	33	116	18

Cadbury Heath had 3 points deducted.
Shrewton United and Westbury United each had 1 point deducted.
Frome Town were promoted to the Southern League. Almondsbury changed their name to Almondsbury U.W.E. after agreeing a tie-in with the University of Western England.

2009-10

Premier Division

Bideford	38	27	6	5	93	37	87
Willand Rovers	38	24	11	3	79	30	83
Ilfracombe Town	38	21	10	7	64	45	73
Bishop Sutton	38	19	6	13	69	55	63
Welton Rovers	38	16	13	9	66	52	61
Street	38	19	4	15	65	62	61
Bristol Manor Farm	38	16	11	11	70	55	59
Bitton	38	16	8	14	58	55	56
Brislington	38	14	9	15	44	48	51
Dawlish Town	38	14	9	15	57	63	51
Longwell Green Sports	38	13	10	15	50	63	49
Hallen	38	13	8	17	52	55	47
Wellington	38	13	7	18	63	72	46
Larkhall Athletic	38	12	10	16	61	72	46
Barnstaple Town	38	13	6	19	67	76	45
Radstock Town	38	12	5	21	44	63	41
Corsham Town	38	11	5	22	51	64	38
Sherborne Town	38	9	9	20	63	80	36
Melksham Town	*38*	*10*	*5*	*23*	*41*	*84*	*35*
Calne Town	*38*	*8*	*8*	*22*	*51*	*77*	*32*

First Division

Wells City	38	29	4	5	76	33	91
Odd Down	38	25	6	7	75	43	81
Gillingham Town	38	23	8	7	95	51	77
Bradford Town	38	21	10	7	82	50	73
Westbury United	38	22	5	11	81	49	71
Oldland Abbotonians	38	20	10	8	82	42	70
Hengrove Athletic	38	20	8	10	75	43	68
Keynsham Town	38	22	5	11	68	45	68
Shrewton United	38	18	5	15	76	67	59
Bridport	38	16	6	16	65	66	54
Cadbury Heath	38	15	8	15	62	64	53
Portishead Town	38	14	6	18	53	59	48
Almondsbury U.W.E.	38	13	4	21	79	84	43
Elmore	38	13	4	21	66	93	43
Clevedon United	38	12	6	20	58	72	42
Chard Town	38	7	11	20	40	74	32
Shepton Mallet	38	8	6	24	33	78	30
Roman Glass St. George	38	5	11	22	38	72	26
Devizes Town	38	8	2	28	40	104	26
Minehead Town	38	3	7	28	39	94	16

Keynsham Town had 3 points deducted.
Bideford were promoted to the Southern League. Clevedon United and Minehead Town both moved to the Somerset County League. Merthyr Town joined as a re-formed club after Merthyr Tydfil of the Southern League were liquidated.

2010-11

Premier Division

Larkhall Athletic	36	25	4	7	83	46	79
Bitton	36	21	7	8	71	37	70
Ilfracombe Town	36	20	7	9	59	37	67
Willand Rovers	36	18	11	7	69	40	65
Bishop Sutton	36	18	9	9	66	38	63
Dawlish Town	36	17	10	9	78	65	61
Bristol Manor Farm	36	18	7	11	73	63	61
Odd Down	36	17	8	11	60	47	59
Wells City	36	16	7	13	67	55	55
Corsham Town	36	14	9	13	48	49	51
Barnstaple Town	36	15	6	15	65	74	51
Radstock Town	36	15	3	18	59	56	48
Street	36	12	9	15	50	61	45
Sherborne Town	36	13	4	19	58	70	43
Brislington	36	9	11	16	36	56	38
Hallen	36	10	6	20	56	79	36
Longwell Green Sports	36	7	5	24	35	79	26
Wellington	*36*	*5*	*6*	*25*	*48*	*87*	*21*
Welton Rovers	*36*	*4*	*7*	*25*	*38*	*80*	*19*

Dawlish Town folded on 23rd July 2011 due to financial problems.

First Division

Merthyr Town	36	29	3	4	118	33	90
Oldland Abbotonians	36	22	10	4	93	46	76
Bridport	36	23	3	10	74	44	72
Cadbury Heath	36	20	9	7	88	49	68
Devizes Town	36	21	2	13	63	65	65
Bradford Town	36	18	7	11	84	62	61
Gillingham Town	36	18	6	12	73	57	60
Melksham Town	36	14	13	9	63	51	55
Shrewton United	36	15	6	15	71	79	51
Hengrove Athletic	36	13	7	16	52	58	46
Calne Town	36	14	6	16	72	56	44
Almondsbury U.W.E.	36	11	11	14	55	64	44
Chard Town	36	11	8	17	57	68	41
Shepton Mallet	36	11	5	20	47	76	38
Roman Glass St. George	36	10	6	20	43	76	36
Keynsham Town	36	9	8	19	45	61	35
Westbury United	36	9	3	24	45	82	30
Portishead Town	36	6	11	19	48	84	29
Elmore	36	5	2	29	47	127	17

Calne Town had 4 points deducted. Cadbury Heath had 1 point deducted.

2011-12

Premier Division

Merthyr Town	34	22	9	3	96	32	75
Bitton	34	23	4	7	74	35	73
Larkhall Athletic	34	21	4	9	67	29	67
Hallen	34	19	8	7	59	41	65
Willand Rovers	34	18	7	9	62	37	61
Bishop Sutton	34	16	10	8	60	37	58
Brislington	34	14	11	9	49	34	53
Bristol Manor Farm	34	13	8	13	63	57	47
Odd Down	34	13	9	12	54	48	47
Street	34	14	4	16	56	58	46
Ilfracombe Town	34	12	8	14	52	52	44
Wells City	34	13	5	16	54	66	44
Longwell Green Sports	34	10	8	16	30	47	38
Bridport	34	10	4	20	42	81	34
Barnstaple Town	34	9	5	20	45	66	32
Radstock Town	34	8	3	23	33	74	27
Sherborne Town	*34*	*8*	*3*	*23*	*36*	*91*	*27*
Corsham Town	*34*	*6*	*4*	*24*	*21*	*68*	*22*

Odd Down had 1 point deducted.

First Division

	P	W	D	L	F	A	Pts
Cadbury Heath	36	25	9	2	88	32	84
Melksham Town	36	24	6	6	77	42	78
Gillingham Town	36	22	6	8	94	52	72
Calne Town	36	21	7	8	60	34	70
Bradford Town	36	16	10	10	72	44	58
Chard Town	36	15	7	14	62	54	52
Welton Rovers	36	14	8	14	61	57	49
Roman Glass St. George	36	13	10	13	48	51	49
Almondsbury U.W.E.	36	14	6	16	70	67	48
Hengrove Athletic	36	12	10	14	53	59	46
Oldland Abbotonians	36	11	11	14	52	53	44
Portishead Town	36	12	8	16	48	61	44
Keynsham Town	36	11	13	12	52	59	43
Elmore	36	12	6	18	51	64	42
Shrewton United	36	10	9	17	63	88	39
Shepton Mallet	36	9	10	17	59	84	37
Westbury United	36	10	5	21	48	65	35
Wellington	36	9	5	22	40	84	32
Devizes Town	36	5	8	23	34	82	23

Keynsham Town had 3 points deducted. Welton Rovers 1 point deducted. Merthyr Town were promoted to the Southern League. Buckland Athletic joined from the South-West Peninsula League, Winterbourne United joined from the Hellenic League, Cheddar joined from the Somerset County League, Warminster Town joined from the Wessex League and Cribbs Friends Life joined from the Gloucestershire County League.

2012-13

Premier Division

	P	W	D	L	F	A	Pts
Bishop Sutton	38	24	10	4	94	34	82
Brislington	38	22	10	6	73	42	76
Gillingham Town	38	23	4	11	93	59	73
Cadbury Heath	38	22	4	12	85	53	70
Larkhall Athletic	38	21	6	11	77	50	69
Street	38	18	6	14	74	62	60
Bitton	38	17	8	13	60	63	59
Odd Down	38	16	10	12	84	58	58
Hallen	38	17	6	15	78	68	57
Buckland Athletic	38	15	10	13	77	59	55
Willand Rovers	38	15	10	13	52	53	55
Winterbourne United	38	15	4	19	66	84	49
Melksham Town	38	14	6	18	62	74	48
Bridport	38	11	14	13	55	63	47
Longwell Green Sports	38	12	9	17	49	64	45
Ilfracombe Town	38	13	5	20	52	70	44
Radstock Town	38	10	10	18	60	85	40
Bristol Manor Farm	38	11	6	21	55	72	39
Wells City	*38*	*7*	*6*	*25*	*57*	*90*	*27*
Barnstaple Town	*38*	*3*	*4*	*31*	*23*	*123*	*13*

First Division

	P	W	D	L	F	A	Pts
Sherborne Town	*40*	*28*	*9*	*3*	*116*	*53*	*93*
Hengrove Athletic	*40*	*29*	*4*	*7*	*93*	*34*	*91*
Bradford Town	40	26	5	9	103	48	83
Corsham Town	40	24	8	8	92	55	80
Oldland Abbotonians	40	24	7	9	77	37	79
Chard Town	40	24	5	11	94	58	77
Shepton Mallet	40	21	7	12	85	63	70
Cribbs Friends Life	40	19	8	13	79	55	65
Calne Town	40	16	11	13	67	59	59
Almondsbury U.W.E.	40	15	8	17	67	65	53
Cheddar	40	15	3	22	76	85	48
Elmore	40	14	7	19	88	100	48
Keynsham Town	40	15	6	19	59	73	48
Portishead Town	40	15	3	22	63	82	48
Warminster Town	40	10	11	19	60	82	41
Welton Rovers	40	11	7	22	54	88	40
Roman Glass St. George	40	9	10	21	49	76	37
Wellington	40	9	6	25	61	99	33
Westbury United	40	8	8	24	46	82	32
Shrewton United	40	8	6	26	43	105	30
Devizes Town	40	8	5	27	65	138	29

Keynsham Town had 3 points deducted.
Elmore had 1 point deducted.
Elmore moved to the South-West Peninsula League and Shrewton United moved to the Wiltshire League. Slimbridge joined from the Hellenic League, Wincanton Town joined from the Dorset Premier League, Chippenham Park joined from the Wiltshire League and Ashton & Backwell United joined from the Somerset County League. Cribbs Friends Life changed their name to Cribbs.

2013-14

Premier Division

	P	W	D	L	F	A	Pts
Larkhall Athletic	40	34	5	1	114	33	107
Bristol Manor Farm	40	26	8	6	104	32	86
Gillingham Town	40	23	7	10	87	47	76
Odd Down	40	22	8	10	76	45	74
Street	40	21	5	14	75	65	68
Bitton	40	19	8	13	75	58	65
Melksham Town	40	20	5	15	74	67	65
Willand Rovers	40	18	6	16	69	63	60
Sherborne Town	40	18	5	17	74	70	59
Brislington	40	16	11	13	61	59	59
Buckland Athletic	40	16	10	14	72	51	58
Bridport	40	15	8	17	78	81	53
Cadbury Heath	40	15	5	20	77	80	50
Longwell Green Sports	40	11	14	15	52	69	47
Hallen	40	11	11	18	55	75	44
Slimbridge	40	12	7	21	53	70	43
Winterbourne United	40	13	6	21	77	104	42
Ilfracombe Town	40	10	3	27	47	93	33
Bishop Sutton	40	8	8	24	47	92	32
Radstock Town	*40*	*10*	*4*	*26*	*51*	*110*	*31*
Hengrove Athletic	*40*	*8*	*4*	*28*	*33*	*87*	*28*

Winterbourne United and Radstock Town each had 3 points deducted.

First Division

	P	W	D	L	F	A	Pts
Bradford Town	**42**	**32**	**6**	**4**	**143**	**43**	**102**
Shepton Mallet	**42**	**26**	**11**	**5**	**113**	**52**	**89**
Barnstaple Town	42	26	5	11	102	62	83
Wincanton Town	42	23	8	11	116	70	77
Cribbs	42	23	8	11	89	61	77
Welton Rovers	42	21	11	10	82	56	74
Corsham Town	42	20	10	12	62	71	70
Wellington	42	18	10	14	65	64	64
Almondsbury U.W.E.	42	19	7	16	77	77	64
Chippenham Park	42	19	6	17	64	72	63
Devizes Town	42	19	7	16	71	72	60
Roman Glass St. George	42	16	5	21	78	91	53
Calne Town	42	14	10	18	74	70	52
Ashton & Backwell United	42	15	7	20	49	63	52
Chard Town	42	14	9	19	56	58	51
Wells City	42	14	8	20	63	75	50
Cheddar	42	12	9	21	66	92	45
Warminster Town	42	11	9	22	54	88	42
Keynsham Town	42	12	6	24	56	94	42
Westbury United	42	11	8	23	50	75	41
Oldland Abbotonians	42	5	10	27	54	104	25
Portishead Town	42	5	4	33	34	108	19

Devizes Town had 4 points deducted.
Larkhall Athletic were promoted to the Southern League. Ilfracombe Town resigned from the league and their reserves who were playing in the North Devon League, became the first team.

2014-15

Premier Division

Melksham Town	36	23	7	6	89	41	76
Buckland Athletic	36	23	2	11	90	41	71
Slimbridge	36	20	6	10	55	36	66
Bristol Manor Farm	36	18	9	9	67	40	63
Odd Down	36	18	8	10	78	56	62
Willand Rovers	36	18	7	11	78	60	61
Bitton	36	17	7	12	67	52	58
Bradford Town	36	17	6	13	71	61	57
Shepton Mallet	36	16	7	13	70	70	55
Brislington	36	14	10	12	64	45	52
Sherborne Town	36	13	11	12	62	53	50
Cadbury Heath	36	15	5	16	71	83	50
Street	36	12	8	16	64	64	44
Bridport	36	13	5	18	44	66	44
Gillingham Town	36	13	4	19	66	68	43
Longwell Green Sports	36	12	5	19	49	67	41
Hallen	36	8	7	21	41	70	31
Winterbourne United	36	8	4	24	49	93	28
Bishop Sutton	*36*	*4*	*2*	*30*	*30*	*139*	*14*

First Division

Barnstaple Town	42	30	10	2	128	27	100
Welton Rovers	42	28	9	5	85	41	93
Cribbs	42	26	12	4	88	43	90
Wincanton Town	42	24	4	14	101	77	76
Chard Town	42	21	7	14	74	68	70
Almondsbury U.W.E.	42	21	6	15	77	67	69
Wellington	42	20	8	14	70	62	68
Ashton & Backwell United	42	19	10	13	81	62	67
Corsham Town	42	19	7	16	79	67	64
Cheddar	42	19	9	14	92	85	63
Chippenham Park	42	15	10	17	68	62	55
Hengrove Athletic	42	15	10	17	75	75	55
Radstock Town	42	15	10	17	73	73	55
Oldland Abbotonians	42	15	10	17	58	70	55
Calne Town	42	13	12	17	63	85	51
Warminster Town	42	12	9	21	63	74	45
Keynsham Town	42	11	9	22	62	109	42
Devizes Town	42	11	6	25	59	83	39
Wells City	42	9	10	23	62	84	37
Roman Glass St. George	42	7	15	20	39	74	36
Portishead Town	42	8	5	29	39	88	29
Westbury United	42	6	8	28	52	112	26

Cheddar had 3 points deducted.
Barnstaple Town were awarded a home win after Devizes Town failed to appear for the game on 2nd May 2015.
Slimbridge were promoted to the Southern League from where Clevedon Town were demoted. Chipping Sodbury Town joined from the Gloucestershire County League.

SOUTH-WESTERN LEAGUE

The South-Western League was formed in 1951 to accommodate clubs from Cornwall and Devon. Several of its founder members came from the Cornwall Senior League while others came from Devon-based leagues such as the Plymouth & District League although Torquay United Reserves moved from the Southern League.

Abbreviation: ECPL = East Cornwall Premier League.

Several of the published tables contained errors in the goals scored record. Additional research has succeeded in correcting many of these, totals that still do not balance are shown below the relevant columns in italics.

1951-52

Torquay United Reserves	22	16	4	2	77	22	36
St. Blazey	22	12	2	8	77	56	26
St. Austell	22	11	3	8	49	43	25
Barnstaple Town Reserves	22	11	2	9	62	55	24
Newquay	22	9	5	8	67	69	23
Plymouth Argyle "A"	22	7	7	8	45	41	21
Saltash United	22	10	1	11	47	53	21
Penzance	22	7	6	9	48	51	20
Falmouth Town	22	6	7	9	37	53	19
Newton Abbot	22	6	6	10	46	49	18
Truro City	22	6	6	10	45	59	18
Bideford Reserves	22	5	3	14	36	85	13

Tavistock joined from the Plymouth & District League and Wadebridge Town also joined, extending the league to 14 clubs.

1952-53

Torquay United Reserves	26	21	1	4	100	32	43
Saltash United	26	16	4	6	78	55	36
Wadebridge Town	26	12	8	6	76	62	32
Bideford Reserves	26	14	2	10	73	54	30
Newton Abbot	26	13	4	9	63	52	30
Penzance	26	11	4	11	62	64	26
Plymouth Argyle "A"	26	11	3	12	72	65	25
St. Austell	26	9	7	10	48	59	25
Newquay	26	10	4	12	66	68	24
St. Blazey	26	8	5	13	72	69	21
Barnstaple Town Reserves	26	8	5	13	60	62	21
Tavistock	26	8	5	13	51	76	21
Truro City	26	7	2	17	48	95	16
Falmouth Town	26	6	2	18	45	95	14
					914	*908*	

Newton Abbot left but Bodmin Town, Helston Athletic, Ilfracombe Town Reserves and United Services joined, extending the league to 17 clubs.

1953-54

Saltash United	32	21	3	8	93	68	45
Plymouth Argyle "A"	32	20	3	9	98	48	43
St. Austell	32	18	6	8	92	58	42
Tavistock	32	18	5	9	76	53	41
Wadebridge Town	32	16	7	9	86	76	39
St. Blazey	32	16	6	10	95	72	38
Torquay United Reserves	32	13	8	11	62	55	34
Newquay	32	15	4	13	86	80	34
Truro City	32	12	9	11	63	68	33
Helston Athletic	32	13	5	14	81	80	31
Penzance	32	11	7	14	56	73	29
United Services	32	10	8	14	69	79	28
Barnstaple Town Reserves	32	10	7	15	67	71	27
Bideford Reserves	32	11	2	19	65	88	24
Bodmin Town	32	10	2	20	50	74	22
Falmouth Town	32	5	8	19	37	81	18
Ilfracombe Town Reserves	32	6	4	22	50	110	16
					1226	*1234*	

Ilfracombe Town Reserves and United Services left, reducing the league to 15 clubs.

1954-55

St. Blazey	28	21	3	4	102	46	45
Truro City	28	18	5	5	70	41	41
Torquay United Reserves	28	17	5	6	73	36	39
Penzance	28	13	8	7	71	53	34
Tavistock	28	14	3	11	89	71	31
Bodmin Town	28	11	8	9	58	51	30
Newquay	28	11	4	13	69	76	26
Saltash United	28	10	6	12	84	93	26
Wadebridge Town	28	11	4	13	64	83	26
St. Austell	28	9	6	13	46	68	24
Helston Athletic	28	9	6	13	46	48	24
Barnstaple Town Reserves	28	9	5	14	59	69	23
Plymouth Argyle "A"	28	7	5	16	55	77	19
Bideford Reserves	28	8	3	17	58	88	19
Falmouth Town	28	4	5	19	47	92	13
					991	992	

Torquay United Reserves left to join the Western League and Barnstaple Town Reserves also left. They were replaced by Camelford and Bugle.

1955-56

Penzance	28	20	4	4	103	50	44
St. Blazey	28	16	5	7	84	60	37
Plymouth Argyle "A"	28	17	2	9	84	49	36
Newquay	28	16	4	8	87	59	36
Bodmin Town	28	14	4	10	83	69	32
Tavistock	28	13	6	9	83	76	32
Wadebridge Town	28	14	4	10	67	63	32
Truro City	28	13	4	11	66	63	30
Falmouth Town	28	12	4	12	84	84	28
Saltash United	28	10	5	13	70	89	25
St. Austell	28	8	6	14	51	61	22
Camelford	28	9	4	15	54	73	22
Helston Athletic	28	7	5	16	36	70	19
Bideford Reserves	28	6	4	18	61	92	16
Bugle	28	3	3	22	46	101	9

1956-57

Penzance	28	17	5	6	110	43	39
St. Blazey	28	16	5	7	107	73	37
Falmouth Town	28	16	4	8	78	46	36
Plymouth Argyle "A"	28	14	4	10	59	58	32
Newquay	28	14	3	11	89	55	31
Tavistock	28	14	3	11	80	70	31
Truro City	28	14	3	11	78	79	31
St. Austell	28	12	5	11	67	60	29
Saltash United	28	12	4	12	92	78	28
Helston Athletic	28	11	3	14	43	69	25
Bugle	28	10	5	13	67	97	25
Bodmin Town	28	11	3	14	80	70	23
Bideford Reserves	28	9	4	15	54	80	22
Wadebridge Town	28	8	5	15	62	99	21
Camelford	28	2	4	22	40	129	8

Bodmin Town had 2 points deducted.
Bideford Reserves left, reducing the league to 14 clubs.

1957-58

St. Blazey	26	20	2	4	106	49	42
Newquay	26	18	3	5	88	34	39
Penzance	26	15	5	6	67	38	35
Truro City	26	15	5	6	61	36	35
Plymouth Argyle "A"	26	15	4	7	111	46	34
Bodmin Town	26	15	4	7	64	42	34
St. Austell	26	11	4	11	59	59	26
Falmouth Town	26	10	6	10	57	58	26
Saltash United	26	11	3	12	66	81	25
Wadebridge Town	26	6	6	14	42	60	18
Camelford	26	8	2	16	48	108	18
Bugle	26	6	1	19	46	94	13
Helston Athletic	26	3	4	19	36	79	10
Tavistock	26	3	3	20	38	105	9

Launceston and Exeter City Reserves joined, extending the league to 16 clubs.

1958-59

Newquay	30	23	3	4	123	45	49
Falmouth Town	30	22	3	5	121	42	47
Truro City	30	21	5	4	98	53	47
Bodmin Town	30	18	1	11	73	67	37
Plymouth Argyle "A"	30	16	4	10	88	50	36
St. Austell	30	18	0	12	81	68	36
Penzance	30	15	3	12	89	65	33
Launceston	30	13	7	10	77	70	33
St. Blazey	30	13	3	14	80	101	29
Exeter City Reserves	30	10	6	14	56	75	26
Wadebridge Town	30	10	3	17	77	80	23
Helston Athletic	30	8	4	18	58	86	20
Camelford	30	7	5	18	51	88	19
Saltash United	30	8	2	20	52	113	18
Bugle	30	8	0	22	53	86	16
Tavistock	30	4	3	23	47	130	11
					1224	1219	

Saltash United left the League to join the ECPL.
Newton Abbott Spurs joined the League.

1959-60

Newquay	30	19	7	4	92	46	45
Plymouth Argyle "A"	30	21	4	5	91	28	44
St. Blazey	30	19	1	10	113	69	39
Truro City	30	17	5	8	100	63	39
Falmouth Town	30	15	6	9	73	43	36
Exeter City Reserves	30	15	6	9	75	48	36
Launceston	30	14	5	11	81	62	33
Camelford	30	13	4	13	61	73	30
Penzance	30	12	4	14	73	65	28
Wadebridge Town	30	11	6	13	79	87	28
Bodmin Town	30	13	2	15	62	87	28
St. Austell	30	11	2	17	64	81	24
Helston Athletic	30	10	4	16	65	84	24
Newton Abbott Spurs	30	6	4	20	43	92	16
Tavistock	30	6	4	20	48	103	16
Bugle	30	5	2	23	42	131	12

Plymouth Argyle "A" had 2 points deducted for fielding an ineligible player.
Exeter City Reserves left to join the Western League.
The League was reduced to 15 clubs.

1960-61

Truro City	28	19	6	3	110	36	44
Plymouth Argyle "A"	28	18	3	7	97	54	39
St. Blazey	28	16	4	8	97	43	36
Falmouth Town	28	15	5	8	87	37	35
Bugle	28	13	9	6	79	55	35
Newquay	28	13	6	9	89	59	32
Helston Athletic	28	15	2	11	63	55	32
St. Austell	28	13	4	11	62	67	30
Penzance	28	12	5	11	68	69	29
Wadebridge Town	28	12	3	13	58	64	27
Camelford	28	9	5	14	47	67	23
Launceston	28	9	5	14	68	86	23
Newton Abbott Spurs	28	9	3	16	48	71	21
Bodmin Town	28	2	3	23	41	142	7
Tavistock	28	2	3	23	31	135	7
					1045	1040	

Nanpean Rovers joined the League but Launceston and Tavistock left.
The League was reduced to 14 clubs.

1961-62

Falmouth Town	26	20	3	3	97	31	43
St. Blazey	26	19	1	6	89	45	39
Truro City	26	17	3	6	77	51	37
Newquay	26	16	3	7	86	47	35
Bugle	26	14	3	9	81	57	31
Nanpean Rovers	26	12	6	8	75	52	30
St. Austell	26	14	1	11	79	61	29
Penzance	26	9	6	11	62	65	24
Wadebridge Town	26	11	1	14	62	70	23
Newton Abbott Spurs	26	8	4	14	45	72	20
Bodmin Town	26	8	2	16	50	98	18
Plymouth Argyle "A"	26	6	5	15	61	83	17
Helston Athletic	26	7	1	18	48	94	15
Camelford	26	1	1	24	21	107	3

Bodmin Town left the League but Saltash United joined from the ECPL and Launceston and Torpoint Athletic also joined which increased the League to 16 clubs.

1962-63

St. Blazey	30	20	6	4	115	51	46
Truro City	30	22	1	7	98	54	45
Falmouth Town	30	20	4	6	119	50	44
Torpoint Athletic	30	19	3	8	92	59	41
Penzance	30	16	4	10	98	63	36
St. Austell	30	12	8	10	89	84	32
Plymouth Argyle "A"	30	13	5	12	77	89	31
Newton Abbott Spurs	30	14	3	13	61	78	31
Helston Athletic	30	12	5	13	76	79	29
Launceston	30	12	4	14	72	71	28
Saltash United	30	11	5	14	89	99	27
Newquay	30	12	3	15	77	89	27
Bugle	30	11	2	17	71	85	24
Nanpean Rovers	30	9	2	19	81	106	20
Wadebridge Town	30	4	5	21	52	103	13
Camelford	30	1	4	25	38	145	6

Camelford left the League and were replaced by St. Luke's College.

1963-64

St. Blazey	30	22	5	3	119	39	49
St. Austell	30	19	5	6	108	58	43
Newquay	30	19	1	10	88	58	39
Falmouth Town	30	16	5	9	83	51	37
Penzance	30	17	3	10	83	64	37
Torpoint Athletic	30	15	5	10	83	78	35
Plymouth Argyle "A"	30	16	2	12	93	64	34
St. Luke's College	30	13	4	13	80	74	30
Newton Abbott Spurs	30	13	3	14	59	69	29
Nanpean Rovers	30	12	4	14	85	88	28
Truro City	30	11	4	15	76	82	26
Wadebridge Town	30	7	9	14	64	79	23
Saltash United	30	8	5	17	63	119	21
Helston Athletic	30	8	3	19	42	81	19
Launceston	30	6	6	18	57	115	18
Bugle	30	2	8	20	57	121	12

1964-65

Torpoint Athletic	30	23	5	2	117	41	51
Falmouth Town	30	24	4	2	130	28	50
Helston Athletic	30	19	6	5	88	50	44
St. Blazey	30	19	3	8	87	55	41
St. Austell	30	18	4	8	118	73	40
Wadebridge Town	30	16	4	10	84	71	36
St. Luke's College	30	15	5	10	95	56	35
Plymouth Argyle "A"	30	13	2	15	89	86	28
Penzance	30	12	4	14	60	73	28
Truro City	30	12	2	16	64	77	26
Newton Abbott Spurs	30	8	7	15	44	69	23
Newquay	30	9	3	18	60	75	21
Saltash United	30	9	2	19	64	102	20
Launceston	30	6	2	22	45	114	14
Nanpean Rovers	30	5	2	23	53	120	12
Bugle	30	4	1	25	31	139	9

Falmouth Town had 2 points deducted for fielding an unregistered player. Plymouth Argyle "A" left to join the Western League. The League was reduced to 15 clubs.

1965-66

Falmouth Town	28	25	0	3	117	36	50
St. Austell	28	20	2	6	103	51	42
Truro City	28	19	3	6	93	51	41
Torpoint Athletic	28	17	3	8	102	66	37
Helston Athletic	28	14	4	10	69	56	32
St. Blazey	28	14	2	12	95	63	30
St. Luke's College	28	15	0	13	82	66	30
Wadebridge Town	28	13	3	12	75	63	29
Saltash United	28	10	3	15	53	97	23
Penzance	28	9	4	15	52	72	22
Nanpean Rovers	28	8	5	15	69	96	21
Newton Abbott Spurs	28	8	3	17	44	86	19
Newquay	28	6	6	16	36	78	18
Bugle	28	7	2	19	58	100	16
Launceston	28	4	2	22	39	106	10

St. Luke's College left to join the Western League and Launceston left to join the ECPL. Liskeard Athletic joined from the Plymouth & District League which reduced the League to 14 clubs.

1966-67

Torpoint Athletic	26	19	5	2	104	48	43
Truro City	26	20	2	4	88	31	42
St. Blazey	26	17	6	3	87	35	40
Falmouth Town	26	17	3	6	88	36	37
St. Austell	26	16	2	8	69	55	34
Newquay	26	12	5	9	49	48	29
Penzance	26	11	3	12	57	57	25
Helston Athletic	26	10	4	12	56	52	24
Wadebridge Town	26	10	3	13	50	64	23
Liskeard Athletic	26	9	5	12	55	74	23
Bugle	26	8	4	14	47	77	20
Newton Abbott Spurs	26	4	4	18	35	67	12
Saltash United	26	3	1	22	46	95	7
Nanpean Rovers	26	2	1	23	32	124	5

Porthleven joined from the Cornwall Combination and the League increased to 15 clubs.

1967-68

	P	W	D	L	F	A	Pts
Falmouth Town	28	22	3	3	79	29	47
Truro City	28	20	5	3	111	33	45
Torpoint Athletic	28	18	4	6	87	40	40
St. Austell	28	17	5	6	85	41	39
Porthleven	28	17	4	7	71	40	38
Wadebridge Town	28	16	3	9	84	49	35
Penzance	28	16	1	11	77	60	33
St. Blazey	28	14	4	10	64	57	32
Newton Abbott Spurs	28	9	4	15	30	71	22
Liskeard Athletic	28	9	3	16	54	73	21
Nanpean Rovers	28	9	2	17	54	74	20
Helston Athletic	28	5	5	18	41	72	15
Newquay	28	4	6	18	54	88	14
Bugle	28	4	4	20	42	127	12
Saltash United	28	2	3	23	38	117	7

Tavistock and St. Luke's College Reserves joined so the League increased to 17 clubs.

1968-69

	P	W	D	L	F	A	Pts
St. Austell	32	24	4	4	132	35	52
Wadebridge Town	32	21	6	5	99	52	48
Falmouth Town	32	21	5	6	93	45	47
Truro City	32	21	3	8	100	37	45
Saltash United	32	20	3	9	97	58	43
Newquay	32	16	5	11	88	61	37
Torpoint Athletic	32	15	6	11	86	53	36
Tavistock	32	15	6	11	83	73	36
St. Blazey	32	14	7	11	86	62	35
Penzance	32	13	6	13	61	66	32
Porthleven	32	14	3	15	69	66	31
Nanpean Rovers	32	11	4	17	68	77	26
Liskeard Athletic	32	12	1	19	83	97	25
St. Luke's College Reserves	32	8	4	20	57	94	20
Helston Athletic	32	4	4	24	33	181	12
Newton Abbott Spurs	32	4	3	25	29	125	11
Bugle	32	2	4	26	38	120	8

Bodmin Town joined from the ECPL and the League increased to 18 clubs.

1969-70

	P	W	D	L	F	A	Pts
Truro City	34	26	4	4	122	35	56
Falmouth Town	34	25	4	5	119	39	54
Wadebridge Town	34	18	5	11	89	57	41
Liskeard Athletic	34	17	7	10	88	59	41
St. Austell	34	18	4	12	82	53	40
Newquay	34	17	6	11	91	67	40
St. Blazey	34	15	10	9	73	56	40
Torpoint Athletic	34	14	11	9	79	72	39
Saltash United	34	17	4	13	76	67	38
Bugle	34	14	6	14	84	69	34
Nanpean Rovers	34	12	7	15	68	88	31
Tavistock	34	12	4	18	59	85	28
Helston Athletic	34	10	7	17	53	93	27
Bodmin Town	34	11	5	18	72	119	27
Porthleven	34	9	8	17	50	72	26
Penzance	34	7	5	22	58	93	19
St. Luke's College Reserves	34	7	5	22	49	90	19
Newton Abbott Spurs	34	4	4	26	33	136	12
					1345	1350	

1970-71

	P	W	D	L	F	A	Pts
Falmouth Town	34	31	3	0	130	21	65
Truro City	34	25	4	5	104	52	54
St. Austell	34	19	7	8	88	53	45
Newquay	34	17	7	10	82	54	41
Bodmin Town	34	18	5	11	98	70	41
St. Blazey	34	18	5	11	99	78	41
Tavistock	34	17	5	12	71	66	39
Porthleven	34	15	8	11	90	60	38
Wadebridge Town	34	15	6	13	85	75	36
Liskeard Athletic	34	13	9	12	73	61	35
Saltash United	34	14	5	15	66	70	33
Penzance	34	12	6	16	71	77	30
St. Luke's College Reserves	34	11	5	18	51	70	27
Bugle	34	8	6	20	52	98	22
Torpoint Athletic	34	7	4	23	59	95	18
Newton Abbott Spurs	34	6	6	22	60	129	18
Nanpean Rovers	34	6	4	24	46	119	16
Helston Athletic	34	4	5	25	48	125	13

Newton Abbott Spurs left the League and were replaced by Holsworthy.

1971-72

	P	W	D	L	F	A	Pts
Falmouth Town	34	29	3	2	144	31	61
St. Austell	34	25	5	4	96	25	55
Bodmin Town	34	24	6	4	107	38	54
Wadebridge Town	34	23	7	4	93	39	53
Holsworthy	34	23	4	7	76	33	50
Newquay	34	16	8	10	64	46	40
Penzance	34	14	7	13	67	56	35
Liskeard Athletic	34	13	7	14	62	50	33
Saltash United	34	13	6	15	59	74	32
Truro City	34	10	10	14	64	64	30
Porthleven	34	11	6	17	71	79	28
Bugle	34	11	6	17	64	78	28
Tavistock	34	10	8	16	54	77	28
Torpoint Athletic	34	8	8	18	50	82	24
St. Blazey	34	7	7	20	35	74	21
St. Luke's College Reserves	34	5	8	21	30	97	18
Helston Athletic	34	7	2	25	42	103	16
Nanpean Rovers	34	2	2	30	23	155	6

Helston Athletic left to join the Cornwall Combination and the League was reduced to 17 clubs.

1972-73

	P	W	D	L	F	A	Pts
Falmouth Town	32	30	1	1	136	20	61
St. Austell	32	24	2	6	94	33	50
Penzance	32	24	2	6	95	44	50
Holsworthy	32	19	5	8	67	34	43
Bodmin Town	32	17	7	8	68	49	41
Truro City	32	16	7	9	62	54	39
Wadebridge Town	32	16	5	11	70	49	37
Porthleven	32	13	4	15	64	73	30
Liskeard Athletic	32	11	6	15	56	52	28
Saltash United	32	11	6	15	65	70	28
Newquay	32	12	2	18	58	77	26
Tavistock	32	10	6	16	53	74	26
St. Blazey	32	11	3	18	63	80	25
Torpoint Athletic	32	8	7	17	76	97	23
St. Luke's College Reserves	32	7	3	22	53	99	17
Nanpean Rovers	32	4	4	24	31	122	12
Bugle	32	3	2	27	30	114	6

Bugle had 2 points deducted.
Nanpean Rovers left and the League was reduced to 16 clubs.

1973-74

Falmouth Town	30	26	2	2	143	29	54
Saltash United	30	18	7	5	100	40	43
Wadebridge Town	30	18	5	7	73	47	41
St. Blazey	30	17	4	9	69	55	38
Newquay	30	15	8	7	57	46	38
Porthleven	30	12	12	6	60	43	36
Bodmin Town	30	14	6	10	56	46	34
Penzance	30	13	8	9	54(57)	50	32
Holsworthy	30	10	12	8	61	62	32
Liskeard Athletic	30	9	11	10	55	63	29
St. Austell	30	10	5	15	48	62	25
Truro City	30	8	6	16	56	76	22
Tavistock	30	6	6	18	30	72	18
Torpoint Athletic	30	5	4	21	45	93	14
Bugle	30	6	2	22	37	107	14
St. Luke's College Reserves	30	2	4	24	32	88	8

Penzance had three goals and two points deducted.
Falmouth Town left to join the Western League. Elmore and Ottery St. Mary joined from the Devon & Exeter League, Exeter City Reserves joined from the Western League and Illogan RBL also joined. The League was increased to 19 clubs.

1974-75

Penzance	36	24	11	1	113	35	59
Saltash United	36	27	4	5	127	37	58
Wadebridge Town	36	26	5	5	111	55	57
Liskeard Athletic	36	21	6	9	72	44	48
Exeter City Reserves	36	20	6	10	61	38	46
Ottery St. Mary	36	20	4	12	92	67	44
Tavistock	36	15	10	11	63	53	40
Newquay	36	16	6	14	68	49	38
Elmore	36	16	6	14	66	55	38
Porthleven	36	15	8	13	80	73	38
Holsworthy	36	13	8	15	69	63	34
Torpoint Athletic	36	12	8	16	63	81	32
St. Austell	36	11	10	15	45	58	32
Bodmin Town	36	11	10	15	45	64	32
Illogan RBL	36	11	6	19	65	94	28
Truro City	36	8	4	24	51	110	20
St. Luke's College Reserves	36	5	8	23	38	94	18
St. Blazey	36	5	3	28	47	112	13
Bugle	36	2	5	29	35	129	9

Exeter City Reserves left to join the Western League and Truro City left to join the Cornwall Combination. They were replaced by Plymouth Argyle "A" from the Plymouth & District League and Louis International.

1975-76

Saltash United	36	30	4	2	119	25	64
Liskeard Athletic	36	22	10	4	90	35	54
Bodmin Town	36	21	8	7	79	33	50
Elmore	36	21	8	7	71	56	50
Wadebridge Town	36	22	3	11	96	50	47
Louis International	35	16	13	6	67	37	47
Holsworthy	36	19	6	11	70	44	44
Penzance	36	15	8	13	66	60	38
Tavistock	36	15	7	14	58	60	37
Ottery St. Mary	36	14	8	14	60	54	35
Newquay	36	15	4	17	64	54	34
Illogan RBL	36	12	8	16	61	66	32
Plymouth Argyle "A"	36	12	10	14	50	51	30
Porthleven	35	12	5	18	52	92	29
St. Luke's College Reserves	36	9	2	25	45	78	20
St. Blazey	36	7	5	24	48	103	19
Torpoint Athletic	36	7	5	24	48	104	19
St. Austell	36	5	5	26	47	100	15
Bugle	36	5	5	26	33	126	15
						1224	1228

Plymouth Argyle "A" had 4 points deducted for fielding ineligible players. Louis International were awarded two points when Porthleven failed to appear for their game and Ottery St. Mary had 1 point deducted.
Ottery St. Mary and Saltash United left to join the Western League and

Plymouth Command joined from the Plymouth & District League. The League was reduced to 18 clubs.

1976-77

Liskeard Athletic	34	24	8	2	82	34	56
Bodmin Town	34	19	10	5	75	40	48
Tavistock	34	18	9	7	65	37	45
Holsworthy	34	20	5	9	58	37	45
Newquay	34	20	5	9	87	45	43
Elmore	34	18	7	9	76	51	43
Wadebridge Town	34	17	8	9	77	45	42
Plymouth Command	34	16	4	14	59	48	36
Penzance	34	12	11	11	56	43	35
Torpoint Athletic	34	13	9	12	51	55	35
Illogan RBL	34	11	9	14	59	68	30
Louis International	34	11	8	15	45	59	30
Plymouth Argyle "A"	34	11	7	16	40	54	29
Bugle	34	11	6	17	49	66	28
St. Blazey	34	8	6	20	48	86	22
Porthleven	34	5	6	23	28	75	16
St. Luke's College Reserves	34	4	7	23	35	77	15
St. Austell	34	4	3	27	43	113	11

Newquay had 2 points deducted for fielding ineligible players.
Illogan RBL had 1 point deducted for fielding ineligible players.
Porthleven left to join the Cornwall Combination and St. Luke's College Reserves also left the League. Newton Abbot Dynamoes joined from the South Devon League so the League was reduced to 17 clubs.

1977-78

Newquay	32	24	5	3	88	33	53
Liskeard Athletic	32	19	9	4	73	32	47
Wadebridge Town	32	20	6	6	79	40	46
Torpoint Athletic	32	17	7	8	59	40	41
Bodmin Town	32	17	5	10	67	43	39
St. Blazey	32	14	5	13	62	67	33
St. Austell	32	13	6	13	64	44	32
Elmore	32	10	12	10	53	53	32
Illogan RBL	32	12	7	13	59	72	31
Bugle	32	13	5	14	47	64	31
Holsworthy	32	10	10	12	50	49	30
Penzance	32	13	4	15	56	62	30
Louis International	32	12	5	15	50	59	29
Tavistock	32	8	5	19	38	68	21
Plymouth Command	32	6	5	21	48	78	17
Newton Abbot Dynamoes	32	5	6	21	34	61	16
Plymouth Argyle "A"	32	6	4	22	33	95	16

Elmore left to join the Western League and Plymouth Argyle "A" also left. Torrington joined from the Devon & Exeter League and Plymouth Civil Service, Appledore and Truro City also joined. League increased to 19 clubs.

1978-79

Liskeard Athletic	36	26	5	5	98	42	57
Wadebridge Town	36	23	7	6	91	36	53
Newquay	36	22	9	5	74	33	53
Plymouth Civil Service	36	20	7	9	71	45	47
St. Blazey	36	17	7	12	60	49	41
Torpoint Athletic	36	16	9	11	73	69	41
Louis International	36	15	10	11	57	52	40
Truro City	36	15	9	12	69	57	39
Holsworthy	36	15	8	13	66	59	38
St. Austell	36	15	7	14	57	59	37
Tavistock	36	11	11	14	61	64	33
Penzance	36	11	10	15	63	65	32
Bugle	36	11	7	18	43	71	29
Appledore	36	10	8	18	47	58	28
Bodmin Town	36	9	7	20	43	81	25
Illogan RBL	36	6	12	18	58	88	24
Torrington	36	8	9	19	50	80	23
Newton Abbot Dynamoes	36	8	6	22	33	59	22
Plymouth Command	36	6	8	22	34	82	20
						1148	1149

Torrington had 2 points deducted.
Liskeard Athletic leftto join the Western League and were replaced by
Launceston.

1979-80

Newquay	36	24	9	3	110	34	57
Wadebridge Town	36	23	10	3	95	29	56
Penzance	36	21	7	8	80	47	49
Plymouth Civil Service	36	19	8	9	83	43	46
St. Blazey	36	19	6	11	77	65	44
Tavistock	36	15	12	9	60	47	42
Appledore	36	16	9	11	56	41	41
Louis International	36	15	11	10	57	55	41
Newton Abbot Dynamoes	36	13	12	11	54	48	38
Torpoint Athletic	36	15	8	13	69	73	38
St. Austell	36	14	8	14	55	63	36
Truro City	36	14	6	16	65	59	34
Launceston	36	13	4	19	57	71	30
Holsworthy	36	10	8	18	43	60	28
Torrington	36	8	11	17	50	67	27
Bodmin Town	36	10	5	21	57	82	25
Plymouth Command	36	6	6	24	37	81	18
Illogan RBL	37	7	4	25	40	106	18
Bugle	36	5	6	25	30	104	16

Louis International left the League but Millbrook and Plymouth Argyle "A"
joined. The League was increased to 20 clubs.

1980-81

St. Blazey	38	26	8	4	71	24	60
Torrington	38	23	7	8	74	43	53
Newquay	38	20	10	8	67	38	50
Wadebridge Town	38	21	8	9	73	44	50
Plymouth Civil Service	38	17	12	9	69	44	46
Appledore	38	16	11	11	63	45	43
Torpoint Athletic	38	17	7	14	64	63	41
Penzance	38	16	7	15	77	62	39
Holsworthy	38	12	14	12	49	49	38
Millbrook	38	12	13	13	56	54	37
Bugle	38	14	9	15	58	58	37
Plymouth Argyle "A"	38	16	4	18	68	63	36
Truro City	38	14	9	15	55	68	36
Newton Abbot Dynamoes	38	13	8	17	42	53	34
Launceston	38	12	7	19	60	65	31
Tavistock	38	10	10	18	40	63	30
Plymouth Command	38	11	8	19	60	79	28
St. Austell	38	7	10	21	49	90	24
Bodmin Town	38	6	10	22	41	77	22
Illogan RBL	38	6	10	22	36	90	22

Plymouth Command had 2 points deducted.
Truro City had 1 point deducted.
Illogan RBL left and were replaced by Clyst Rovers who moved from Sunday
football. Newton Abbot Dynamoes changed their name to Newton Abbot.

1981-82

Newquay	36	24	5	7	89	43	53
Millbrook	36	23	6	7	75	38	52
Torpoint Athletic	36	22	7	7	106	66	51
St. Blazey	36	23	4	9	81	44	50
Torrington	36	21	6	9	74	38	48
Wadebridge Town	36	18	10	8	77	39	46
Plymouth Civil Service	36	21	3	12	53	40	45
Penzance	36	19	5	12	63	48	43
Bugle	36	14	10	12	78	70	38
Launceston	36	14	8	14	75	65	36
St. Austell	36	10	10	16	47	70	30
Plymouth Argyle "A"	36	12	5	19	69	76	29
Tavistock	36	10	9	17	51	72	29
Newton Abbot	36	10	8	18	38	51	28
Appledore	36	10	8	18	49	72	28
Clyst Rovers	36	7	10	19	41	78	24
Bodmin Town	36	8	7	21	54	85	23
Truro City	36	5	7	24	40	89	17
Holsworthy	36	1	12	23	32	108	14

Plymouth Command withdrew from the League on 6th April 1982 due to
the Falkland Islands crisis and their results were deleted from the table.
They rejoined for the 1982-83 season. Plymouth Argyle "A" left and were
replaced by Teignmouth from the South Devon League.

1982-83

St. Blazey	38	28	6	4	114	33	62
Torrington	38	24	5	9	105	53	53
Wadebridge Town	38	21	9	8	85	41	51
Millbrook	38	21	7	10	87	49	49
Bugle	38	22	5	11	77	53	49
Launceston	38	19	8	11	69	37	46
Newton Abbot	38	15	13	10	69	58	43
Plymouth Civil Service	38	17	9	12	65	56	43
Teignmouth	38	18	5	15	93	69	41
St. Austell	38	15	11	12	63	55	41
Penzance	38	18	5	15	62	65	41
Torpoint Athletic	38	15	8	15	69	72	38
Newquay	38	15	8	15	61	64	38
Appledore	38	14	8	16	66	76	36
Bodmin Town	38	8	10	20	56	97	26
Tavistock	38	8	10	20	43	86	26
Holsworthy	38	7	11	20	43	80	25
Plymouth Command	38	6	9	23	53	112	21
Clyst Rovers	38	6	8	24	56	106	20
Truro City	38	3	5	30	36	110	11

**Goal difference replaced goal average to decide
places for teams with equal points from the next
season.**

1983-84

Newquay	38	26	8	4	87	26	60
Launceston	38	24	6	8	99	54	54
Millbrook	38	22	8	8	79	37	52
Bugle	38	24	9	5	68	33	52
St. Austell	38	22	6	10	85	49	50
Newton Abbot	38	21	6	11	83	51	48
St. Blazey	38	17	13	8	88	64	47
Appledore	38	20	6	12	76	54	46
Wadebridge Town	38	18	8	12	74	56	44
Torpoint Athletic	38	16	10	12	66	65	42
Plymouth Civil Service	38	17	5	16	78	58	39
Torrington	38	13	9	16	57	56	35
Truro City	38	14	9	15	63	75	34
Tavistock	38	13	4	21	52	69	30
Holsworthy	38	11	6	21	51	65	28
Clyst Rovers	38	10	8	20	61	77	28
Teignmouth	38	9	7	22	50	89	25
Penzance	38	5	7	26	43	94	17
Plymouth Command	38	3	5	30	40	130	11
Bodmin Town	38	3	4	31	45	145	10
						1345	1347

Bugle had 5 points deducted. Truro City had 3 points deducted.
Torrington left to join the Western League and Plymouth Command also
left the League.
Falmouth Town joined from the Cornwall Combination.
The League was reduced to 19 clubs.

1985-86

Falmouth Town	38	27	6	5	113	42	60
Newquay	38	24	7	7	94	55	55
Millbrook	38	23	7	8	88	41	53
Bodmin Town	38	25	3	10	84	44	53
Bugle	38	19	11	8	71	40	49
Truro City	38	21	5	12	85	64	47
Wadebridge Town	38	19	7	12	77	47	45
St. Austell	38	19	7	12	74	63	45
St. Blazey	38	14	13	11	77	47	41
Newton Abbot	38	14	13	11	58	54	41
Clyst Rovers	38	14	8	16	74	89	36
Torpoint Athletic	38	12	11	15	71	93	35
Torquay United Reserves	38	12	7	19	69	80	31
Appledore-Bideford AAC	38	11	8	19	52	71	30
Penryn Athletic	38	11	6	21	66	97	28
Tavistock	38	12	3	23	54	91	27
Penzance	38	8	9	21	51	96	25
Teignmouth	38	9	6	23	46	67	24
Launceston	38	7	10	21	49	85	24
Holsworthy	38	4	3	31	41	128	11

Penryn Athletic left to join the Cornwall Combination.
The League was reduced to 19 clubs.

1984-85

Bugle	36	28	4	4	102	32	60
St. Blazey	36	23	9	4	91	36	55
Newquay	36	20	10	6	86	38	50
Wadebridge Town	36	20	8	8	65	37	48
Millbrook	36	19	8	9	63	36	46
Falmouth Town	36	17	8	11	91	59	42
Appledore	36	18	6	12	63	43	42
Truro City	36	17	6	13	60	51	41
Torpoint Athletic	36	12	16	8	53	47	40
Newton Abbot	36	17	5	14	67	47	39
Clyst Rovers	36	12	10	14	56	65	34
Tavistock	36	13	8	15	39	70	34
Plymouth Civil Service	36	11	9	16	47	64	31
Teignmouth	36	12	5	19	58	74	29
Launceston	36	11	7	18	57	73	28
St. Austell	36	10	8	18	52	75	28
Penzance	36	6	8	22	36	75	20
Bodmin Town	36	3	3	30	33	120	9
Holsworthy	36	1	6	29	30	108	8
						1149	1150

Launceston had 1 point deducted.
Truro City had an additional point awarded.
Plymouth Civil Service left the League but Penryn Athletic joined from the
Cornwall Combination and Torquay United Reserves also joined.
Appledore changed their name to Appledore-Bideford AAC.
The League was increased to 20 clubs.

1986-87

Falmouth Town	36	28	6	2	112	26	62
St. Blazey	36	27	6	3	93	26	60
Millbrook	36	25	7	4	84	29	57
Wadebridge Town	36	19	12	5	60	34	50
Bodmin Town	36	20	9	7	75	38	47
St. Austell	36	19	7	10	73	41	45
Torquay United Reserves	36	15	10	11	62	56	40
Newquay	36	14	10	12	60	52	38
Newton Abbot	36	13	11	12	51	56	37
Clyst Rovers	36	13	8	15	56	69	34
Truro City	36	9	14	13	53	55	32
Bugle	36	9	7	20	46	88	25
Teignmouth	36	9	7	20	39	83	25
Appledore-Bideford AAC	36	10	4	22	47	62	24
Torpoint Athletic	36	8	7	21	48	80	23
Tavistock	36	6	10	20	34	64	22
Launceston	36	7	8	21	49	81	22
Holsworthy	36	7	8	21	44	97	22
Penzance	36	4	9	23	41	96	17
						1127	1133

Bodmin Town had 2 points deducted.
Oak Villa joined, increasing the League to 20 clubs.

1987-88

	P	W	D	L	F	A	Pts
Newquay	38	28	9	1	97	18	65
Falmouth Town	38	27	8	3	106	42	62
St. Blazey	38	24	8	6	94	49	56
Bodmin Town	38	21	8	9	77	46	50
Millbrook	38	20	9	9	86	57	49
St. Austell	38	18	10	10	83	49	46
Wadebridge Town	38	20	4	14	69	41	44
Truro City	38	15	12	11	51	47	42
Torquay United Reserves	38	16	8	14	62	49	40
Teignmouth	38	14	10	14	51	46	38
Newton Abbot	38	14	10	14	58	55	38
Appledore-Bideford AAC	38	14	9	15	43	55	37
Launceston	38	13	10	15	55	59	36
Torpoint Athletic	38	9	10	19	59	74	28
Penzance	38	9	7	22	49	84	25
Oak Villa	38	7	10	21	57	84	24
Holsworthy	38	8	7	23	40	103	23
Tavistock	38	8	4	26	36	92	20
Clyst Rovers	38	5	10	23	46	111	20
Bugle	38	5	7	26	49	107	17

Torquay United Reserves left to join the Capital Finance League and Teignmouth left and joined the South Devon League.
The League was reduced to 18 clubs.

1988-89

	P	W	D	L	F	A	Pts
Falmouth Town	34	24	7	3	95	27	55
St. Blazey	34	23	7	4	73	29	53
Bodmin Town	34	22	9	3	69	29	53
Newquay	34	22	8	4	68	24	52
Launceston	34	14	15	5	45	26	43
Truro City	34	16	8	10	60	51	40
Wadebridge Town	34	14	12	8	57	48	40
Torpoint Athletic	34	12	10	12	52	72	34
Tavistock	34	10	10	14	48	57	30
Millbrook	34	12	5	17	48	57	29
Oak Villa	34	10	9	15	42	61	29
St. Austell	34	8	9	17	32	52	25
Newton Abbot	34	10	5	19	41	63	25
Clyst Rovers	34	7	10	17	40	66	24
Bugle	34	7	9	18	34	50	23
Penzance	34	7	8	19	45	72	22
Holsworthy	34	5	10	19	33	66	20
Appledore-Bideford AAC	34	5	5	24	44	76	15

Oak Villa left and joined the Plymouth & District League and Newton Abbot left and joined the South Devon League. Porthleven joined from the Cornwall Combination. The League was reduced to 17 clubs.

1989-90

	P	W	D	L	F	A	Pts
Falmouth Town	32	26	2	4	99	29	54
St. Blazey	32	21	8	3	84	40	50
Bodmin Town	32	18	8	6	73	28	44
Newquay	32	17	10	5	66	32	44
Bugle	32	16	7	9	55	44	39
Millbrook	32	16	4	12	61	42	36
Launceston	32	14	7	11	55	45	35
Clyst Rovers	32	14	5	13	42	56	33
Tavistock	32	14	4	14	53	57	32
Truro City	32	11	9	12	55	52	31
Appledore-Bideford AAC	32	13	4	15	43	53	30
Wadebridge Town	32	10	9	13	49	53	29
St. Austell	32	8	6	18	39	71	22
Torpoint Athletic	32	6	7	19	35	69	19
Penzance	32	5	8	19	37	79	18
Porthleven	32	5	7	20	53	91	17
Holsworthy	32	4	3	25	27	85	11

1990-91

	P	W	D	L	F	A	Pts
Bodmin Town	32	25	5	2	87	31	55
St. Blazey	32	22	8	2	105	29	52
Falmouth Town	32	18	9	5	82	39	45
Newquay	32	20	5	7	73	40	45
St. Austell	32	17	7	8	83	46	41
Torpoint Athletic	32	16	8	8	66	37	40
Truro City	32	16	6	10	67	44	38
Bugle	32	16	6	10	57	37	38
Appledore-Bideford AAC	32	13	5	14	66	59	31
Wadebridge Town	32	10	8	14	47	52	28
Millbrook	32	12	3	17	70	79	27
Tavistock	32	8	9	15	46	67	25
Porthleven	32	11	2	19	52	72	24
Clyst Rovers	32	10	1	21	43	100	21
Launceston	32	6	6	18	46	75	20
Holsworthy	32	3	4	25	32	110	10
Penzance	32	1	2	29	31	136	4

Devon & Cornwall Police joined, increasing the league to 18 clubs.

1991-92

	P	W	D	L	F	A	Pts
Falmouth Town	34	26	5	3	91	20	57
Newquay	34	23	5	6	88	31	51
Bugle	34	16	9	9	65	46	41
Truro City	34	14	11	9	74	49	39
Bodmin Town	34	15	9	10	53	51	39
Clyst Rovers	34	15	8	11	59	60	38
Appledore-Bideford AAC	34	16	5	13	78	56	37
Porthleven	34	14	8	12	77	69	36
St. Blazey	34	15	6	13	72	67	36
Torpoint Athletic	34	14	7	13	49	50	35
Holsworthy	34	9	16	9	37	46	34
Wadebridge Town	34	12	7	15	45	52	31
St. Austell	34	10	8	16	45	63	28
Millbrook	34	9	9	16	45	70	27
Launceston	34	8	6	20	45	73	22
Devon & Cornwall Police	34	7	8	19	43	78	22
Tavistock	34	8	5	21	53	79	21
Penzance	34	7	4	23	35	94	18

Bugle left and joined the ECPL and Clyst Rovers left and joined the Western League. Mullion joined from the Cornwall Combination.
The League was reduced to 17 clubs.

1992-93

	P	W	D	L	F	A	Pts
Truro City	32	23	3	6	72	28	49
Bodmin Town	32	20	6	6	84	46	46
Newquay	32	20	5	7	75	39	45
Launceston	32	17	10	5	81	41	44
St. Blazey	32	14	9	9	71	65	37
Falmouth Town	32	15	6	11	77	51	36
Holsworthy	32	12	8	12	49	54	32
Tavistock	32	11	7	14	53	77	29
Mullion	32	9	10	13	51	61	28
Appledore-Bideford AAC	32	10	8	14	56	73	28
Penzance	32	10	6	16	65	69	26
Devon & Cornwall Police	32	12	5	15	61	69	26
Porthleven	32	9	7	16	69	82	25
Wadebridge Town	32	8	9	15	49	87	25
Millbrook	32	8	8	16	50	69	24
Torpoint Athletic	32	8	7	17	44	68	23
St. Austell	32	7	4	21	61	89	18

Devon & Cornwall Police had 3 points deducted.
Okehampton Argyle joined from the Devon & Exeter League.
The League was increased to 18 clubs.

Three points were awarded for a win from the next season onwards.

1993-94

Bodmin Town	34	26	2	6	103	27	80
Newquay	34	24	8	2	92	33	80
Truro City	34	25	4	5	98	31	79
Falmouth Town	34	20	10	4	75	43	70
Launceston	34	19	7	8	86	43	64
Porthleven	34	16	6	12	71	66	54
Torpoint Athletic	34	14	10	10	67	59	52
St. Austell	34	14	6	14	71	57	48
Holsworthy	34	13	9	12	44	50	48
Tavistock	34	13	7	14	70	69	46
St. Blazey	34	12	9	13	76	59	45
Mullion	34	11	6	17	56	77	39
Devon & Cornwall Police	34	8	10	16	54	70	34
Appledore-Bideford AAC	34	8	8	18	44	75	32
Millbrook	34	6	7	21	48	86	25
Wadebridge Town	34	6	5	23	34	94	23
Penzance	34	5	6	23	54	107	21
Okehampton Argyle	34	3	6	25	19	116	15

1994-95

Launceston	34	26	6	2	115	24	84
Bodmin Town	34	25	4	5	89	36	79
Truro City	34	23	4	7	93	45	73
Falmouth Town	34	22	5	7	106	45	71
Torpoint Athletic	34	21	5	8	78	40	68
Porthleven	34	16	9	9	84	54	57
Millbrook	34	14	11	9	68	58	53
Holsworthy	34	14	9	11	44	44	51
Wadebridge Town	34	14	7	13	66	75	49
Tavistock	34	12	8	14	46	71	43
Appledore-Bideford AAC	34	10	4	20	55	79	34
Mullion	34	8	10	16	46	77	34
Newquay	34	9	6	19	66	86	33
St. Blazey	34	9	6	19	56	74	33
Okehampton Argyle	34	8	4	22	49	100	28
Devon & Cornwall Police	34	8	3	23	52	95	27
Penzance	34	6	7	21	35	79	25
St. Austell	34	4	6	24	31	97	18

Tavistock had 1 point deducted. Mullion left to join the Cornwall Combination and Devon & Cornwall Police also left. They were replaced by Liskeard Athletic and Saltash United, both from the Western League.

1995-96

Truro City	34	26	4	4	99	27	82
Torpoint Athletic	34	23	8	3	81	32	77
Falmouth Town	34	22	4	8	87	37	70
Launceston	34	20	9	5	95	29	69
Bodmin Town	34	18	10	6	91	36	64
Penzance	34	18	5	11	64	43	59
Newquay	34	18	4	12	73	54	58
Holsworthy	34	17	5	12	58	43	56
Wadebridge Town	34	16	5	13	65	55	53
Saltash United	34	14	8	12	66	67	50
Porthleven	34	13	5	16	61	66	44
St. Austell	34	10	5	19	57	79	35
Millbrook	34	9	7	18	40	59	34
Liskeard Athletic	34	9	6	19	58	96	33
Appledore-Bideford AAC	34	7	7	20	43	80	28
Tavistock	34	6	6	22	55	99	24
St. Blazey	34	4	4	26	38	106	16
Okehampton Argyle	34	4	2	28	24	143	14
					1155	1151	

Okehampton Argyle left to join the Devon & Exeter League and Appledore-Bideford AAC left to join the Devon County League. The League was reduced to 16 clubs.

1996-97

Falmouth Town	30	24	0	6	90	27	72
Truro City	30	22	6	2	68	25	72
Porthleven	30	20	6	4	70	28	66
Bodmin Town	30	16	6	8	60	34	54
Saltash United	30	15	8	7	63	42	53
Penzance	30	14	7	9	62	37	49
Liskeard Athletic	30	13	7	10	39	31	46
Torpoint Athletic	30	11	9	10	52	49	42
Tavistock	30	11	4	15	48	71	37
Newquay	30	10	6	14	44	63	36
Holsworthy	30	8	8	14	28	43	32
St. Blazey	30	9	5	16	51	70	32
St. Austell	30	8	4	18	38	59	28
Millbrook	30	5	7	18	32	70	22
Wadebridge Town	30	4	6	20	21	49	18
Launceston	30	4	3	23	26	94	15

1997-98

Truro City	30	23	3	4	76	15	72
Falmouth Town	30	22	5	3	76	33	71
Porthleven	30	20	6	4	88	24	66
St. Blazey	30	16	3	11	60	39	51
Torpoint Athletic	30	15	4	11	71	56	49
Millbrook	30	14	7	9	52	42	49
Bodmin Town	30	15	4	11	51	48	49
Penzance	30	13	8	9	54	46	47
Saltash United	30	14	3	13	63	60	45
Holsworthy	30	13	5	12	61	67	44
Wadebridge Town	30	11	2	17	40	53	35
Liskeard Athletic	30	7	6	17	45	64	27
Newquay	30	8	3	19	37	73	27
St. Austell	30	5	8	17	33	82	23
Tavistock	30	3	6	21	38	87	15
Launceston	30	3	3	24	27	83	12

Plymouth Parkway joined from the Devon County League. The League was increased to 17 clubs.

1998-99

St. Blazey	32	23	5	4	69	25	74
Porthleven	32	22	7	3	102	36	73
Truro City	32	18	8	6	65	37	62
Falmouth Town	32	17	8	7	57	35	59
Wadebridge Town	32	17	6	9	64	34	57
Millbrook	32	17	5	10	55	32	56
Saltash United	32	15	7	10	56	45	52
Bodmin Town	32	15	5	12	65	57	50
Penzance	32	12	7	13	58	62	43
Holsworthy	32	11	8	13	50	56	41
Plymouth Parkway	32	10	6	16	50	74	36
Liskeard Athletic	32	8	9	15	47	62	33
Tavistock	32	8	8	16	32	47	32
Newquay	32	10	2	20	40	64	32
St. Austell	32	7	5	20	29	67	26
Torpoint Athletic	32	5	5	22	39	73	20
Launceston	32	4	5	23	33	105	17

Callington Town joined from the ECPL. The League was increased to 18 clubs.

1999-2000

	P	W	D	L	F	A	Pts
Falmouth Town	34	24	8	2	88	25	80
St. Blazey	34	25	5	4	97	36	80
Porthleven	34	23	9	2	91	41	78
Liskeard Athletic	34	18	7	9	80	40	61
Millbrook	34	17	9	8	68	47	60
Saltash United	34	18	3	13	61	50	57
Wadebridge Town	34	17	4	13	66	59	55
Tavistock	34	14	9	11	51	46	51
Plymouth Parkway	34	15	6	13	57	73	51
Newquay	34	14	5	15	67	76	47
Bodmin Town	34	14	4	16	60	64	46
Truro City	34	10	5	19	55	71	35
Penzance	34	10	4	20	51	76	34
Torpoint Athletic	34	9	6	19	53	74	33
Holsworthy	34	7	10	17	51	63	31
Callington Town	34	7	6	21	41	85	27
Launceston	34	5	5	24	35	95	20
St. Austell	34	4	5	25	31	82	17

Penryn Athletic joined from the Cornwall Combination.
The League was increased to 19 clubs.

2000-01

	P	W	D	L	F	A	Pts
St. Blazey	36	27	6	3	124	33	87
Porthleven	36	25	8	3	90	26	83
Liskeard Athletic	36	24	7	5	97	55	79
Holsworthy	36	24	3	9	84	44	75
Millbrook	36	22	6	8	94	45	72
Saltash United	36	21	8	7	85	43	71
Falmouth Town	36	18	10	8	72	46	64
Penzance	36	16	9	11	65	59	57
Tavistock	36	14	8	14	50	52	50
Torpoint Athletic	36	14	7	15	56	60	49
Plymouth Parkway	36	12	4	20	53	77	40
Callington Town	36	11	6	19	63	93	39
Newquay	36	10	8	18	58	81	38
Truro City	36	11	4	21	58	81	37
Penryn Athletic	36	10	5	21	49	80	35
St. Austell	36	7	6	23	41	76	27
Launceston	36	8	3	25	39	92	27
Wadebridge Town	36	6	4	26	51	115	22
Bodmin Town	36	5	2	29	39	110	17

2001-02

	P	W	D	L	F	A	Pts
St. Blazey	36	33	3	0	120	25	102
Porthleven	36	27	4	5	105	32	85
Liskeard Athletic	36	25	4	7	121	53	79
Holsworthy	36	24	5	7	94	47	77
Plymouth Parkway	36	21	6	9	88	50	69
Penzance	36	16	8	12	79	62	56
Falmouth Town	36	16	6	14	82	86	54
Tavistock	36	15	7	14	61	53	52
Saltash United	36	15	5	16	62	76	50
Newquay	36	14	7	15	76	68	49
Bodmin Town	36	13	9	14	66	81	48
Torpoint Athletic	36	13	6	17	67	74	45
Wadebridge Town	36	13	6	17	58	70	45
Launceston	36	12	2	22	65	91	38
Millbrook	36	8	7	21	44	93	31
Callington Town	36	8	5	23	57	112	29
Truro City	36	6	10	20	57	82	28
Penryn Athletic	36	8	3	25	42	84	27
St. Austell	36	2	3	31	20	125	9

2002-03

	P	W	D	L	F	A	Pts
St. Blazey	36	30	5	1	126	23	95
Tavistock	36	24	5	7	87	41	77
Porthleven	36	23	5	8	95	48	74
Plymouth Parkway	36	23	4	9	83	55	73
Liskeard Athletic	36	21	4	11	95	59	67
Wadebridge Town	36	17	9	10	61	46	60
Launceston	36	18	6	12	79	78	60
Holsworthy	36	17	7	12	59	48	58
Saltash United	36	17	3	16	79	68	54
Falmouth Town	36	16	5	15	60	61	53
Newquay	36	13	4	19	64	77	43
Penzance	36	12	5	19	53	55	41
Torpoint Athletic	36	11	8	17	48	69	41
Millbrook	36	12	4	20	56	80	40
Callington Town	36	11	6	19	64	80	39
Truro City	36	9	6	21	44	74	33
Penryn Athletic	36	7	7	22	51	84	28
St. Austell	36	7	6	23	45	108	27
Bodmin Town	36	3	3	30	30	125	12

Holsworthy left and joined the Devon County League.
The League was reduced to 18 clubs.

2003-04

	P	W	D	L	F	A	Pts
St. Blazey	34	27	5	2	90	26	86
Bodmin Town	34	26	4	4	88	29	82
Porthleven	34	19	5	10	68	46	62
Millbrook	34	14	14	6	75	42	56
Saltash United	34	16	8	10	62	58	56
St. Austell	34	16	6	12	58	45	54
Wadebridge Town	34	14	11	9	57	39	53
Penzance	34	14	8	12	50	46	50
Plymouth Parkway	34	12	9	13	51	60	45
Tavistock	34	12	7	15	52	71	43
Launceston	34	11	8	15	52	67	41
Liskeard Athletic	34	11	6	17	43	50	39
Falmouth Town	34	11	5	18	52	72	38
Torpoint Athletic	34	10	6	18	53	72	36
Truro City	34	7	10	17	47	69	31
Penryn Athletic	34	9	4	21	67	90	31
Newquay	34	7	5	22	41	81	26
Callington Town	34	7	5	22	50	93	26

Saltash United left and joined the Western League.
The League was reduced to 17 clubs.

2004-05

	P	W	D	L	F	A	Pts
St. Blazey	32	26	3	3	109	25	81
Bodmin Town	32	24	2	6	102	23	74
Millbrook	32	21	7	4	77	39	70
Falmouth Town	32	20	6	6	76	30	66
Liskeard Athletic	32	20	6	6	80	39	66
Truro City	32	17	4	11	66	49	55
Wadebridge Town	32	15	8	9	56	44	53
Plymouth Parkway	32	14	6	12	50	46	48
St. Austell	32	14	3	15	69	73	45
Launceston	32	12	6	14	59	62	42
Newquay	32	10	6	16	48	64	36
Torpoint Athletic	32	9	5	18	47	81	32
Penryn Athletic	32	8	6	18	45	85	30
Penzance	32	6	8	18	48	78	26
Tavistock	32	4	8	20	48	88	20
Callington Town	32	5	2	25	37	120	17
Porthleven	32	3	2	27	30	108	11

Goonhavern Athletic joined from the Cornwall Combination.
The League was increased to 18 clubs.

2005-06

Bodmin Town	34	25	6	3	89	31	81
Truro City	34	22	7	5	78	29	70
Falmouth Town	34	22	5	7	88	42	70
Liskeard Athletic	34	20	9	5	93	34	69
St. Blazey	34	19	12	3	92	44	69
Penryn Athletic	34	21	3	10	98	47	66
Plymouth Parkway	34	19	8	7	78	54	65
Wadebridge Town	34	17	5	12	47	46	56
Tavistock	34	15	6	13	67	59	51
Porthleven	34	12	5	17	50	62	41
Launceston	34	11	7	16	51	66	40
Millbrook	34	10	9	15	37	54	39
Penzance	34	10	4	20	52	74	34
Newquay	34	7	9	18	44	76	30
Goonhavern Athletic	34	6	6	22	31	80	24
Callington Town	34	5	3	26	31	88	18
Torpoint Athletic	34	4	6	24	23	85	18
St. Austell	34	5	2	27	39	117	17

Truro City had 3 points deducted. Falmouth Town had 1 point deducted. Truro City left and joined the Western League. Saltash United joined from the Western League and Plymouth Argyle "A" joined as a newly formed team. League increased to 19 clubs.

2006-07

St. Blazey	36	25	7	4	94	37	82
Liskeard Athletic	36	25	7	4	88	34	82
Saltash United	36	25	6	5	88	30	81
Bodmin Town	36	24	7	5	82	21	79
Plymouth Argyle "A"	36	22	8	6	91	34	74
Plymouth Parkway	36	17	7	12	81	63	58
Tavistock	36	16	8	12	75	57	56
Launceston	36	16	7	13	82	48	55
Porthleven	36	16	7	13	61	64	55
Falmouth Town	36	14	7	15	63	55	49
Torpoint Athletic	36	13	6	17	52	63	45
Newquay	36	13	4	19	65	82	43
Penryn Athletic	36	12	6	18	66	74	42
Callington Town	36	10	9	17	54	60	39
Wadebridge Town	36	8	9	19	47	63	33
Penzance	36	6	10	20	47	84	28
Millbrook	36	7	5	24	41	101	26
St. Austell	36	5	5	26	34	116	20
Goonhavern Athletic	36	4	3	29	29	154	15

At the end of the season, the South-Western League merged with the Devon County League to form the South West Peninsula League. St. Blazey, Liskeard Athletic, Saltash United, Bodmin Town, Plymouth Parkway, Tavistock, Launceston, Falmouth Town and Torpoint Athletic joined the new league's Premier Division while Porthleven, Newquay, Penryn Athletic, Callington Town, Wadebridge Town, Penzance, Millbrook, St. Austell and Goonhavern Athletic joined the new league's Division One (West). Plymouth Argyle "A" did not join the new league.

DEVON COUNTY LEAGUE

Formation

The Devon County League was formed in 1992 to cover the whole of Devon and provide a logical step between the various local leagues and the Western League.

Its 16 founder members were drawn from three different leagues:

Devon & Exeter League, Premier Division (5) – Alphington, Cullompton Rangers, Newton St. Cyres, Topsham Town and Willand Rovers.

South Devon League, Premier Division (4) – Buckfastleigh Rangers, Northern Telecomm (Paignton), Stoke Gabriel and Teignmouth

South Devon League, First Division (2) – Chagford and Newton Abbot

Plymouth & District League, Premier Division (4) – Elburton Villa, Ivybridge Town, Plymstock United and Weston Mill Oak Villa

Plymouth & District League, First Division (1) – E.A.F. Plymouth

A few of the published tables contained errors. Additional research has succeeded in correcting all but one of these, the totals that still do not balance are shown below the relevant columns in italics.

1992-93

Buckfastleigh Rangers	30	25	4	1	86	21	79
Newton Abbot	30	21	5	4	91	31	68
Northern Telecomm (Paignton)	30	20	5	5	81	38	65
Weston Mill Oak Villa	30	16	6	8	57	46	54
Newton St. Cyres	30	15	7	8	61	44	52
Stoke Gabriel	30	15	7	8	62	47	52
Alphington	30	13	8	9	50	37	47
Elburton Villa	30	12	6	12	62	49	42
Willand Rovers	30	11	5	14	67	70	38
Teignmouth	30	9	8	13	52	60	35
Plymstock United	30	10	5	15	47	61	35
Chagford	30	8	4	18	38	82	28
Cullompton Rangers	30	7	4	19	33	64	25
Topsham Town	30	6	6	18	46	75	24
Ivybridge Town	30	3	6	21	34	84	15
EAF Plymouth	30	3	6	21	36	94	15

EAF Plymouth changed their name to Plymouth Parkway.

1993-94

Newton Abbot	30	23	3	4	122	28	72
Stoke Gabriel	30	19	6	5	85	37	63
Plymouth Parkway	30	19	4	7	71	44	61
Weston Mill Oak Villa	30	16	7	7	71	38	55
Willand Rovers	30	16	6	8	70	58	54
Northern Telecom (Paignton)	30	16	4	10	81	54	52
Buckfastleigh Rangers	30	17	1	12	59	50	52
Plymstock United	30	14	4	12	52	51	46
Alphington	30	11	8	11	65	61	41
Elburton Villa	30	12	3	15	54	55	39
Teignmouth	30	9	4	17	46	79	31
Cullompton Rangers	30	7	7	16	49	68	28
Newton St. Cyres	30	7	5	18	38	86	26
Ivybridge Town	30	7	5	18	39	95	26
Chagford	30	6	5	19	52	70	23
Topsham Town	30	3	4	23	23	95	13
					977	*969*	

Ottery St. Mary joined from the Western League.

1994-95

Stoke Gabriel	32	27	2	3	116	18	83
Alphington	32	23	3	6	77	35	72
Northern Telecom (Paignton)	32	17	3	12	66	57	54
Plymouth Parkway	32	15	8	9	74	54	53
Willand Rovers	32	15	7	10	72	58	52
Plymstock United	32	15	7	10	76	52	52
Weston Mill Oak Villa	32	15	7	10	74	56	52
Topsham Town	32	12	8	12	72	65	44
Cullompton Rangers	32	12	7	13	60	54	43
Chagford	32	13	6	13	53	53	42
Newton Abbot	32	10	7	15	62	69	37
Ottery St. Mary	32	10	9	13	62	81	35
Buckfastleigh Rangers	32	8	6	18	58	106	30
Teignmouth	32	9	2	21	54	89	29
Newton St. Cyres	32	6	10	16	41	82	28
Elburton Villa	32	7	7	18	45	87	25
Ivybridge Town	32	5	7	20	55	101	22

Chagford and Elburton Villa each had 3 points deducted.
Ottery St. Mary had 4 points deducted.
Northern Telecom (Paignton) disbanded. Budleigh Salterton joined from the Devon & Exeter League, Dartmouth United joined from the South Devon League and Plymouth Command joined from the Plymouth & District League.

1995-96

Budleigh Salterton	36	21	10	5	96	41	73
Stoke Gabriel	36	22	7	7	91	36	73
Willand Rovers	36	22	6	8	73	41	72
Dartmouth United	36	22	6	8	80	52	72
Alphington	36	19	6	11	85	46	63
Topsham Town	36	17	9	10	86	60	60
Teignmouth	36	19	3	14	93	67	60
Newton Abbot	36	16	8	12	66	55	56
Plymouth Command	36	16	6	14	68	58	54
Buckfastleigh Rangers	36	12	11	13	62	66	47
Cullompton Rangers	36	13	7	16	46	57	46
Elburton Villa	36	13	7	16	56	81	46
Plymouth Parkway	36	11	12	13	72	77	45
Plymstock United	36	12	8	16	54	63	44
Newton St. Cyres	36	9	7	20	51	89	34
Ivybridge Town	36	10	4	22	55	95	34
Weston Mill Oak Villa	36	9	6	21	57	92	33
Ottery St. Mary	36	8	6	22	43	111	30
Chagford	36	4	5	27	48	95	17

Chagford moved to the South Devon League. Appledore & Bideford AAC joined from the South-Western League and Newton Abbot Spurs joined from the South Devon League.

1996-97

Stoke Gabriel	38	25	10	3	95	39	85
Dartmouth United	38	24	6	8	88	45	78
Willand Rovers	38	22	7	9	101	52	73
Topsham Town	38	21	9	8	87	51	72
Budleigh Salterton	38	22	4	12	82	47	70
Appledore & Bideford AAC	38	21	5	12	116	49	68
Cullompton Rangers	38	22	2	14	77	60	68
Buckfastleigh Rangers	38	18	7	13	79	61	61
Newton Abbot	38	16	12	10	77	62	60
Plymouth Parkway	38	18	4	16	88	58	58
Plymouth Command	38	17	6	15	78	62	57
Ottery St. Mary	38	15	9	14	88	78	54
Alphington	38	15	8	15	62	80	50
Newton Abbot Spurs	38	14	6	18	87	71	48
Weston Mill Oak Villa	38	12	6	20	76	87	42
Elburton Villa	38	10	7	21	59	81	37
Newton St. Cyres	38	9	6	23	54	99	33
Plymstock United	38	7	5	26	51	129	25
Ivybridge Town	38	8	1	29	52	152	25
Teignmouth	38	4	0	34	40	174	3

Alphington had 3 points deducted. Teignmouth had 9 points deducted.

1997-98

Topsham Town	38	27	4	7	97	30	85
Cullompton Rangers	38	25	7	6	95	35	82
Newton Abbot	38	25	6	7	84	40	81
Willand Rovers	38	22	9	7	88	32	75
Stoke Gabriel	38	20	9	9	85	41	69
Appledore & Bideford AAC	38	20	6	12	94	71	66
Plymouth Command	38	19	9	10	97	77	66
Budleigh Salterton	38	19	7	12	84	66	64
Dartmouth United	38	18	9	11	82	54	63
Plymouth Parkway	38	17	11	10	87	57	62
Ottery St. Mary	38	18	6	14	72	61	60
Newton St. Cyres	38	13	7	18	63	79	46
Alphington	38	10	11	17	56	79	41
Buckfastleigh Rangers	38	11	7	20	56	85	40
Newton Abbot Spurs	38	10	7	21	63	81	37
Teignmouth	38	11	1	26	59	122	31
Elburton Villa	38	8	6	24	45	86	30
Weston Mill Oak Villa	38	9	3	26	51	98	30
Plymstock United	38	7	4	27	57	114	25
Ivybridge Town	38	6	1	31	50	157	16

Teignmouth and Ivybridge Town each had 3 points deducted.
Weston Mill Oak Villa changed their name to Vospers Oak Villa. Appledore & Bideford AAC changed their name to Appledore. Plymouth Parkway moved to the South-Western League. Crediton United joined from the Western League.

1998-99

Willand Rovers	38	28	6	4	101	33	90
Cullompton Rangers	38	26	7	5	84	40	85
Budleigh Salterton	38	25	7	6	115	47	82
Vospers Oak Villa	38	21	8	9	107	55	71
Ottery St. Mary	38	20	6	12	71	50	66
Appledore	38	18	10	10	90	57	64
Stoke Gabriel	38	16	13	9	84	62	61
Dartmouth United	38	18	7	13	75	66	61
Newton Abbot Spurs	38	17	7	14	67	70	58
Buckfastleigh Rangers	38	17	6	15	97	61	57
Crediton United	38	18	3	17	67	64	57
Topsham Town	38	14	10	14	82	66	52
Newton Abbot	38	13	12	13	57	52	51
Newton St. Cyres	38	14	8	16	62	66	50
Ivybridge Town	38	14	3	21	79	93	45
Alphington	38	10	6	22	61	100	36
Plymstock United	38	6	10	22	41	80	28
Elburton Villa	38	7	5	26	48	98	26
Plymouth Command	38	6	5	27	44	109	23
Teignmouth	38	2	1	35	40	203	7

Dartmouth United merged with Dartmouth Y.M.R.C. to form Dartmouth. Plymouth Command moved to the Plymouth & District League and Teignmouth moved to the South Devon League. Exeter Civil Service joined from the Devon & Exeter League and Heavitree United joined from the Western League.

1999-2000

Budleigh Salterton	38	25	6	7	102	51	81
Stoke Gabriel	38	26	2	10	92	48	80
Newton Abbot Spurs	38	23	8	7	84	45	77
Alphington	38	23	4	11	82	62	73
Vospers Oak Villa	38	23	3	12	117	70	72
Ivybridge Town	38	22	6	10	99	56	72
Willand Rovers	38	20	8	10	83	44	65
Dartmouth	38	20	5	13	95	58	65
Ottery St. Mary	38	17	13	8	80	55	64
Cullompton Rangers	38	18	4	16	95	74	58
Newton Abbot	38	17	5	16	81	71	56
Exeter Civil Service	38	15	10	13	77	76	55
Appledore	38	13	12	13	63	71	51
Plymstock United	38	12	6	20	52	69	42
Buckfastleigh Rangers	38	10	6	22	43	75	36
Topsham Town	38	9	4	25	53	89	31
Crediton United	38	7	6	25	53	117	27
Heavitree United	38	7	6	25	50	118	27
Elburton Villa	38	5	7	26	58	139	27
Newton St. Cyres	38	5	5	28	52	123	20

Willand Rovers had 3 points deducted.
Newton St. Cyres moved to the Devon & Exeter League and Buckland Athletic joined from the Devon & Exeter League.

2000-01

Willand Rovers	38	26	9	3	98	41	87
Buckland Athletic	38	24	5	9	107	54	77
Alphington	38	21	10	7	87	58	73
Heavitree United	38	22	5	11	97	61	71
Dartmouth	38	19	11	8	108	60	68
Vospers Oak Villa	38	20	6	12	80	61	66
Ottery St. Mary	38	20	5	13	82	57	65
Budleigh Salterton	38	19	8	11	77	60	65
Newton Abbot Spurs	38	16	12	10	89	57	60
Newton Abbot	38	17	8	13	96	58	59
Elburton Villa	38	14	8	16	59	83	50
Ivybridge Town	38	13	10	15	74	74	49
Cullompton Rangers	38	11	12	15	51	69	45
Appledore	38	12	6	20	73	87	42
Topsham Town	38	10	6	22	67	105	36
Crediton United	38	10	6	22	61	103	36
Exeter Civil Service	38	8	9	21	55	82	33
Buckfastleigh Rangers	38	9	3	26	39	118	30
Stoke Gabriel	38	7	8	23	57	93	27
Plymstock United	38	4	9	25	47	123	21

Willand Rovers moved to the Western League and Dartington Sports joined from the South Devon League.

2001-02

Dartmouth	38	28	7	3	125	45	91
Newton Abbot	38	25	8	5	107	45	83
Vospers Oak Villa	38	24	4	10	82	38	76
Ivybridge Town	38	23	6	9	109	59	75
Newton Abbot Spurs	38	23	1	14	74	63	70
Buckland Athletic	38	19	9	10	91	59	66
Budleigh Salterton	38	20	2	16	70	87	62
Topsham Town	38	18	7	13	95	72	58
Ottery St. Mary	38	16	7	15	76	52	55
Alphington	38	15	8	15	65	86	53
Heavitree United	38	16	4	18	71	76	52
Cullompton Rangers	38	14	7	17	64	67	49
Exeter Civil Service	38	13	9	16	60	72	48
Elburton Villa	38	14	6	18	64	82	48
Plymstock United	38	13	7	18	61	71	46
Dartington Sports	38	11	9	18	63	75	42
Stoke Gabriel	38	10	4	24	63	104	34
Crediton United	38	9	5	24	52	74	32
Appledore	38	8	7	23	57	84	27
Buckfastleigh Rangers	38	2	1	35	32	170	4

Topsham Town and Buckfastleigh Rangers each had 3 points deducted. Buckfastleigh Rangers moved to the South Devon League and University of Exeter joined from the Devon & Exeter League.

2002-03

Dartmouth	38	29	5	4	96	32	92
Ivybridge Town	38	26	8	4	135	55	86
Buckland Athletic	38	23	6	9	88	47	75
Vospers Oak Villa	38	21	4	13	72	57	67
Alphington	38	19	7	12	80	54	64
Newton Abbot Spurs	38	19	6	13	62	49	60
University of Exeter	38	19	3	16	85	76	60
Newton Abbot	38	16	11	11	67	57	59
Plymstock United	38	14	13	11	72	58	55
Cullompton Rangers	38	15	8	15	56	65	53
Ottery St. Mary	38	15	6	17	63	74	51
Heavitree United	38	14	6	18	71	84	48
Dartington Sports	38	13	7	18	79	70	46
Appledore	38	12	9	17	51	69	45
Elburton Villa	38	11	10	17	67	69	43
Budleigh Salterton	38	12	8	18	58	77	43
Exeter Civil Service	38	9	13	16	46	79	40
Stoke Gabriel	38	7	6	25	58	92	27
Crediton United	38	7	5	26	30	109	26
Topsham Town	38	7	3	28	29	92	24

Budleigh Salterton had 1 point deducted.
Newton Abbot Spurs had 3 points deducted.
Holsworthy joined from the South-Western League.

2003-04

Holsworthy	40	26	11	3	100	40	89
Ivybridge Town	40	25	9	6	115	49	84
Vospers Oak Villa	40	25	6	9	105	53	81
Elburton Villa	40	23	7	10	93	65	76
Dartington Sports	40	22	8	10	123	71	74
Ottery St. Mary	40	20	8	12	87	64	71
Newton Abbot	40	22	4	14	79	63	70
Buckland Athletic	40	21	6	13	86	63	69
Dartmouth	40	16	10	14	88	64	58
Crediton United	40	15	12	13	78	70	57
University of Exeter	40	17	3	20	64	63	54
Budleigh Salterton	40	13	15	12	66	69	54
Plymstock United	40	13	13	14	61	63	52
Alphington	40	12	10	18	55	73	46
Appledore	40	13	6	21	54	79	45
Cullompton Rangers	40	10	14	16	71	71	44
Stoke Gabriel	40	12	7	21	53	92	43
Newton Abbot Spurs	40	9	10	21	55	103	37
Exeter Civil Service	40	5	12	23	37	79	27
Heavitree United	40	6	5	29	50	139	23
Topsham Town	40	4	6	30	28	115	13

Ottery St. Mary had 3 points added.
Topsham Town had 5 points deducted.
Topsham Town moved to the Devon & Exeter League. Heavitree United merged with Heavitree Social Club from the Devon & Exeter League Senior Division Three and moved to the Premier Division of the Devon & Exeter League as Heavitree United Social Club. Teignmouth joined from the South Devon League and St. Loyes joined from the Devon & Exeter League.

2004-05

Teignmouth	40	30	5	5	106	44	95
Plymstock United	40	27	6	7	107	41	87
Dartmouth	40	25	6	9	90	52	81
Ivybridge Town	40	22	9	9	110	60	75
Vospers Oak Villa	40	23	4	13	95	61	72
Newton Abbot	40	20	8	12	89	52	70
Buckland Athletic	40	19	12	9	78	52	69
Dartington Sports	40	20	9	11	76	53	69
Elburton Villa	40	20	6	14	95	63	66
Budleigh Salterton	40	20	6	14	81	78	66
Newton Abbot Spurs	40	18	7	15	90	71	61
Ottery St. Mary	40	16	9	15	70	71	57
St. Loyes	40	16	5	19	65	80	53
Holsworthy	40	15	5	20	67	63	50
University of Exeter	40	13	6	21	74	85	45
Cullompton Rangers	40	11	10	19	68	89	43
Alphington	40	12	3	25	44	93	39
Appledore	40	11	3	26	59	99	36
Crediton United	40	10	5	25	52	115	35
Stoke Gabriel	40	6	0	34	49	137	18
Exeter Civil Service	40	1	6	33	27	133	6

Newton Abbot had 2 points added.
Vospers Oak Villa had 1 point deducted.
Exeter Civil Service had 3 points deducted.
Dartington Sports merged with Totnes Town of the South Devon League and continued in the Devon County League as Totnes and Dartington SC.
Exeter Civil Service moved to the Devon & Exeter League.

2005-06

Ivybridge Town	38	31	4	3	122	38	97
Plymstock United	38	23	8	7	93	41	77
Holsworthy	38	23	5	10	90	67	74
Ottery St. Mary	38	21	7	10	85	60	70
Dartmouth	38	21	7	10	79	56	70
Newton Abbot	38	20	6	12	83	49	66
Budleigh Salterton	38	20	5	13	78	59	65
Newton Abbot Spurs	38	19	7	12	75	58	64
Teignmouth	38	18	9	11	90	66	63
Totnes & Dartington SC	38	17	8	13	78	62	59
Elburton Villa	38	15	6	17	59	59	54
Crediton United	38	16	4	18	53	65	52
Buckland Athletic	38	14	6	18	63	82	48
Alphington	38	13	7	18	56	79	46
Vospers Oak Villa	38	12	7	19	68	75	43
University of Exeter	38	14	2	22	66	71	40
Cullompton Rangers	38	10	4	24	56	95	34
Appledore	38	10	2	26	45	95	32
Stoke Gabriel	38	4	6	28	42	117	18
St. Loyes	38	2	4	32	31	118	10

Elburton Villa had 3 points added.
University of Exeter had 4 points deducted.
St. Loyes moved to the Devon & Exeter League, swapping places with Witheridge.

2006-07

Dartmouth	38	27	6	5	100	36	87
Newton Abbot	38	25	6	7	85	39	81
Elburton Villa	38	25	5	8	83	48	80
Budleigh Salterton	38	24	6	8	87	47	78
Holsworthy	38	21	6	11	86	71	69
University of Exeter	38	20	7	11	83	51	67
Cullompton Rangers	38	21	3	14	91	68	66
Ivybridge Town	38	18	9	11	94	52	63
Newton Abbot Spurs	38	17	12	9	70	55	63
Ottery St. Mary	38	16	7	15	68	61	55
Witheridge	38	12	9	17	64	78	45
Buckland Athletic	38	13	5	20	57	71	44
Appledore	38	12	8	18	49	69	44
Totnes & Dartington SC	38	11	10	17	73	87	43
Crediton United	38	12	5	21	47	73	41
Plymstock United	38	11	4	23	52	78	37
Vospers Oak Villa	38	10	6	22	46	80	36
Alphington	38	10	5	23	64	76	35
Stoke Gabriel	38	8	3	27	43	99	27
Teignmouth	38	5	2	31	37	140	17

At the end of this season, the Devon County League closed down as it merged with the South-Western League to form the new South West Peninsula League.

Dartmouth, Elburton Villa, Holsworthy, Cullompton Rangers, Ivybridge Town, Newton Abbot Spurs, Witheridge and Buckland Athletic joined the new league's Premier Division while Newton Abbot, Budleigh Salterton, University of Exeter, Ottery St. Mary, Appledore, Totnes & Dartington SC, Crediton United, Plymstock United, Alphington, Stoke Gabriel and Teignmouth joined the new league's Division One (East) and Vospers Oak Villa joined Division One (West).

SOUTH WEST PENINSULA LEAGUE

The South West Peninsula League was formed in 2007 by a merger of the Devon County League and the South-Western League. It would act as a feeder competition to the Western League.

There were three divisions in the new league.

The 18-club Premier Division consisted of 9 clubs from the South-Western League – Bodmin Town, Falmouth Town, Launceston, Liskeard Athletic, Plymouth Parkway, Saltash United, St. Blazey, Tavistock and Torpoint Athletic; plus 8 clubs from the Devon County League – Buckland Athletic, Cullompton Rangers, Dartmouth, Elburton Villa, Holsworthy, Ivybridge Town, Newton Abbot Spurs and Witheridge, plus Clyst Rovers from the Western League.

The 17-club Division One (East) consisted of 11 clubs from the Devon County League – Alphington, Appledore, Budleigh Salterton, Crediton United, Newton Abbot, Ottery St. Mary, Plymstock United, Stoke Gabriel, Teignmouth, Totnes & Dartington SC and University of Exeter; plus 3 clubs from the Devon & Exeter League – Axminster Town, Exmouth Town and Okehampton Argyle and 3 clubs from the South Devon League – Buckfastleigh Rangers, Galmpton United and Liverton United.

The 16-club Division One (West) consisted of 9 clubs from the South-Western League – Callington Town, Goonhavern Athletic, Millbrook, Newquay, Penryn Athletic, Penzance, Porthleven, St. Austell and Wadebridge Town; plus 3 clubs from the Cornwall Combination – Hayle, Mousehole and Wendron United; 3 clubs from the East Cornwall League – Camelford, Dobwalls and Foxhole Stars; and Vospers Oak Villa from the Devon County League.

Promoted clubs shown are in bold type and relegated clubs are shown in bold-italic type.

2007-08

Premier Division

Bodmin Town	34	25	6	3	91	32	81
Saltash United	34	22	5	7	83	38	71
Plymouth Parkway	34	21	7	6	88	49	70
Falmouth Town	34	18	8	8	87	41	62
Launceston	34	19	4	11	76	55	61
Torpoint Athletic	34	18	7	9	57	49	61
Dartmouth	34	17	8	9	64	54	59
St. Blazey	34	14	9	11	74	61	51
Witheridge	34	14	6	14	70	56	48
Tavistock	34	15	3	16	66	80	48
Ivybridge Town	34	11	5	18	54	76	38
Newton Abbot Spurs	34	10	7	17	55	86	37
Liskeard Athletic	34	11	3	20	64	64	36
Buckland Athletic	34	8	7	19	53	66	31
Elburton Villa	34	6	12	16	58	68	30
Holsworthy	34	6	10	18	46	77	28
Clyst Rovers	34	7	3	24	42	99	24
Cullompton Rangers	34	6	6	22	32	109	24

Division One (East)

Budleigh Salterton	32	25	5	2	84	21	80
Plymstock United	32	20	4	8	88	43	64
Newton Abbot	32	19	6	7	69	37	63
Stoke Gabriel	32	20	3	9	65	35	63
Exmouth Town	32	19	6	7	60	36	63
University of Exeter	32	19	3	10	89	39	60
Totnes & Dartington SC	32	15	10	7	63	39	55
Appledore	32	15	6	11	71	53	51
Ottery St. Mary	32	13	9	10	65	62	48
Axminster Town	32	12	7	13	55	63	43
Okehampton Argyle	32	8	8	16	54	76	32
Alphington	32	9	3	20	51	85	30
Liverton United	32	6	11	15	45	52	29
Galmpton United	32	7	8	17	56	74	29
Teignmouth	32	7	3	22	38	102	24
Crediton United	32	4	6	22	48	91	18
Buckfastleigh Rangers	32	4	2	26	28	121	14

Plymstock United transferred to Division One (West). Exeter Civil Service joined from the Devon & Exeter League, Bovey Tracey joined from the South Devon League and Royal Marines joined as a new club. Galmpton United merged with Torbay Gentlemen of the South Devon League to form Galmpton United & Torbay Gentlemen.

Division One (West)

Wadebridge Town	30	23	4	3	74	31	73
Porthleven	30	22	5	3	98	30	71
Mousehole	30	14	9	7	66	58	51
Camelford	30	14	8	8	63	50	50
Penryn Athletic	30	12	11	7	66	40	47
Newquay	30	15	2	13	70	49	47
Vospers Oak Villa	30	14	4	12	51	49	46
Hayle	30	11	11	8	53	39	44
Dobwalls	30	14	2	14	71	59	44
Foxhole Stars	30	13	2	15	62	68	41
Penzance	30	11	7	12	57	62	40
Millbrook	30	10	8	12	52	48	38
Wendron United	30	8	7	15	43	63	31
Callington Town	30	7	2	21	49	79	23
Goonhavern Athletic	30	4	6	20	34	99	18
St. Austell	30	3	2	25	28	113	8

St. Austell had 3 points deducted.
Truro City Reserves joined from the Cornwall Combination and Godolphin Atlantic joined from the East Cornwall League. Goonhavern Athletic moved to the One and All Mining League.

Division One (East)

Exeter Civil Service	32	22	6	4	80	39	72
Bovey Tracey	32	23	2	7	86	37	71
Stoke Gabriel	32	21	2	9	89	41	65
Appledore	32	20	4	8	76	40	64
Galmpton United & Torbay Gents	32	18	3	11	71	57	57
University of Exeter	32	16	6	10	65	58	54
Royal Marines	32	15	4	13	94	59	49
Axminster Town	32	15	4	13	68	67	49
Budleigh Salterton	32	14	6	12	68	58	48
Teignmouth	32	15	1	16	66	60	46
Alphington	32	13	3	16	61	70	42
Totnes & Dartington SC	32	10	8	14	62	72	38
Crediton United	32	10	5	17	48	58	35
Okehampton Argyle	32	7	8	17	51	97	29
Exmouth Town	32	8	4	20	46	95	28
Liverton United	32	7	3	22	47	82	24
Ottery St. Mary	32	2	3	27	25	113	9

Buckfastleigh Rangers resigned in January 2009 and their record at the time was deleted:

	18	4	7	7	32	41	19

Their reserves continued to play in the South Devon League and effectively became the first team. Bickleigh joined from the Devon & Exeter League.

2008-09

Premier Division

Bodmin Town	36	27	5	4	88	25	86
Plymouth Parkway	36	22	7	7	99	46	73
Buckland Athletic	36	21	9	6	79	39	72
Ivybridge Town	36	21	8	7	88	61	71
Saltash United	36	20	8	8	98	53	68
Tavistock	36	20	5	11	70	58	63
Dartmouth	36	18	5	13	72	70	59
Cullompton Rangers	36	18	2	16	80	70	56
Torpoint Athletic	36	16	5	15	75	79	53
Launceston	36	14	6	16	72	70	48
Witheridge	36	13	8	15	64	54	47
St. Blazey	36	11	10	15	64	74	43
Wadebridge Town	36	11	8	17	54	71	41
Falmouth Town	36	10	6	20	48	73	36
Holsworthy	36	9	6	21	48	103	33
Liskeard Athletic	36	9	5	22	39	69	32
Clyst Rovers	36	9	4	23	58	104	31
Elburton Villa	36	7	6	23	55	88	27
Newton Abbot Spurs	*36*	*7*	*5*	*24*	*36*	*80*	*26*

Tavistock had 2 points deducted.
Newton Abbot were expelled on 6th November 2008 after they failed to fulfil 2 fixtures and their record was deleted when it stood as follows:

7	2	0	5	10	19	6

The players had refused to play because they had not been paid expenses. The club later disbanded.
Newton Abbot Spurs were relegated to Division One (East).

Division One (West)

Penzance	32	24	3	5	107	39	75
Newquay	32	23	2	7	98	46	71
St. Austell	32	21	7	4	90	40	70
Penryn Athletic	32	20	2	10	72	50	62
Callington Town	32	19	4	9	75	46	61
Porthleven	32	19	2	11	95	59	59
Dobwalls	32	15	4	13	63	51	49
Camelford	32	13	6	13	59	66	45
Foxhole Stars	32	12	8	12	69	66	44
Truro City Reserves	32	13	5	14	56	68	44
Godolphin Atlantic	32	13	4	15	56	63	43
Mousehole	32	11	3	18	55	79	36
Hayle	32	9	7	16	65	72	34
Plymstock United	32	7	5	20	45	77	26
Vospers Oak Villa	32	6	4	22	44	93	22
Wendron United	32	5	5	22	31	97	20
Millbrook	32	5	3	24	40	108	18

Perranporth joined from the Cornwall Combination.

2009-10

Premier Division

Buckland Athletic	36	27	6	3	121	46	87
Bodmin Town	36	28	3	5	98	31	87
Falmouth Town	36	23	4	9	87	41	73
St. Blazey	36	22	3	11	81	53	69
Tavistock	36	21	3	12	77	52	66
Plymouth Parkway	36	19	7	10	89	53	64
Penzance	36	18	7	11	68	54	61
Torpoint Athletic	36	17	10	9	65	55	61
Saltash United	36	16	10	10	74	49	58
Witheridge	36	17	4	15	83	72	55
Launceston	36	14	5	17	65	67	47
Ivybridge Town	36	11	10	15	57	67	43
Elburton Villa	36	10	11	15	57	78	41
Wadebridge Town	36	10	5	21	53	76	35
Dartmouth	36	10	5	21	48	78	35
Liskeard Athletic	36	7	8	21	54	82	29
Bovey Tracey	36	5	8	23	50	109	23
Cullompton Rangers	36	6	3	27	39	100	21
Holsworthy	*36*	*2*	*6*	*28*	*37*	*140*	*12*

Clyst Rovers resigned from the league on 5th March 2010 and their record at the time was deleted:

	20	2	2	16	20	49	8

They later disbanded. Their ground was to be built upon as part of the Skypark Business Park and the club originally had planned to find a new ground. However, a series of delays to the project meant that they did not have access to the funds needed for a new ground and a series of short term leases meant they were unable to maintain the current ground properly. Holsworthy were relegated to Division One (West).

Division One (East)

Royal Marines	**34**	**26**	**3**	**5**	**110**	**46**	**81**
Stoke Gabriel	34	22	3	9	92	43	69
Liverton United	34	19	8	7	82	47	65
Galmpton United & Torbay Gents	34	18	6	10	83	50	60
Appledore	34	18	3	13	89	69	57
Alphington	34	18	3	13	75	55	57
Totnes & Dartington SC	34	17	5	12	69	50	56
Exmouth Town	34	16	5	13	79	68	53
Budleigh Salterton	34	15	6	13	67	55	51
Exeter Civil Service	34	16	3	15	62	69	51
Teignmouth	34	15	5	14	81	77	50
University of Exeter	34	12	5	17	60	68	41
Newton Abbot Spurs	34	12	4	18	64	86	40
Crediton United	34	10	5	19	59	86	35
Axminster Town	34	11	2	21	56	96	35
Okehampton Argyle	34	10	4	20	67	101	34
Ottery St. Mary	34	5	7	22	48	127	22
Bickleigh	34	6	3	25	50	100	21

Okehampton Argyle transferred to Division One (West).

Division One (West)

Perranporth	30	20	4	6	78	35	64
St. Austell	**30**	**20**	**2**	**8**	**81**	**39**	**62**
Hayle	30	18	2	10	68	37	56
Penryn Athletic	30	17	3	10	69	45	54
Newquay	30	16	4	10	79	62	52
Godolphin Atlantic	30	14	7	9	66	51	49
Plymstock United	30	14	7	9	56	41	49
Camelford	30	14	5	11	62	51	47
Dobwalls	30	13	7	10	55	46	46
Callington Town	30	12	7	11	57	50	43
Porthleven	30	11	6	13	64	67	39
Vospers Oak Villa	30	11	4	15	50	62	37
Foxhole Stars	30	7	7	16	41	78	28
Truro City Reserves	30	6	4	20	35	73	22
Millbrook	30	6	4	20	34	87	22
Mousehole	30	1	7	22	18	89	10

Wendron United resigned from the league and their record was deleted when it stood as follows:

	13	0	0	13	1	60	0

The club had lost its experienced players and could not compete effectively. The reserves, playing in the Cornwall Combination, became the first team. Millbrook moved to the East Cornwall League.

2010-11

Premier Division

Buckland Athletic	38	31	3	4	131	49	96
Bodmin Town	38	27	7	4	98	38	88
Plymouth Parkway	38	27	5	6	118	49	86
Torpoint Athletic	38	24	7	7	113	54	79
Falmouth Town	38	24	5	9	112	60	77
Saltash United	38	17	6	15	82	70	57
Ivybridge Town	38	17	5	16	98	77	56
St. Blazey	38	16	8	14	83	72	56
Penzance	38	16	6	16	74	73	54
St. Austell	38	16	6	16	98	98	54
Launceston	38	15	8	15	76	84	53
Liskeard Athletic	38	13	8	17	59	69	47
Tavistock	38	13	6	19	58	79	45
Witheridge	38	11	9	18	66	86	42
Royal Marines	38	12	6	20	67	95	42
Cullompton Rangers	38	10	6	22	57	127	36
Bovey Tracey	38	8	9	21	58	104	33
Dartmouth	38	8	6	24	59	111	30
Elburton Villa	38	7	6	25	58	98	27
Wadebridge Town	*38*	*5*	*4*	*29*	*44*	*116*	*19*

Wadebridge Town were relegated to Division One (West).

Division One (East)

Liverton United	30	24	5	1	100	19	77
Budleigh Salterton	30	17	9	4	71	31	60
Stoke Gabriel	30	17	8	5	72	47	59
Teignmouth	30	16	5	9	68	46	53
Galmpton United & Torbay Gents	30	15	5	10	68	55	50
Appledore	30	14	7	9	48	37	49
Alphington	30	12	7	11	49	42	43
University of Exeter	30	12	6	12	60	54	42
Totnes & Dartington SC	30	13	2	15	55	69	41
Bickleigh	30	11	5	14	40	50	38
Exmouth Town	30	10	5	15	54	59	35
Exeter Civil Service	30	9	8	13	41	67	35
Ottery St. Mary	30	9	2	19	40	82	29
Newton Abbot Spurs	30	6	8	16	41	64	26
Crediton United	30	6	4	20	40	73	22
Axminster Town	30	4	4	22	29	81	16

Bickleigh resigned and the reserves, playing in the Devon & Exeter League, became the first team. Sidmouth Town joined from the Devon & Exeter League. Galmpton United & Torbay Gentlemen changed their name to Galmpton United.

Division One (West)

Camelford	**30**	**20**	**8**	**2**	**85**	**27**	**68**
Godolphin Atlantic	30	20	5	5	73	37	65
Callington Town	30	20	4	6	85	41	64
Vospers Oak Villa	30	16	8	6	72	40	56
Penryn Athletic	30	15	6	9	76	56	51
Porthleven	30	14	7	9	53	48	49
Plymstock United	30	14	6	10	63	48	48
Perranporth	30	14	6	10	54	40	48
Newquay	30	15	1	14	76	68	46
Holsworthy	30	10	5	15	40	67	35
Dobwalls	30	8	8	14	44	52	32
Truro City Reserves	30	9	3	18	39	76	30
Foxhole Stars	30	7	4	19	41	79	25
Mousehole	30	5	6	19	39	84	21
Okehampton Argyle	30	5	5	20	47	81	20
Hayle	30	4	6	20	30	73	18

Okehampton Argyle transferred to Division One (East). Helston Athletic joined from the Cornwall Combination and St. Dennis joined from the East Cornwall League.

2011-12

Premier Division

	P	W	D	L	F	A	Pts
Bodmin Town	38	36	0	2	145	34	108
Buckland Athletic	38	28	5	5	123	56	89
Falmouth Town	38	24	6	8	122	58	78
Saltash United	38	24	5	9	113	59	77
Launceston	38	22	6	10	78	47	72
Plymouth Parkway	38	22	4	12	94	53	70
Liskeard Athletic	38	21	5	12	74	57	68
St. Austell	38	19	5	14	79	64	62
Camelford	38	18	3	17	63	64	57
Tavistock	38	15	8	15	79	75	53
Elburton Villa	38	16	5	17	66	71	53
Torpoint Athletic	38	16	3	19	49	74	51
Witheridge	38	15	4	19	59	69	49
Dartmouth	38	13	7	18	57	73	48
Cullompton Rangers	38	11	6	21	65	79	39
Bovey Tracey	38	10	7	21	47	86	37
Penzance	38	8	3	27	40	110	27
St. Blazey	38	8	2	28	41	100	26
Ivybridge Town	38	7	4	27	53	118	25
Royal Marines	38	2	2	34	26	126	6

Dartmouth had 2 points added and Royal Marines had 2 points deducted. Buckland Athletic moved to the Western League. Dartmouth resigned just before the start of the 2012-13 season because of difficulty attracting and keeping players of the required standard. Their reserves (in the South Devon League) became the first team. Royal Marines were to be relegated to Division One (East) but disbanded instead.

Division One (East)

	P	W	D	L	F	A	Pts
Liverton United	32	26	2	4	99	30	80
Stoke Gabriel	32	22	5	5	109	57	71
Galmpton United	32	20	5	7	83	53	65
Crediton United	32	19	4	9	81	58	61
Exmouth Town	32	18	5	9	77	40	59
Alphington	32	18	4	10	73	53	58
Teignmouth	32	16	6	10	81	60	54
Okehampton Argyle	32	13	10	9	62	55	49
Newton Abbot Spurs	32	13	8	11	67	63	47
Totnes & Dartington SC	32	13	5	14	67	68	44
Budleigh Salterton	32	11	7	14	56	75	40
Appledore	32	11	3	18	48	53	36
Exeter Civil Service	32	10	6	16	46	63	36
Sidmouth Town	32	11	1	20	47	75	34
University of Exeter	32	7	8	17	54	71	29
Axminster Town	32	2	1	29	33	124	7
Ottery St. Mary	32	1	2	29	28	113	5

Ottery St. Mary moved to the Devon & Exeter League because of the costs involved in competing in the South West Peninsula League.

Division One (West)

	P	W	D	L	F	A	Pts
Newquay	32	28	3	1	127	33	87
Helston Athletic	32	22	7	3	89	39	73
Penryn Athletic	32	22	4	6	94	34	70
Godolphin Atlantic	32	18	8	6	64	29	62
Vospers Oak Villa	32	17	10	5	90	37	61
Callington Town	32	17	3	12	66	54	54
Truro City Reserves	32	15	6	11	70	54	51
Plymstock United	32	13	4	15	56	59	45
St. Dennis	32	12	6	14	65	66	42
Dobwalls	32	13	3	16	64	66	42
Wadebridge Town	32	11	8	13	71	61	41
Porthleven	32	13	2	17	55	82	41
Hayle	32	10	6	16	55	64	36
Foxhole Stars	32	8	7	17	50	75	31
Holsworthy	32	8	2	22	46	58	26
Perranporth	32	2	3	27	19	149	7
Mousehole	32	2	0	30	26	147	6

Plymstock United had 2 points added and Perranporth had 2 points deducted. Plymstock United transferred to Division One (East). Sticker joined from the East Cornwall League.

2012-13

Premier Division

	P	W	D	L	F	A	Pts
Bodmin Town	36	28	6	2	127	28	90
Plymouth Parkway	36	24	6	6	89	45	78
Elburton Villa	36	24	5	7	95	53	77
St. Austell	36	23	5	8	89	45	74
Launceston	36	19	4	13	64	46	61
Saltash United	36	17	9	10	77	43	60
Witheridge	36	17	6	13	84	58	57
St. Blazey	36	16	8	12	79	57	56
Camelford	36	16	7	13	76	53	55
Tavistock	36	17	2	17	73	71	53
Liverton United	36	15	5	16	75	72	50
Newquay	36	15	4	17	68	62	49
Ivybridge Town	36	14	4	18	65	75	46
Torpoint Athletic	36	12	9	15	59	68	45
Bovey Tracey	36	11	9	16	49	84	42
Falmouth Town	36	8	6	22	48	87	30
Cullompton Rangers	36	8	3	25	44	106	27
Liskeard Athletic	36	5	6	25	44	108	20
Penzance	36	0	2	34	22	166	2

Liskeard Athletic had 1 point deducted.
Penzance were relegated to Division One (West) and Liverton United were voluntarily relegated to Division One (East) as they believed they would be uncompetitive in the Premier Division. Elmore joined from the Western League.

Division One (East)

	P	W	D	L	F	A	Pts
Exmouth Town	30	23	6	1	88	27	75
Stoke Gabriel	30	19	7	4	100	49	66
Budleigh Salterton	30	18	4	8	73	58	58
Newton Abbot Spurs	30	17	6	7	80	52	57
Appledore	30	17	5	8	67	42	56
Galmpton United	30	14	3	13	58	64	47
Teignmouth	30	14	3	13	73	71	45
Exeter Civil Service	30	11	10	9	55	56	43
Okehampton Argyle	30	11	5	14	59	69	38
University of Exeter	30	8	11	11	63	68	35
Axminster Town	30	10	7	13	56	59	33
Totnes & Dartington SC	30	9	5	16	62	68	32
Alphington	30	9	5	16	39	65	32
Plymstock United	30	7	4	19	50	76	25
Sidmouth Town	30	3	7	20	33	66	16
Crediton United	30	4	4	22	29	95	12

Stoke Gabriel and Galmpton United both had 2 points added. Axminster Town and Crediton United both had 4 points deducted. Exeter Civil Service changed their name to Exwick Villa.

Division One (West)

	P	W	D	L	F	A	Pts
Godolphin Atlantic	30	27	2	1	99	21	83
Helston Athletic	30	21	5	4	135	37	68
Wadebridge Town	30	21	3	6	112	40	66
Sticker	30	18	4	8	68	45	58
Callington Town	30	16	7	7	87	32	57
St. Dennis	30	18	2	10	89	62	56
Penryn Athletic	30	16	5	9	79	55	53
Dobwalls	30	16	5	9	75	63	53
Perranporth	30	13	2	15	64	70	41
Hayle	30	11	7	12	59	49	40
Porthleven	30	11	3	16	40	65	36
Truro City Reserves	30	11	1	18	49	68	24
Holsworthy	30	7	0	23	40	101	21
Vospers Oak Villa	30	6	1	23	46	90	19
Mousehole	30	3	0	27	24	123	9
Foxhole Stars	30	1	1	28	19	164	0

Callington Town had 2 points added. Truro City Reserves had 10 points deducted and Foxhole Stars had 4 points deducted.
Hayle replaced their reserves in the Cornwall Combination as they thought they would be uncompetitive in the South West Peninsula League after losing their manager and many players. Bude Town joined from the East Cornwall League.

2013-14

Premier Division

Plymouth Parkway	38	29	3	6	121	33	90
Exmouth Town	38	26	8	4	85	28	86
Saltash United	38	27	4	7	104	33	85
Ivybridge Town	38	24	5	9	98	60	77
Godolphin Atlantic	38	23	6	9	75	50	75
Witheridge	38	23	4	11	83	49	73
Bodmin Town	38	22	7	9	75	41	73
Launceston	38	22	5	11	92	61	71
St. Austell	38	20	8	10	99	58	68
Torpoint Athletic	38	17	8	13	70	56	59
Newquay	38	15	4	19	78	91	49
Elburton Villa	38	14	6	18	64	92	48
St. Blazey	38	14	4	20	72	72	46
Camelford	38	14	4	20	59	79	46
Bovey Tracey	38	13	7	18	62	95	46
Falmouth Town	38	8	5	25	46	84	29
Elmore	38	6	8	24	62	110	26
Cullompton Rangers	38	4	6	28	45	117	18
Tavistock	*38*	*2*	*5*	*31*	*34*	*107*	*11*
Liskeard Athletic	*38*	*1*	*5*	*32*	*32*	*140*	*8*

Tavistock were relegated to Division One (East) and Liskeard Athletic were relegated to Division One (West).

Division One (East)

Stoke Gabriel	**30**	**23**	**5**	**2**	**100**	**21**	**74**
Teignmouth	30	19	7	4	81	38	64
Galmpton United	30	19	5	6	78	50	62
Exwick Villa	30	17	6	7	82	51	57
Totnes & Dartington SC	30	13	6	11	71	65	45
Crediton United	30	12	6	12	60	59	42
University of Exeter	30	12	5	13	58	56	41
Alphington	30	11	7	12	64	71	40
Budleigh Salterton	30	11	6	13	64	60	39
Appledore	30	10	6	14	53	49	36
Newton Abbot Spurs	30	10	5	15	55	54	35
Axminster Town	30	8	7	15	52	68	31
Sidmouth Town	30	7	8	15	41	58	29
Okehampton Argyle	30	7	7	16	47	79	28
Liverton United	30	7	4	19	43	119	25
Plymstock United	30	6	6	18	40	91	24

St. Martins joined from the Devon & Exeter League and Brixham joined from the South Devon League.

Division One (West)

Callington Town	**30**	**25**	**1**	**4**	**87**	**41**	**76**
Mousehole	30	23	0	7	68	42	69
Helston Athletic	30	20	1	9	101	50	61
Sticker	30	17	4	9	85	51	55
Penryn Athletic	30	16	6	8	68	43	54
Truro City Reserves	30	17	1	12	76	60	52
Wadebridge Town	30	15	4	11	76	52	49
Dobwalls	30	15	2	13	63	54	47
St. Dennis	30	14	3	13	71	63	45
Vospers Oak Villa	30	13	6	11	59	59	45
Porthleven	30	8	7	15	54	70	31
Perranporth	30	7	4	19	46	68	25
Bude Town	30	6	5	19	43	78	23
Penzance	30	6	5	19	41	87	23
Holsworthy	30	7	0	23	37	101	21
Foxhole Stars	30	6	1	23	27	83	19

Truro City disbanded their reserve side. Foxhole Stars resigned because they could not field a strong enough team and so the reserves, playing in the Duchy League, became their first team. Illogan RBL joined from the Cornwall Combination and Millbrook joined from the East Cornwall League.

2014-15

Premier Division

St. Austell	36	30	3	3	103	31	93
Bodmin Town	36	25	6	5	98	42	81
Saltash United	36	26	2	8	81	59	80
Ivybridge Town	36	23	5	8	91	39	74
Plymouth Parkway	36	23	4	9	128	48	73
Witheridge	36	18	7	11	88	59	61
Godolphin Atlantic	36	18	6	12	72	54	60
Exmouth Town	36	14	13	9	63	50	55
St. Blazey	36	14	7	15	58	70	49
Launceston	36	13	9	14	56	67	48
Callington Town	36	13	7	16	48	54	46
Cullompton Rangers	36	14	4	18	58	70	46
Torpoint Athletic	36	13	7	16	51	67	46
Stoke Gabriel	36	12	4	20	53	74	40
Newquay	36	8	6	22	50	79	30
Falmouth Town	36	7	9	20	45	80	30
Camelford	36	7	5	24	51	90	26
Elburton Villa	36	5	8	23	39	109	23
Bovey Tracey	*36*	*1*	*4*	*31*	*33*	*124*	*4*

Bovey Tracey could not raise a team for their game at St. Austell. St. Austell were awarded a win and Bovey Tracey had 3 points deducted.
Elmore resigned from the league on 23rd September 2014 because they were finding it difficult to raise a team of the standard needed. Their record at the time was deleted: 7   0   1   6   7   30   1
Their reserves continued to play in the Devon & Exeter League and became their first team. Bovey Tracey were relegated to Division One (East).

Division One (East)

Tavistock	**34**	**24**	**5**	**5**	**79**	**31**	**77**
Appledore	34	24	5	5	70	32	77
Teignmouth	34	21	6	7	102	48	69
University of Exeter	34	20	8	6	102	45	68
St. Martins	34	21	4	9	79	41	67
Galmpton United	34	18	7	9	83	53	58
Alphington	34	15	6	13	66	70	51
Okehampton Argyle	34	15	5	14	71	79	50
Brixham	34	11	8	15	63	62	41
Sidmouth Town	34	12	5	17	71	94	41
Crediton United	34	12	2	20	58	79	38
Totnes & Dartington SC	34	10	5	19	74	89	35
Budleigh Salterton	34	9	8	17	56	84	35
Plymstock United	34	11	2	21	59	94	35
Liverton United	34	10	4	20	61	96	34
Exwick Villa	34	10	3	21	50	76	33
Newton Abbot Spurs	34	8	6	20	59	87	30
Axminster Town	34	8	5	21	62	105	29

Galmpton United had 3 points deducted.
Plymstock United transferred to Division One (West). Tiverton Town Reserves joined from the Devon & Exeter League.

Division One (West)

Helston Athletic	**30**	**22**	**2**	**6**	**104**	**39**	**68**
Vospers Oak Villa	30	20	5	5	73	43	65
Penryn Athletic	30	19	6	5	71	33	63
St. Dennis	30	20	3	7	67	37	63
Sticker	30	18	4	8	73	50	58
Liskeard Athletic	30	15	6	9	58	53	51
Mousehole	30	14	5	11	70	42	47
Bude Town	30	15	2	13	68	55	47
Illogan RBL	30	13	5	12	59	53	44
Wadebridge Town	30	13	2	15	69	65	41
Porthleven	30	10	5	15	68	74	35
Dobwalls	30	10	4	16	56	71	34
Holsworthy	30	7	7	16	55	71	28
Penzance	30	6	4	20	47	82	22
Millbrook	30	3	5	22	40	133	14
Perranporth	30	1	3	26	30	107	6

Perranporth moved to the Cornwall Combination, swapping places with Wendron United. Plymouth Argyle re-formed their reserve side which joined the division.

GLOUCESTERSHIRE COUNTY LEAGUE

Until the Gloucestershire County League was formed in 1968, clubs in the north and south of the county had their own competitions. The Avon Premier Combination was the principal competition for those in the Bristol area while the Gloucestershire Northern Senior League catered for those in the north. The new Gloucestershire County League combined many of the top clubs from these two competitions.

Abbreviations:

APC = Avon Premier Combination

BPC=Bristol Premier Combination

GNSL = Gloucestershire Northern Senior League

Several of the published tables contained errors in the goals scored record. Additional research has succeeded in correcting many of these, totals that still do not balance are shown below the relevant columns in italics.

1968-69

Stonehouse	30	26	4	0	102	27	56
Bristol St. George	30	20	6	4	91	34	46
Hanham Athletic	30	16	7	7	85	48	39
Yate Y.M.C.A.	30	16	6	8	74	45	38
Cirencester Town	30	15	4	11	70	52	34
Forest Green Rovers	30	13	8	9	43	44	34
Old Patchwegians	30	11	7	12	49	64	29
Sharpness	30	11	6	13	58	58	28
Cinderford Town Reserves	30	12	4	14	56	59	28
Cadbury Heath	30	10	8	12	37	52	28
Charlton Kings	30	10	7	13	51	63	27
Gloucester City Reserves	30	10	6	14	51	72	26
Matson Athletic	30	9	2	19	44	71	20
Thornbury	30	5	8	17	45	71	18
Bristol Rovers "A"	30	6	6	18	41	79	18
Brimscombe	30	3	5	22	27	85	11

Cinderford Town joined from the West Midlands League, replacing their reserves. Cirencester Town left and joined the Hellenic League and were replaced by Old Georgians. Yate Y.M.C.A. changed their name to Yate Town.

1969-70

Bristol St. George	30	23	7	0	97	23	53
Cinderford Town	30	20	8	2	76	22	48
Forest Green Rovers	30	18	7	5	84	48	43
Sharpness	30	18	5	7	71	53	41
Old Georgians	30	13	6	11	57	47	32
Yate Town	30	12	6	12	48	54	30
Stonehouse	30	9	11	10	62	62	29
Cadbury Heath	30	11	6	13	43	50	28
Hanham Athletic	30	8	10	12	45	55	26
Bristol Rovers "A"	30	8	10	12	62	92	26
Matson Athletic	30	9	6	15	45	60	24
Old Patchwegians	30	8	8	14	30	45	24
Gloucester City Reserves	30	9	4	17	52	64	22
Thornbury	30	8	5	17	49	68	21
Brimscombe	30	5	8	17	30	67	18
Charlton Kings	30	6	3	21	35	76	15

Gloucester City Reserves left but Lydbrook Athletic joined from the Midland Combination and Clifton St. Vincent and Worrall Hill also joined, increasing the league to 18 clubs.

1970-71

Cadbury Heath	34	25	6	3	89	24	56
Sharpness	34	24	7	3	80	33	55
Forest Green Rovers	34	25	3	6	96	45	53
Cinderford Town	34	23	5	6	85	30	51
Worrall Hill	34	14	14	6	46	24	42
Old Georgians	34	18	5	11	77	49	41
Stonehouse	34	17	5	12	73	51	39
Old Patchwegians	34	12	8	14	52	63	32
Clifton St. Vincent	34	10	9	15	50	68	29
Bristol St. George	34	11	6	17	55	62	28
Matson Athletic	34	9	9	16	41	53	27
Yate Town	34	9	9	16	44	61	27
Hanham Athletic	34	11	4	19	41	68	26
Brimscombe	34	9	6	19	32	63	24
Bristol Rovers "A"	34	8	7	19	44	68	23
Charlton Kings	34	8	6	20	44	77	22
Thornbury	34	7	8	19	34	79	22
Lydbrook Athletic	34	5	5	24	25	90	15

1971-72

Cadbury Heath	34	25	7	2	94	26	57
Cinderford Town	34	20	12	2	77	30	52
Bristol St. George	34	20	6	8	86	38	46
Forest Green Rovers	34	18	6	10	62	48	42
Old Georgians	34	16	7	11	60	50	39
Stonehouse	34	15	9	10	68	59	39
Worrall Hill	34	14	7	13	58	53	35
Bristol Rovers "A"	34	13	8	13	63	57	34
Sharpness	34	11	12	11	56	54	34
Matson Athletic	34	15	4	15	54	59	34
Charlton Kings	34	14	6	14	55	67	34
Old Patchwegians	34	9	11	14	42	53	29
Brimscombe	34	11	6	17	52	71	28
Clifton St. Vincent	34	9	7	18	49	68	25
Yate Town	34	9	7	18	36	56	25
Lydbrook Athletic	34	9	5	20	33	60	23
Thornbury	34	3	14	17	37	74	20
Hanham Athletic	34	5	6	23	42	101	16

1972-73

Cadbury Heath	34	27	4	3	102	27	58
Bristol St. George	34	24	5	5	89	44	53
Cinderford Town	34	18	10	6	76	34	46
Old Georgians	34	19	8	7	84	51	46
Charlton Kings	34	19	6	9	66	43	44
Thornbury	34	13	13	8	59	52	39
Sharpness	34	14	8	12	58	55	36
Stonehouse	34	12	12	10	61	71	36
Forest Green Rovers	34	11	12	11	60	57	34
Matson Athletic	34	12	9	13	59	53	33
Worrall Hill	34	10	11	13	49	48	31
Bristol Rovers "A"	34	11	8	15	48	57	30
Old Patchwegians	34	12	5	17	41	55	29
Yate Town	34	10	6	18	53	54	26
Lydbrook Athletic	34	8	5	21	51	96	21
Hanham Athletic	34	7	7	20	54	98	19
Clifton St. Vincent	34	4	8	22	41	87	16
Brimscombe	34	5	3	26	46	115	13

Hanham Athletic had 2 points deducted for fielding an ineligible player.
Brimscombe left to join the GNSL and were replaced by Wilton Rovers.
Old Patchwegians changed their name to Patchway.

1973-74

Cadbury Heath	34	26	6	2	87	28	58
Cinderford Town	34	26	4	4	89	25	56
Matson Athletic	34	21	7	6	79	48	49
Bristol Rovers "A"	34	18	7	9	79	56	43
Worrall Hill	34	16	8	10	59	46	40
Old Georgians	34	16	7	11	64	56	39
Sharpness	34	14	9	11	63	60	37
Yate Town	34	16	4	14	56	48	36
Hanham Athletic	34	14	9	11	62	49	35
Forest Green Rovers	34	14	5	15	49	55	33
Patchway	34	9	13	12	48	52	31
Charlton Kings	34	13	5	16	46	51	31
Bristol St. George	34	11	6	17	47	58	28
Thornbury	34	8	9	17	42	57	25
Stonehouse	34	7	8	19	47	75	22
Lydbrook Athletic	34	6	8	20	48	87	20
Clifton St. Vincent	34	8	4	22	37	69	20
Wilton Rovers	34	2	3	29	19	101	7

Hanham Athletic had 2 points deducted for fielding an ineligible player.
Cinderford Town left to join the Midland Combination and were replaced
by Oldland (Decora).

1974-75

Matson Athletic	34	25	4	5	91	36	54
Cadbury Heath	34	24	5	5	95	25	53
Yate Town	34	20	6	8	57	36	46
Lydbrook Athletic	34	16	12	6	78	47	44
Worrall Hill	34	16	8	10	42	38	40
Forest Green Rovers	34	16	7	11	72	62	39
Oldland (Decora)	34	14	10	10	53	48	38
Clifton St. Vincent	34	13	8	13	52	56	34
Patchway	34	12	8	14	36	41	32
Sharpness	34	14	3	17	74	79	31
Old Georgians	34	12	6	16	57	68	30
Bristol St. George	34	11	8	15	42	54	30
Charlton Kings	34	11	6	17	48	58	28
Stonehouse	34	11	6	17	52	63	28
Thornbury Town	34	9	8	17	43	65	26
Hanham Athletic	34	9	5	20	41	66	23
Bristol Rovers "A"	34	8	5	21	41	82	21
Wilton Rovers	34	2	11	21	35	85	15

Forest Green Rovers left to join the Hellenic League and Cadbury Heath left
to join the Midland Combination. They were replaced by Almondsbury
Greenway from the APC and Shortwood United from the GNSL.

1975-76

Matson Athletic	34	29	2	3	102	20	60
Almondsbury Greenway	34	23	6	5	84	35	52
Oldland (Decora)	34	21	7	6	68	36	49
Bristol St. George	34	17	9	8	70	44	43
Yate Town	34	17	8	9	78	47	42
Worrall Hill	34	15	7	12	66	53	37
Patchway	34	13	11	10	45	45	37
Thornbury Town	34	16	4	14	75	41	36
Old Georgians	34	12	8	14	45	44	32
Lydbrook Athletic	34	12	6	16	41	58	30
Wilton Rovers	34	9	12	13	37	51	30
Clifton St. Vincent	34	10	5	19	42	74	25
Bristol Rovers "A"	34	9	7	18	48	81	25
Charlton Kings	34	7	10	17	40	58	24
Hanham Athletic	34	7	10	17	48	87	24
Shortwood United	34	8	8	18	50	90	24
Sharpness	34	7	9	18	35	65	23
Stonehouse	34	5	9	20	40	85	19

Bristol Rovers "A" left the League which was reduced to 17 clubs.

1976-77

Almondsbury Greenway	32	26	4	2	90	22	56
Matson Athletic	32	21	5	6	78	25	47
Old Georgians	32	20	7	5	54	27	47
Oldland (Decora)	32	20	4	8	67	41	44
Yate Town	32	18	6	8	71	37	42
Worrall Hill	32	16	7	9	60	43	39
Sharpness	32	12	10	10	52	43	34
Shortwood United	32	11	9	12	52	54	31
Hanham Athletic	32	12	6	14	40	41	30
Bristol St. George	32	12	4	16	50	52	28
Clifton St. Vincent	32	12	4	16	48	65	28
Charlton Kings	32	8	7	17	42	69	23
Patchway	32	9	5	18	41	68	23
Wilton Rovers	32	7	9	16	36	62	23
Lydbrook Athletic	32	6	7	19	38	68	19
Thornbury Town	32	3	10	19	41	86	14
Stonehouse	32	5	4	23	32	83	14

Thornbury Town had 2 points deducted for fielding an ineligible player.
Thornbury Town left but Gloucester City Reserves and Hambrook both
joined, increasing the league to 18 clubs.

1977-78

Almondsbury Greenway	34	28	2	4	112	28	58
Hambrook	34	22	6	6	55	36	50
Matson Athletic	34	21	4	9	83	45	46
Old Georgians	34	20	6	8	62	36	46
Yate Town	34	20	4	10	77	46	44
Worrall Hill	34	17	8	9	60	39	42
Shortwood United	34	14	9	11	63	57	37
Oldland (Decora)	34	13	9	12	59	61	35
Patchway	34	10	12	12	56	66	32
Bristol St. George	34	11	8	15	61	61	30
Gloucester City Reserves	34	12	6	16	45	65	30
Stonehouse	34	10	9	15	50	72	29
Hanham Athletic	34	11	6	17	46	68	28
Wilton Rovers	34	9	9	16	48	48	27
Sharpness	34	10	7	17	52	60	27
Charlton Kings	34	8	5	21	32	76	21
Lydbrook Athletic	34	6	8	20	53	87	20
Clifton St. Vincent	34	4	2	28	24	91	10

Port of Bristol joined from the Bristol & Suburban League but Charlton
Kings and Clifton St. Vincent left, reducing the league to 17 clubs.

1978-79

Almondsbury Greenway	32	23	3	6	112	36	49
Hambrook	32	22	4	6	73	44	48
Worrall Hill	32	18	7	7	64	45	43
Port of Bristol	32	16	10	6	72	45	42
Matson Athletic	32	16	9	7	67	44	41
Sharpness	32	16	3	13	64	48	35
Yate Town	32	13	9	10	58	44	35
Hanham Athletic	32	15	5	12	55	44	35
Old Georgians	32	13	9	10	53	48	35
Stonehouse	32	12	10	10	47	55	34
Bristol St. George	32	10	5	17	45	54	25
Lydbrook Athletic	32	8	9	15	42	69	25
Patchway	32	7	9	16	39	75	23
Wilton Rovers	32	9	4	19	33	68	22
Oldland (Decora)	32	6	9	17	33	61	21
Shortwood United	32	3	10	19	43	88	16
Gloucester City Reserves	32	3	9	20	33	65	15

Worrall Hill left to join the Hellenic League but Frampton United and Newent Town both joined, increasing the league to 18 clubs.

1979-80

Almondsbury Greenway	34	24	5	5	123	44	53
Shortwood United	34	19	8	7	89	60	46
Sharpness	34	13	15	6	53	42	41
Matson Athletic	34	14	12	8	67	54	40
Yate Town	34	15	10	9	66	57	40
Port of Bristol	34	15	8	11	78	52	38
Hambrook	34	12	12	10	52	42	36
Bristol St. George	34	11	14	9	51	42	36
Oldland (Decora)	34	12	11	11	58	59	35
Frampton United	34	13	8	13	59	72	34
Newent Town	34	11	9	14	53	57	31
Hanham Athletic	34	8	14	12	50	61	30
Lydbrook Athletic	34	10	10	14	47	59	30
Old Georgians	34	10	9	15	43	65	29
Stonehouse	34	11	4	19	46	80	26
Gloucester City Reserves	34	9	7	18	45	74	25
Wilton Rovers	34	3	18	13	25	42	24
Patchway	34	4	10	20	43	86	18

Patchway left and were replaced by Cadbury Heath from the APC. Bristol St. George became Immediate Bristol St. George.

1980-81

Almondsbury Greenway	34	27	4	3	108	45	58
Shortwood United	34	23	3	8	73	37	49
Wilton Rovers	34	22	4	8	72	43	48
Port of Bristol	34	17	9	8	65	45	43
Matson Athletic	34	18	5	11	85	54	41
Sharpness	34	13	11	10	49	39	37
Immediate Bristol St. George	34	14	9	11	51	44	37
Lydbrook Athletic	34	12	12	10	55	53	36
Gloucester City Reserves	34	16	4	14	63	71	36
Frampton United	34	15	5	14	59	56	35
Yate Town	34	15	4	15	62	55	34
Hambrook	34	15	4	15	52	51	34
Newent Town	34	11	9	14	49	57	31
Oldland (Decora)	34	8	12	14	39	57	28
Hanham Athletic	34	9	2	23	47	79	20
Old Georgians	34	5	7	22	26	64	17
Cadbury Heath	34	5	7	22	27	68	17
Stonehouse	34	3	5	26	43	107	11

Gloucester City Reserves left, reducing the league to 17 clubs.

Goal difference replaced goal average to decide places for teams with equal points from the next season onwards.

1981-82

Shortwood United	32	22	6	4	92	49	50
Almondsbury Greenway	32	21	7	4	88	32	49
Lydbrook Athletic	32	17	11	4	69	36	45
Wilton Rovers	32	18	6	8	66	44	42
Immediate Bristol St. George	32	19	5	8	75	42	41
Port of Bristol	32	16	6	10	70	53	38
Old Georgians	32	16	6	10	56	39	38
Hambrook	32	13	8	11	54	57	34
Sharpness	32	11	10	11	60	49	32
Oldland (Decora)	32	10	9	13	44	57	29
Hanham Athletic	32	6	15	11	41	50	27
Yate Town	32	8	8	16	53	81	24
Newent Town	32	7	9	16	29	54	23
Matson Athletic	32	8	6	18	43	72	22
Frampton United	32	6	8	18	41	60	20
Cadbury Heath	32	4	8	20	27	74	16
Stonehouse	32	3	6	23	34	93	12

Immediate Bristol St. George had 2 points deducted after fielding an ineligible player.
Almondsbury Greenway and Shortwood United left to join the Hellenic League and Matson Athletic also left. They were replaced by Avon St. Philips from the APC, Harrow Hill from the GNSL and Lawrence Weston Hallen.

1982-83

Old Georgians	32	26	3	3	73	23	55
Port of Bristol	32	20	7	5	64	33	47
Lawrence Weston Hallen	32	18	6	8	52	29	42
Hanham Athletic	32	16	10	6	49	28	42
Sharpness	32	14	8	10	51	48	36
Wilton Rovers	32	13	7	12	51	44	33
Hambrook	32	12	8	12	49	38	32
Avon St. Philips	32	11	10	11	53	50	32
Immediate Bristol St. George	32	11	9	12	57	48	31
Harrow Hill	32	13	3	16	55	63	29
Lydbrook Athletic	32	11	7	14	45	55	29
Frampton United	32	9	10	13	44	49	28
Yate Town	32	10	7	15	44	60	27
Oldland (Decora)	32	10	6	16	41	50	26
Cadbury Heath	32	7	8	17	52	72	22
Newent Town	32	6	10	16	41	65	22
Stonehouse	32	3	5	24	28	94	11

Yate Town left to join the Hellenic League but Frampton Athletic from the APC and Wotton Rovers from the GNSL both joined, increasing the league to 18 clubs. Immediate Bristol St. George became Bristol St. George and Hanham Athletic became Mount Hill Hanham Athletic.

1983-84

Sharpness	34	29	4	1	116	26	62
Old Georgians	34	24	7	3	76	29	55
Bristol St. George	34	17	9	8	61	40	43
Port of Bristol	34	14	11	9	50	41	39
Avon St. Philips	34	15	8	11	65	59	38
Lawrence Weston Hallen	34	16	4	14	54	51	36
Hambrook	34	14	6	14	43	46	34
Frampton Athletic	34	15	3	16	61	60	33
Oldland (Decora)	34	12	9	13	59	61	33
Hanham Mount Hill Athletic	34	12	9	13	47	50	33
Harrow Hill	34	11	9	14	40	48	31
Wotton Rovers	34	10	10	14	43	51	30
Wilton Rovers	34	10	9	15	41	61	29
Frampton United	34	9	9	16	43	58	27
Newent Town	34	10	7	17	48	65	27
Lydbrook Athletic	34	10	6	18	57	63	26
Cadbury Heath	34	6	10	18	35	64	22
Stonehouse	34	4	6	24	38	104	14

Sharpness left to join the Hellenic League. Ellwood from the GNSL and Cinderford Town from the Midland Combination joined, increasing the league to 19 clubs. Hanham Mount Hill Athletic reverted to Hanham Athletic and Cadbury Heath became Cadbury Heath St. Josephs.

1984-85

Old Georgians	36	23	10	3	109	46	56
Port of Bristol	36	20	10	6	78	42	50
Hanham Athletic	36	18	10	8	62	36	46
Lydbrook Athletic	36	19	7	10	80	51	45
Lawrence Weston Hallen	36	16	12	8	64	49	44
Ellwood	36	18	7	11	70	56	43
Cinderford Town	36	16	11	9	44	32	43
Harrow Hill	36	16	8	12	74	58	40
Hambrook	36	16	8	12	56	56	40
Avon St. Philips	36	11	11	14	54	54	33
Frampton United	36	10	13	13	43	55	33
Wotton Rovers	36	8	15	13	47	60	31
Cadbury Heath St. Josephs	36	10	9	17	52	67	29
Stonehouse	36	10	9	17	49	71	29
Newent Town	36	10	9	17	38	67	29
Oldland (Decora)	36	9	8	19	38	63	26
Bristol St. George	36	7	11	18	57	76	25
Wilton Rovers	36	9	6	21	52	72	24
Frampton Athletic	36	6	6	24	44	100	18

Frampton Athletic left to join the APC and Wilton Rovers left to join the GNSL. They were replaced by Brimscombe & Thrupp from the GNSL and Patchway from the APC.

1985-86

Patchway	36	27	5	4	80	20	59
Old Georgians	36	22	9	5	80	25	53
Ellwood	36	21	8	7	78	45	50
Brimscombe & Thrupp	36	19	9	8	54	45	47
Wotton Rovers	36	17	11	8	53	42	45
Cinderford Town	36	16	10	10	52	37	42
Lydbrook Athletic	36	17	7	12	66	47	41
Port of Bristol	36	14	12	10	59	46	40
Bristol St. George	36	17	4	15	57	52	38
Harrow Hill	36	14	10	12	66	64	38
Hanham Athletic	36	11	10	15	49	61	32
Avon St. Philips	36	11	8	17	54	66	30
Cadbury Heath St. Josephs	36	12	5	19	54	69	29
Lawrence Weston Hallen	36	8	9	19	44	62	25
Hambrook	36	8	9	19	31	58	25
Stonehouse	36	8	9	19	41	69	25
Frampton United	36	8	8	20	38	59	24
Newent Town	36	7	10	19	39	71	24
Oldland (Decora)	36	3	11	22	42	99	17

Newent Town and Oldland (Decora) left and were replaced by Henbury Old Boys from the APC and Gala Wilton.

1986-87

Old Georgians	36	28	5	3	95	21	61
Ellwood	36	24	6	6	86	43	54
Patchway	36	22	6	8	86	49	50
Bristol St. George	36	15	16	5	67	42	46
Harrow Hill	36	20	5	11	64	43	45
Henbury Old Boys	36	17	8	11	64	42	42
Hanham Athletic	36	16	7	13	53	51	39
Wotton Rovers	36	16	7	13	61	47	39
Lawrence Weston Hallen	36	13	12	11	55	50	38
Cinderford Town	36	15	7	14	60	61	37
Cadbury Heath St. Josephs	36	12	10	14	64	71	34
Port of Bristol	36	12	8	16	47	53	32
Frampton United	36	11	9	16	51	55	31
Brimscombe & Thrupp	36	10	9	17	51	53	29
Gala Wilton	36	11	7	18	43	68	29
Hambrook	36	11	4	21	35	67	26
Stonehouse	36	10	7	19	62	95	24
Lydbrook Athletic	36	4	10	22	35	86	18
Avon St. Philips	36	1	5	30	28	110	7

Stonehouse had 3 points deducted.
Bymacks and D.R.G. (FP) joined but Avon St. Philips, Bristol St. George and Lydbrook Athletic left, reducing the league to 18 clubs. Cadbury Heath St. Josephs reverted to Cadbury Heath.

1987-88

Old Georgians	34	26	4	4	108	45	56
Lawrence Weston Hallen	34	23	9	2	78	29	55
Ellwood	34	22	5	7	77	37	49
Henbury Old Boys	34	21	6	7	83	36	48
Patchway	34	17	8	9	65	42	42
Harrow Hill	34	15	8	11	55	49	38
Hambrook	34	15	6	13	49	47	36
D.R.G. (FP)	34	12	9	13	63	51	33
Port of Bristol	34	11	8	15	55	55	30
Wotton Rovers	34	9	12	13	48	64	30
Brimscombe & Thrupp	34	10	9	15	40	51	29
Frampton United	34	9	10	15	30	51	28
Cadbury Heath	34	10	8	16	39	61	28
Bymacks	34	9	10	15	28	50	28
Cinderford Town	34	11	4	19	49	59	26
Hanham Athletic	34	6	13	15	35	56	25
Gala Wilton	34	8	7	19	39	74	23
Stonehouse	34	1	6	27	33	117	4

Stonehouse had 4 points deducted.
Bymacks disbanded and Gala Wilton and Stonehouse were relegated to the GNSL. They were replaced by Campden Town from the Worcestershire Senior League, Pucklechurch Sports from the APC and Tuffley Rovers from the GNSL.

1988-89 (Three points for a win)

Lawrence Weston Hallen	34	24	5	5	86	28	77
Henbury Old Boys	34	23	7	4	87	33	76
Ellwood	34	24	3	7	76	37	75
Old Georgians	34	18	6	10	77	44	60
Pucklechurch Sports	34	18	6	10	78	53	60
Patchway	34	15	14	5	55	39	59
Harrow Hill	34	12	11	11	43	41	47
Campden Town	34	13	7	14	49	50	46
Port of Bristol	34	12	8	14	45	51	44
Hambrook	34	12	7	15	49	52	43
Tuffley Rovers	34	11	8	15	54	60	39
Cinderford Town	34	10	8	16	57	74	38
D.R.G. (FP)	34	8	13	13	47	62	37
Cadbury Heath	34	9	7	18	44	61	34
Wotton Rovers	34	8	8	18	43	77	32
Frampton United	34	6	13	15	37	51	31
Hanham Athletic	34	7	10	17	40	67	31
Brimscombe & Thrupp	34	1	9	24	22	104	12

Tuffley Rovers had 2 points deducted.
Brimscombe & Thrupp left to join the GNSL and Hanham Athletic left to join the APC. St. Philips Marsh Adult School from the APC and Berkeley Town both joined the League.

1989-90

Ellwood	34	27	3	4	84	32	84
Old Georgians	34	22	6	6	82	39	72
Henbury Old Boys	34	19	6	9	84	48	63
Lawrence Weston Hallen	34	17	9	8	69	57	60
Cadbury Heath	34	18	5	11	69	45	59
Harrow Hill	34	16	8	10	66	40	56
St. Philips Marsh Adult School	34	16	7	11	65	58	55
D.R.G. (FP)	34	14	10	10	66	57	52
Patchway	34	11	8	15	68	64	41
Wotton Rovers	34	12	4	18	45	66	40
Cinderford Town	34	10	9	15	52	60	39
Port of Bristol	34	10	9	15	51	65	39
Hambrook	34	9	10	15	45	56	37
Pucklechurch Sports	34	8	12	14	44	57	36
Tuffley Rovers	34	9	8	17	47	61	35
Berkeley Town	34	8	11	15	32	46	35
Campden Town	34	8	6	20	36	84	30
Frampton United	34	4	5	25	29	84	17

Cinderford Town left to join the Hellenic League and Frampton United left to join the GNSL. They were replaced by Stapleton from the APC and St. Marks C.A.. Lawrence Weston Hallen changed their name to Hallen.

1990-91

Tuffley Rovers	34	23	2	9	87	34	71
Cadbury Heath	34	21	6	7	80	42	69
Ellwood	34	20	7	7	84	46	67
Henbury Old Boys	34	18	11	5	51	32	65
Hallen	34	20	4	10	85	56	64
Patchway	34	18	3	13	71	55	55
St. Philips Marsh Adult School	34	14	10	10	77	55	52
Old Georgians	34	14	7	13	48	64	49
D.R.G. (FP)	34	11	10	13	45	59	43
Hambrook	34	12	6	16	55	58	42
St. Marks C.A.	34	12	5	17	52	63	41
Harrow Hill	34	10	9	15	41	49	39
Port of Bristol	34	8	11	15	54	70	35
Stapleton	34	10	5	19	36	64	35
Wotton Rovers	34	8	9	17	54	73	33
Pucklechurch Sports	34	7	12	15	40	70	33
Campden Town	34	8	5	21	51	80	29
Berkeley Town	34	5	12	17	52	93	27

Dowty Dynamos joined from the GNSL. Berkeley Town left to join the GNSL and Tuffley Rovers left to join the Hellenic League.
The League was reduced to 17 clubs.

1991-92

Patchway Town	32	24	5	3	87	29	77
Cadbury Heath	32	19	11	2	85	27	68
Hallen	32	19	8	5	83	46	65
D.R.G. (FP)	32	18	9	5	56	37	63
Ellwood	32	17	5	10	60	47	56
St. Philips Marsh Adult School	32	14	10	8	70	48	52
Pucklechurch Sports	32	11	11	10	43	49	44
Wotton Rovers	32	12	7	13	59	41	43
Henbury Old Boys	32	12	4	16	53	53	40
Campden Town	32	11	5	16	39	55	38
Stapleton	32	9	7	16	42	66	34
Old Georgians	32	9	7	16	24	50	34
Harrow Hill	32	8	9	15	41	53	33
Hambrook	32	9	6	17	43	56	33
St. Marks C.A.	32	8	8	16	34	59	32
Dowty Dynamos	32	8	6	18	39	71	30
Port of Bristol	32	4	2	26	33	104	14

Port of Bristol left to join the Bristol & Suburban League. Smiths Athletic joined from the GNSL and Winterbourne United joined from the APC.
The League was increased to 18 clubs.

1992-93

Hallen	34	26	2	6	91	35	80
Old Georgians	34	24	5	5	77	37	77
Ellwood	34	21	4	9	93	50	67
D.R.G. (FP)	34	20	3	11	74	42	63
Wotton Rovers	34	16	9	9	61	56	57
Harrow Hill	34	16	6	12	67	54	54
Patchway Town	34	14	11	9	59	43	53
Cadbury Heath	34	15	6	13	52	51	51
Henbury Old Boys	34	13	11	10	52	49	50
Pucklechurch Sports	34	14	4	16	46	56	46
St. Philips Marsh Adult School	34	12	7	15	53	51	43
St. Marks C.A.	34	12	6	16	43	52	42
Campden Town	34	10	10	14	39	55	40
Winterbourne United	34	10	7	17	47	70	37
Dowty Dynamos	34	8	8	18	49	63	32
Smiths Athletic	34	8	8	18	42	62	32
Stapleton	34	6	5	23	42	87	23
Hambrook	34	2	6	26	19	93	12

Hallen left to join the Hellenic League and Hambrook left to join the APC. They were replaced by Endsleigh from the GNSL and Totterdown Athletic from the Bristol & Suburban League. D.R.G. (FP) changed their name to D.R.G.

1993-94

Cadbury Heath	34	24	5	5	68	28	77
Endsleigh	34	23	5	6	78	27	74
St. Philips Marsh Adult School	34	23	4	7	66	22	73
Ellwood	34	18	9	7	67	34	63
Henbury Old Boys	34	18	8	8	67	41	62
Patchway Town	34	16	11	7	67	35	59
Harrow Hill	34	16	5	13	73	42	53
Totterdown Athletic	34	15	7	12	63	56	52
D.R.G.	34	15	5	14	54	50	50
Old Georgians	34	14	6	14	46	53	48
Pucklechurch Sports	34	13	8	13	41	51	47
St. Marks C.A.	34	13	7	14	50	47	46
Wotton Rovers	34	13	3	18	56	56	42
Smiths Athletic	34	11	9	14	50	56	42
Stapleton	33	8	5	20	34	69	29
Winterbourne United	34	7	6	21	42	70	27
Campden Town	33	2	4	27	27	116	10
Dowty Dynamos	34	1	3	30	30	126	6

Stapleton vs Campden Town was not played as Campden Town could not raise a side.
Dowty Dynamos left to join the GNSL, Endsleigh left to join the Hellenic League and Campden Town also left. Broadwell Amateurs joined from the GNSL and Oldland joined from the APC.
The League was reduced to 17 clubs.
Totterdown Athletic merged with Port of Bristol and became Totterdown Port of Bristol.

1994-95

Henbury Old Boys	32	19	10	3	62	29	67
Harrow Hill	32	17	10	5	52	32	61
Pucklechurch Sports	32	17	4	11	49	43	55
Ellwood	32	15	9	8	66	45	54
D.R.G.	32	14	7	11	51	50	49
Old Georgians	32	13	8	11	52	48	47
Cadbury Heath	32	13	8	11	57	54	47
Stapleton	32	13	8	11	45	45	47
Totterdown Port of Bristol	32	12	6	14	48	42	42
St. Marks C.A.	32	10	9	13	41	50	39
Wotton Rovers	32	9	11	12	40	48	38
Broadwell Amateurs	32	10	7	15	40	42	37
Winterbourne United	32	11	3	18	59	66	36
Patchway Town	32	7	11	14	42	52	32
Smiths Athletic	32	8	8	16	37	58	32
Oldland	32	5	15	12	40	58	30
St. Philips Marsh Adult School	32	9	6	17	47	65	30
					828	827	

St. Philips Marsh Adult School had 3 points deducted.
Harrow Hill left to join the Hellenic League, St. Philips Marsh Adult School left to join the BPC and Oldland also left. Broad Plain House Old Boys joined from the Bristol & Suburban League, Bitton and Frampton Athletic both joined from the BPC and Brockworth joined from the GNSL.
The League was increased to 18 clubs.

1995-96

	P	W	D	L	F	A	Pts
D.R.G.	34	23	7	4	74	30	76
Cadbury Heath	34	19	6	9	70	36	63
Broad Plain House Old Boys	34	18	9	7	68	46	63
Brockworth	34	19	5	10	62	42	62
Bitton	34	15	11	8	63	37	56
Frampton Athletic	34	14	9	11	53	49	51
Wotton Rovers	34	14	7	13	54	53	49
Patchway Town	34	13	6	15	51	62	45
Old Georgians	34	11	12	11	49	60	45
Henbury Old Boys	34	11	10	13	49	55	43
St. Marks C.A.	34	11	10	13	68	76	43
Totterdown Port of Bristol	34	11	8	15	58	62	41
Ellwood	34	9	12	13	35	49	39
Broadwell Amateurs	34	9	9	16	38	60	36
Pucklechurch Sports	34	8	11	15	39	63	35
Stapleton	34	8	10	16	38	52	34
Smiths Athletic	34	8	5	21	45	62	29
Winterbourne United	34	6	11	17	43	63	29

Smiths Athletic left to join the GNSL and Winterbourne United also left. They were replaced by Dursley Town from the GNSL and Oldland.

1996-97

	P	W	D	L	F	A	Pts
Old Georgians	34	19	13	2	58	27	70
Bitton	34	19	10	5	68	38	67
Frampton Athletic	34	17	10	7	80	54	61
Henbury Old Boys	34	16	10	8	66	44	58
Cadbury Heath	34	16	9	9	64	44	57
Dursley Town	34	15	11	8	44	33	56
Brockworth	34	15	4	15	47	46	49
D.R.G.	34	12	11	11	63	47	47
Broad Plain House Old Boys	34	13	8	13	52	57	47
Oldland	34	12	7	15	51	73	43
Patchway Town	34	10	10	13	41	51	41
Pucklechurch Sports	34	11	7	16	45	52	40
Stapleton	34	10	9	15	46	59	39
Broadwell Amateurs	34	8	11	15	54	61	35
Wotton Rovers	34	9	8	17	40	63	35
Totterdown Port of Bristol	34	9	6	19	36	57	33
Ellwood	34	8	7	19	39	57	31
St. Marks C.A.	34	9	4	21	40	71	31

Bitton left to join the Western League and St. Marks C.A. left to join the GNSL. They were replaced by Viney St. Swithins and Winterbourne United.

1997-98

	P	W	D	L	F	A	Pts
Cadbury Heath	34	24	5	5	81	27	77
Henbury Old Boys	34	19	8	7	55	31	65
Pucklechurch Sports	34	18	9	7	52	31	63
Dursley Town	34	16	12	6	40	23	60
Patchway Town	34	15	11	8	51	36	56
D.R.G.	34	15	10	9	78	56	55
Wotton Rovers	34	14	8	12	53	58	50
Broadwell Amateurs	34	13	9	12	54	48	48
Viney St. Swithins	34	13	8	13	56	47	47
Frampton Athletic	34	12	11	11	43	46	47
Winterbourne United	34	11	12	11	68	59	45
Totterdown Port of Bristol	34	12	6	16	41	55	42
Old Georgians	34	11	6	17	46	60	39
Brockworth	34	9	10	15	36	58	37
Ellwood	34	9	7	18	38	54	34
Broad Plain House Old Boys	34	8	7	19	39	58	31
Oldland	34	5	8	21	46	82	23
Stapleton	34	6	5	23	31	77	23
					908	906	

Stapleton left to join the BPC and Oldland also left the League. They were replaced by Highridge United from the BPC and Tytherington Rocks from the Bristol Suburban League.

1998-99

	P	W	D	L	F	A	Pts
Cadbury Heath	34	27	4	3	89	32	85
Highridge United	34	21	8	5	79	32	71
Winterbourne United	34	20	7	7	69	35	67
Patchway Town	34	19	10	5	57	37	67
Dursley Town	34	17	7	10	46	31	58
D.R.G.	34	15	8	11	59	48	53
Frampton Athletic	34	14	10	10	57	38	52
Old Georgians	34	16	4	14	51	56	52
Broad Plain House Old Boys	34	14	7	13	57	47	49
Henbury Old Boys	34	13	10	11	51	43	49
Ellwood	34	10	12	12	28	41	42
Broadwell Amateurs	34	11	8	15	32	47	41
Pucklechurch Sports	34	10	7	17	41	55	37
Brockworth	34	9	8	17	31	51	35
Viney St. Swithins	34	8	8	18	33	61	32
Tytherington Rocks	34	7	10	17	47	63	31
Totterdown Port of Bristol	34	4	7	23	33	66	19
Wotton Rovers	34	2	3	29	26	103	9

Wotton Rovers left to join the GNSL and Totterdown Port of Bristol also left. They were replaced by Hardwicke from the GNSL and Roman Glass St. George from the BPC.

1999-2000

	P	W	D	L	F	A	Pts
Highridge United	34	26	5	3	68	29	83
Cadbury Heath	34	22	6	6	81	42	72
Patchway Town	34	19	6	9	70	33	63
Hardwicke	34	18	5	11	62	47	59
D.R.G.	34	16	10	8	63	35	58
Henbury Old Boys	34	17	6	11	51	41	57
Ellwood	34	16	8	10	54	37	56
Tytherington Rocks	34	17	3	14	67	60	54
Winterbourne United	34	13	7	14	73	67	46
Old Georgians	34	13	7	14	47	62	46
Frampton Athletic	34	13	5	16	50	49	44
Roman Glass St. George	34	12	5	17	57	74	41
Viney St. Swithins	34	10	10	14	43	48	40
Broad Plain House Old Boys	34	10	9	15	55	51	39
Pucklechurch Sports	34	11	5	18	47	70	38
Brockworth	34	7	9	18	40	61	30
Broadwell Amateurs	34	6	3	25	38	93	21
Dursley Town	34	4	3	27	29	76	15

Broadwell Amateurs and Dursley Town both left to join the GNSL and Cadbury Heath left to join the Western League. Whitminster joined from the GNSL, AXA joined from the BPC and Totterdown Port of Bristol joined. D.R.G. merged with Stapleton and became D.R.G. Stapleton. Frampton Athletic became Frampton Athletic Rangers.

2000-01

	P	W	D	L	F	A	Pts
Winterbourne United	34	24	4	6	89	48	76
Highridge United	34	22	4	8	71	28	70
Patchway Town	34	20	9	5	66	31	69
Tytherington Rocks	34	17	7	10	75	48	58
Whitminster	34	15	9	10	59	44	54
Brockworth	34	15	9	10	59	52	54
Roman Glass St. George	34	16	6	12	52	49	54
D.R.G. Stapleton	34	12	11	11	59	52	47
Pucklechurch Sports	34	14	5	15	50	47	47
Totterdown Port of Bristol	34	13	7	14	56	63	46
AXA	34	13	5	16	62	72	44
Hardwicke	34	11	7	16	61	70	40
Viney St. Swithins	34	10	10	14	51	63	40
Ellwood	34	10	6	18	46	66	36
Henbury Old Boys	34	10	5	19	46	64	35
Broad Plain House Old Boys	34	9	7	18	43	65	34
Old Georgians	34	9	6	19	45	75	33
Frampton Athletic Rangers	34	7	1	26	40	93	22

Winterbourne United left to join the Hellenic League, Brockworth left to join the GNSL and Frampton Athletic Rangers also left. Almondsbury joined from the Bristol & Suburban League and Slimbridge Town joined from the GNSL. League reduced to 17 clubs.

2001-02

	P	W	D	L	F	A	Pts
Roman Glass St. George	32	22	3	7	83	40	69
Slimbridge Town	32	21	5	6	81	33	68
Highridge United	32	20	8	4	68	33	68
Ellwood	32	19	5	8	57	36	62
Patchway Town	32	15	11	6	55	27	56
Almondsbury	32	17	5	10	65	38	56
D.R.G. Stapleton	32	13	10	9	51	41	49
Henbury Old Boys	32	11	12	9	50	46	45
Tytherington Rocks	32	10	8	14	35	49	38
Viney St. Swithins	32	11	5	16	43	68	38
AXA	32	10	7	15	47	60	37
Whitminster	32	10	7	15	38	61	37
Hardwicke	32	9	5	18	44	56	32
Pucklechurch Sports	32	7	10	15	31	43	31
Old Georgians	32	8	5	19	31	62	29
Totterdown Port of Bristol	32	5	9	18	39	69	24
Broad Plain House Old Boys	32	3	7	22	41	97	16

Broad Plain House Old Boys left to join the Bristol & Suburban League and Slimbridge Town left to join the Hellenic League. Wotton Rovers and Taverners both joined from the GNSL and Thornbury Town joined from the BPC. The League was increased to 18 clubs.

2002-03

	P	W	D	L	F	A	Pts
Patchway Town	34	23	7	4	69	18	76
Henbury Old Boys	34	21	6	7	73	36	69
Wotton Rovers	34	18	11	5	70	39	65
Almondsbury	34	19	5	10	76	49	62
Tytherington Rocks	34	18	3	13	72	57	57
Highridge United	34	17	5	12	54	49	56
Thornbury Town	34	16	7	11	65	48	55
D.R.G. Stapleton	34	13	7	14	62	52	46
AXA	34	13	6	15	59	64	45
Roman Glass St. George	34	12	7	15	53	60	43
Taverners	34	12	6	16	40	46	42
Old Georgians	34	12	5	17	55	70	41
Hardwicke	34	12	5	17	57	84	41
Ellwood	34	9	9	16	36	48	36
Pucklechurch Sports	34	10	4	20	55	88	34
Totterdown Port of Bristol	34	8	9	17	39	53	33
Viney St. Swithins	34	7	10	17	35	62	31
Whitminster	34	6	8	20	44	91	26

Whitminster left to join the Stroud & District League and were replaced by Kings Stanley from the GNSL.

2003-04

	P	W	D	L	F	A	Pts
Almondsbury	34	20	10	4	63	32	70
Tytherington Rocks	34	20	9	5	81	47	69
Patchway Town	34	19	9	6	63	38	63
Taverners	34	17	9	8	53	35	60
Highridge United	34	15	10	9	64	45	55
AXA	34	13	11	10	68	67	50
Thornbury Town	34	13	10	11	51	42	49
Kings Stanley	34	12	13	9	61	53	49
Roman Glass St. George	34	12	12	10	71	63	48
Henbury Old Boys	34	12	7	15	42	52	43
Hardwicke	34	10	11	13	50	64	41
Ellwood	34	10	10	14	54	64	40
Totterdown Port of Bristol	34	10	11	13	58	52	38
Old Georgians	34	8	11	15	64	70	35
Wotton Rovers	34	8	10	16	44	57	34
Pucklechurch Sports	34	8	9	17	44	67	33
D.R.G. Stapleton	34	7	5	22	32	75	23
Viney St. Swithins	34	4	9	21	34	74	21

Patchway Town, Totterdown Port of Bristol and D.R.G. Stapleton all had 3 points deducted.
Almondsbury left to join the Western League and Tytherington Rocks left to join the Hellenic League. Longwell Green Sports joined from the BPC, Sea Mills Park joined from the BPC and Yate Town Reserves joined from the Bristol & Suburban League. The League was increased to 19 clubs.

2004-05

	P	W	D	L	F	A	Pts
Highridge United	36	24	10	2	104	35	82
Longwell Green Sports	36	25	7	4	92	34	82
Ellwood	36	24	5	7	84	36	77
Kings Stanley	36	21	7	8	75	50	70
Roman Glass St. George	36	20	9	7	82	36	69
Patchway Town	36	18	9	9	71	54	63
Thornbury Town	36	17	12	7	64	49	63
Yate Town Reserves	36	17	5	14	84	76	56
Hardwicke	36	17	4	15	70	52	55
Sea Mills Park	36	13	8	15	74	73	47
AXA	36	12	8	16	75	79	44
Totterdown Port of Bristol	36	14	4	18	74	84	46
Wotton Rovers	36	11	9	16	48	65	42
Taverners	36	9	12	15	48	64	39
Henbury Old Boys	36	8	10	18	46	72	34
D.R.G. Stapleton	36	8	4	24	43	96	28
Pucklechurch Sports	36	5	6	25	37	85	21
Old Georgians	36	6	3	27	45	95	21
Viney St. Swithins	36	5	4	27	45	126	19

Henbury Old Boys changed their name to Henbury. Longwell Green Sports left to join the Western League, Old Georgians left and joined the Bristol & Suburban League and Viney St. Swithins left and joined the GNSL. Lydney Town joined from the GNSL. The League was reduced to 17 clubs.

2005-06

	P	W	D	L	F	A	Pts
Lydney Town	32	23	7	2	87	28	76
Highridge United	32	20	6	6	73	31	66
Yate Town Reserves	32	17	8	7	61	36	59
Totterdown Port of Bristol	32	16	8	8	70	46	56
Patchway Town	32	17	5	10	55	39	56
Ellwood	32	15	9	8	60	35	54
Taverners	32	15	6	11	56	46	51
Henbury	32	17	6	9	56	45	50
Roman Glass St. George	32	15	4	13	49	47	49
Thornbury Town	32	13	5	14	56	56	44
Hardwicke	32	12	6	14	60	61	42
AXA	32	10	8	14	56	59	38
Kings Stanley	32	10	7	15	56	62	37
D.R.G. Stapleton	32	7	6	19	44	79	27
Sea Mills Park	32	6	4	22	36	92	22
Wotton Rovers	32	4	4	24	31	103	16
Pucklechurch Sports	32	3	5	24	31	72	14

Henbury had 7 points deducted.
Lydney Town moved to the Hellenic League. Berkeley Town joined from the GNSL and Hanham Athletic joined from the BPC.

2006-07

	P	W	D	L	F	A	Pts
Roman Glass St. George	34	22	8	4	77	36	74
Patchway Town	34	21	8	5	66	36	71
Highridge United	34	20	8	6	72	40	66
Henbury	34	20	4	10	75	47	64
Yate Town Reserves	34	19	6	9	86	34	63
Taverners	34	19	5	10	46	30	62
Ellwood	34	17	2	15	53	54	53
Hanham Athletic	34	14	9	11	46	39	48
Hardwicke	34	14	5	15	48	53	47
Kings Stanley	34	14	4	16	45	57	46
AXA	34	11	11	12	57	61	44
Totterdown Port of Bristol	34	13	4	17	63	63	43
Sea Mills Park	34	11	7	16	48	67	40
D.R.G. Stapleton	34	10	6	18	42	67	36
Berkeley Town	34	9	8	17	44	65	35
Wotton Rovers	34	5	10	19	37	76	24
Thornbury Town	34	5	8	21	37	64	23
Pucklechurch Sports	34	3	7	24	25	78	16

Hanham Athletic had 3 points deducted.
Wotton Rovers had 1 point deducted.
Roman Glass St. George moved to the Western League. Totterdown Port of Bristol resigned and took their reserves' place in the Bristol & Suburban League. Sea Mills Park resigned and took their reserves' place in the Bristol & District League.

2007-08

Team	P	W	D	L	F	A	Pts
Hardwicke	30	23	5	2	74	18	74
Highridge United	30	17	7	6	64	35	57
Hanham Athletic	30	18	5	7	78	33	56
Tuffley Rovers	30	16	5	9	49	39	53
AXA	30	15	7	8	61	43	52
Ellwood	30	15	5	10	65	53	50
Patchway Town	30	13	9	8	61	46	48
Yate Town Reserves	30	13	9	8	47	32	48
Kings Stanley	30	15	4	11	60	51	46
Taverners	30	12	5	13	43	35	41
Thornbury Town	30	7	7	16	31	55	28
Berkeley Town	30	7	7	16	46	76	28
D.R.G. Stapleton	30	5	10	15	36	61	25
Henbury	30	5	8	17	38	60	23
Pucklechurch Sports	30	4	9	17	27	58	21
Wotton Rovers	30	3	2	25	25	110	11

Hanham Athletic and Kings Stanley both had 3 points deducted.
Highridge United had 1 point deducted.
Hardwicke moved to the Hellenic League, Pucklechurch Sport moved to the BPC and Wotton Rovers moved to the GNSL. B & W Avonside joined from the Bristol & Suburban League, Chipping Sodbury Town joined from the BPC and Slimbridge and Bishops Cleeve Reserves both joined from the GNSL.

2008-09

Team	P	W	D	L	F	A	Pts
Slimbridge	32	24	4	4	79	24	76
Kings Stanley	32	22	3	7	76	37	69
Ellwood	32	20	3	9	69	36	63
Bishops Cleeve Reserves	32	18	5	9	63	46	59
Henbury	32	17	6	9	69	46	57
AXA	32	13	10	9	65	67	49
Yate Town Reserves	32	14	6	12	74	53	48
Taverners	32	11	9	12	36	38	42
Thornbury Town	32	11	8	13	50	50	41
B & W Avonside	32	11	7	14	52	55	40
Tuffley Rovers	32	12	4	16	64	70	40
Berkeley Town	32	11	5	16	39	71	38
Highridge United	32	10	5	17	40	55	35
Patchway Town	32	9	7	16	43	60	34
Hanham Athletic	32	7	8	17	46	69	29
D.R.G. Stapleton	32	8	6	18	46	85	27
Chipping Sodbury Town	32	5	2	25	30	79	14

D.R.G. Stapleton and Chipping Sodbury Town both had 3 points deducted.
B & W Avonside changed their name to Rockleaze Avonside. Slimbridge moved to the Hellenic League. Brimscombe & Thrupp and Kingswood both joined from the GNSL.

2009-10

Team	P	W	D	L	F	A	Pts
Thornbury Town	34	22	6	6	90	36	72
Highridge United	34	21	8	5	83	40	71
Tuffley Rovers	34	19	7	8	66	39	64
Yate Town Reserves	34	20	4	10	75	46	61
Brimscombe & Thrupp	34	19	4	11	57	51	61
Kings Stanley	34	17	6	11	70	47	57
Hanham Athletic	34	14	7	13	43	44	49
Chipping Sodbury Town	34	13	9	12	64	51	48
Rockleaze Avonside	34	14	8	12	55	45	45
Kingswood	34	11	11	12	48	49	44
AXA	34	13	2	19	56	88	41
D.R.G. Stapleton	34	11	9	14	41	48	39
Henbury	34	10	8	16	47	56	38
Bishops Cleeve Reserves	34	8	13	13	45	57	37
Berkeley Town	34	8	9	17	45	77	33
Taverners	34	7	11	16	35	52	32
Patchway Town	34	9	4	21	38	75	31
Ellwood	34	2	10	22	33	90	16

Yate Town Reserves and D.R.G. Stapleton both had 3 points deducted.
Rockleaze Avonside had 5 points deducted.
Rockleaze Avonside changed their name to Rockleaze Rangers. Highridge United resigned and took their reserves' place in the BPC.

2010-11

Team	P	W	D	L	F	A	Pts
Brimscombe & Thrupp	32	24	4	4	75	30	76
AXA	32	17	9	6	46	35	60
Chipping Sodbury Town	32	16	10	6	64	35	58
Yate Town Reserves	32	17	7	8	74	48	58
Patchway Town	32	15	7	10	57	46	52
Tuffley Rovers	32	15	4	13	55	55	49
Henbury	32	13	7	12	51	44	46
Kings Stanley	32	14	4	14	60	62	46
D.R.G. Stapleton	32	11	11	10	49	52	43
Taverners	32	10	10	12	52	51	40
Berkeley Town	32	11	6	15	45	60	39
Rockleaze Rangers	32	9	9	14	47	55	36
Thornbury Town	32	9	8	15	48	56	35
Bishops Cleeve Reserves	32	8	8	16	30	45	31
Ellwood	32	9	4	19	31	59	31
Kingswood	32	7	8	17	50	66	29
Hanham Athletic	32	7	5	20	46	81	23

Hanham Athletic had 3 points deducted.
Bishops Cleeve Reserves had 1 point deducted.
AXA changed their name to Cribbs Friends Life. Brimscombe & Thrupp moved to the Hellenic League. Longlevens joined from the GNSL and Bristol Academy joined as a new club.

2011-12

Team	P	W	D	L	F	A	Pts
Cribbs Friends Life	34	24	5	5	90	34	77
Henbury	34	20	7	7	61	45	67
Tuffley Rovers	34	21	2	11	72	44	65
Patchway Town	34	18	5	11	55	34	59
Ellwood	34	16	8	10	64	62	56
D.R.G. Stapleton	34	15	8	11	60	46	53
Bristol Academy	34	13	9	12	61	52	48
Kings Stanley	34	14	6	14	70	71	48
Longlevens	34	14	6	14	57	52	45
Hanham Athletic	34	12	7	15	49	56	43
Kingswood	34	12	6	16	50	61	42
Yate Town Reserves	34	14	3	17	55	74	42
Taverners	34	11	8	15	39	49	41
Bishops Cleeve Reserves	34	9	13	12	51	58	40
Berkeley Town	34	10	8	16	40	57	38
Thornbury Town	34	11	3	20	46	59	36
Rockleaze Rangers	34	10	5	19	53	70	35
Chipping Sodbury Town	34	6	3	25	40	89	21

Longlevens and Yate Town Reserves both had 3 points deducted.
D.R.G. Stapleton changed their name to D.R.G. Frenchay. Cribbs Friends Life moved to the Western League. Southmead CS Athletic joined from the Bristol Suburban League and Frampton United joined from the GNSL.

2012-13

Team	P	W	D	L	F	A	Pts
Longlevens	36	24	5	7	86	44	77
Tuffley Rovers	36	22	6	8	76	47	72
Rockleaze Rangers	36	20	6	10	74	41	66
Southmead CS Athletic	36	21	6	9	85	58	66
Bristol Academy	36	19	9	8	68	44	66
Ellwood	36	17	9	10	67	45	60
Henbury	36	16	6	14	54	57	54
Kings Stanley	36	15	8	13	56	46	53
Patchway Town	36	14	7	15	48	53	49
Hanham Athletic	36	13	9	14	54	58	48
Kingswood	36	13	7	16	42	49	46
Bishops Cleeve Reserves	36	14	2	20	53	65	44
Frampton United	36	12	8	16	56	75	44
Thornbury Town	36	12	4	20	50	66	40
Chipping Sodbury Town	36	11	6	19	52	78	39
Yate Town Reserves	36	9	11	16	53	64	38
Berkeley Town	36	8	7	21	45	92	31
Taverners	36	7	9	20	35	53	30
D.R.G. Frenchay	36	8	9	19	45	64	30

Southmead CS Athletic and D.R.G. Frenchay both had 3 points deducted.

Tuffley Rovers moved to the Hellenic League, Taverners moved to the GNSL and DRG Frenchay moved to the BPC. Gala Wilton joined from the GNSL and Bristol Telephones joined from the Bristol Suburban League.

2013-14

Longlevens	34	26	5	3	105	32	83
Gala Wilton	34	20	6	8	85	45	66
Bristol Telephones	34	19	8	7	91	66	65
Kings Stanley	34	18	10	6	72	41	64
Southmead CS Athletic	34	18	6	10	68	59	57
Patchway Town	34	14	12	8	58	47	54
Frampton United	34	15	7	12	64	48	52
Ellwood	34	13	9	12	50	59	48
Rockleaze Rangers	34	12	5	17	52	62	41
Chipping Sodbury Town	34	11	7	16	67	67	40
Kingswood	34	11	7	16	56	61	40
Henbury	34	12	7	15	47	62	40
Hanham Athletic	34	9	9	16	53	77	36
Bishops Cleeve Reserves	34	10	8	16	65	90	35
Bristol Academy	34	10	5	19	60	87	35
Thornbury Town	34	9	6	19	47	67	33
Yate Town Reserves	34	7	7	20	51	82	28
Berkeley Town	34	8	4	22	47	86	28

Southmead CS Athletic, Henbury and Bishops Cleeve Reserves both had 3 points deducted.
Longlevens moved to the Hellenic League and Bristol Academy withdrew from senior football. Cheltenham Civil Service joined from the GNSL and AEK Boco joined from the BPC.

2014-15

Cheltenham Civil Service	34	25	7	2	101	27	82
AEK Boco	34	23	5	6	77	45	74
Chipping Sodbury Town	34	19	8	7	81	36	65
Thornbury Town	34	18	6	10	67	54	60
Kings Stanley	34	17	8	9	66	47	59
Frampton United	34	15	13	6	56	37	58
Gala Wilton	34	16	9	9	70	54	57
Bristol Telephones	34	17	2	15	107	61	53
Rockleaze Rangers	34	15	8	11	52	50	53
Henbury	34	14	7	13	59	62	49
Kingswood	34	13	4	17	51	56	43
Ellwood	34	13	3	18	46	66	42
Southmead CS Athletic	34	9	5	20	41	83	32
Hanham Athletic	34	9	4	21	36	61	31
Bishops Cleeve Reserves	34	9	4	21	50	88	31
Yate Town Reserves	34	7	9	18	43	66	30
Patchway Town	34	9	3	22	31	75	30
Berkeley Town	34	4	3	27	30	96	15

Berkeley Town moved to the GNSL and Chipping Sodbury Town moved to the Western League. Broadwell Amateurs and Hardwicke both joined from the GNSL.

WESSEX LEAGUE

Formation

The Wessex League was formed in 1986 to provide a platform for ambitious clubs from Hampshire and the surrounding area who might wish to progress to the Southern League. Its 17 founder members were: AFC Totton, Brockenhurst, Eastleigh, Havant Town, Horndean, Lymington Town, Newport (I.O.W.), Portals Athletic, Portsmouth Royal Navy, Romsey Town and Sholing Sports, all from Division One of the Hampshire League, plus:

Bashley from Division Two of the Hampshire League; Bournemouth and Wellworthy Athletic from Division Three of the Hampshire League; Road Sea Southampton from the Southern League Premier Division; Steyning Town who were Sussex County League champions and Thatcham Town from the London-Spartan League.

Some published tables contained errors which have been corrected in the tables below.

1986-87

Bashley	32	24	3	5	71	30	75
Road Sea Southampton	32	22	7	3	70	26	73
AFC Totton	32	20	7	5	62	21	67
Newport (I.O.W.)	32	15	8	9	51	36	53
Havant Town	32	15	7	10	57	48	52
Thatcham Town	32	15	6	11	53	33	51
Wellworthy Athletic	32	14	6	12	48	50	48
Eastleigh	32	14	6	12	40	42	48
Sholing Sports	32	10	8	14	41	45	38
Lymington Town	32	10	8	14	31	37	38
Steyning Town	32	10	8	14	45	47	37
Portals Athletic	32	9	9	14	37	46	36
Portsmouth Royal Navy	32	11	2	19	43	58	35
Horndean	32	8	8	16	42	55	32
Bournemouth	32	7	9	16	33	59	28
Romsey Town	32	7	7	18	25	61	28
Brockenhurst	32	4	5	23	34	89	17

Steyning Town had 1 point deducted.
Road Sea Southampton disbanded and Portals Athletic left. East Cowes Victoria Athletic, Folland Sports and Christchurch joined from the Hampshire League and Wimborne Town joined from the Western League.

1987-88

Bashley	36	26	6	4	91	26	84
Havant Town	36	24	8	4	91	31	80
Romsey Town	36	22	3	11	69	46	69
Newport (I.O.W.)	36	19	8	9	71	37	65
Christchurch	36	17	11	8	50	40	62
Wimborne Town	36	17	8	11	68	53	59
Sholing Sports	36	15	12	9	50	45	57
AFC Totton	36	16	8	12	52	37	56
East Cowes Victoria Athletic	36	15	10	11	49	32	55
Bournemouth	36	14	8	14	55	38	50
Thatcham Town	36	14	7	15	50	53	49
Eastleigh	36	13	8	15	36	39	47
Folland Sports	36	13	7	16	42	48	46
Horndean	36	12	9	15	52	58	45
Wellworthy Athletic	36	12	8	16	46	53	44
Portsmouth Royal Navy	36	11	4	21	39	72	37
Steyning Town	36	6	8	22	24	81	26
Brockenhurst	36	2	8	26	23	93	14
Lymington Town	36	0	7	29	27	103	7

Lymington Town and Wellworthy Athletic merged to form AFC Lymington. Steyning Town moved to the Combined Counties League.

1988-89

Bashley	32	26	4	2	87	24	82
Havant Town	32	21	8	3	67	26	71
Newport (I.O.W.)	32	20	6	6	67	32	66
Thatcham Town	32	17	7	8	60	26	58
AFC Lymington	32	16	9	7	51	32	57
Wimborne Town	32	14	6	12	59	55	48
Romsey Town	32	9	16	7	47	39	43
East Cowes Victoria Athletic	32	11	8	13	44	48	41
Eastleigh	32	10	10	12	39	34	40
Folland Sports	32	10	10	12	46	42	40
Horndean	32	11	5	16	45	70	38
Bournemouth	32	10	6	16	49	64	36
Christchurch	32	9	7	16	40	71	34
AFC Totton	32	8	9	15	39	58	33
Sholing Sports	32	6	6	20	29	65	24
Brockenhurst	32	3	11	18	17	52	20
Portsmouth Royal Navy	32	5	4	23	25	73	19

Bashley moved to the Southern League. B.A.T. Sports joined from the Hampshire League, Fleet Town joined from the Chiltonian League and Bemerton Heath Harlequins joined as a new club after a merger of three junior clubs: Bemerton Athletic, Moon F.C. and Bemerton Boys.

1989-90

Romsey Town	36	25	6	5	84	31	81
Newport (I.O.W.)	36	24	7	5	82	29	79
B.A.T. Sports	36	21	7	8	74	35	70
Wimborne Town	36	20	8	8	83	48	68
AFC Lymington	36	19	8	9	68	44	65
AFC Totton	36	17	8	11	58	45	59
Thatcham Town	36	15	12	9	56	45	57
Bemerton Heath Harlequins	36	16	8	12	61	47	56
Sholing Sports	36	16	8	12	57	51	56
Bournemouth	36	15	9	12	69	70	54
Havant Town	36	13	8	15	49	50	47
Folland Sports	36	13	6	17	42	47	45
East Cowes Victoria Athletic	36	11	10	15	47	54	43
Eastleigh	36	10	11	15	60	66	41
Christchurch	36	10	9	17	47	59	39
Horndean	36	10	6	20	56	75	36
Brockenhurst	36	5	8	23	35	98	23
Fleet Town	36	5	5	26	22	86	20
Portsmouth Royal Navy	36	4	2	30	38	108	14

Folland Sports changed their name to Aerostructures Sports & Social. Newport (I.O.W.) moved to the Southern League. Swanage Town & Herston joined from the Western League and Ryde Sports joined from the Hampshire League.

1990-91

Havant Town	38	24	8	6	76	30	80
Swanage Town & Herston	38	24	6	8	88	41	78
Bournemouth	38	24	4	10	69	33	76
Romsey Town	38	20	11	7	59	35	71
Wimborne Town	38	22	4	12	80	45	70
Thatcham Town	38	19	11	8	68	32	68
Brockenhurst	38	17	8	13	56	51	59
B.A.T. Sports	38	16	10	12	54	48	58
AFC Lymington	38	16	9	13	60	50	57
Fleet Town	38	17	6	15	64	57	57
Ryde Sports	38	17	6	15	62	55	57
Eastleigh	38	13	8	17	40	62	47
East Cowes Victoria Athletic	38	12	10	16	45	52	46
AFC Totton	38	13	6	19	54	70	45
Christchurch	38	11	10	17	37	55	43
Aerostructures Sports & Social	38	11	6	21	32	62	39
Portsmouth Royal Navy	38	10	5	23	51	102	35
Bemerton Heath Harlequins	38	7	11	20	42	59	32
Sholing Sports	38	6	8	24	39	84	26
Horndean	38	5	5	28	39	92	20

Havant Town moved to the Southern League.

1991-92

Wimborne Town	36	25	5	6	82	37	80
AFC Lymington	36	23	5	8	73	39	74
Thatcham Town	36	22	4	10	85	45	70
Romsey Town	36	21	6	9	72	42	69
Swanage Town & Herston	36	20	7	9	78	38	67
Bournemouth	36	20	6	10	73	48	66
Ryde Sports	36	18	8	10	61	51	62
Bemerton Heath Harlequins	36	17	10	9	51	38	61
Aerostructures Sports & Social	36	18	5	13	59	40	59
Eastleigh	36	18	4	14	61	53	58
Fleet Town	36	13	10	13	59	55	49
Brockenhurst	36	12	9	15	47	52	45
Christchurch	36	9	11	16	39	54	38
East Cowes Victoria Athletic	36	9	9	18	36	72	36
Sholing Sports	36	9	7	20	43	81	34
B.A.T. Sports	36	9	4	23	41	57	31
AFC Totton	36	7	8	21	43	71	29
Horndean	36	5	3	28	33	109	18
Portsmouth Royal Navy	36	4	5	27	30	84	17

Gosport Borough joined from the Southern League and Whitchurch United joined from the Hampshire League.

1992-93

AFC Lymington	40	30	7	3	111	27	97
Wimborne Town	40	30	5	5	101	27	95
Bemerton Heath Harlequins	40	27	7	6	77	33	88
Thatcham Town	40	24	10	6	104	45	82
Gosport Borough	40	20	12	8	83	48	72
Ryde Sports	40	21	4	15	79	61	67
Bournemouth	40	18	11	11	83	58	65
Fleet Town	40	17	10	13	79	51	61
Eastleigh	40	17	9	14	68	54	60
Brockenhurst	40	17	7	16	60	56	58
Horndean	40	15	9	16	63	66	54
Aerostructures Sports & Social	40	13	14	13	55	57	53
Christchurch	40	14	7	19	60	73	49
Swanage Town & Herston	40	11	11	18	65	78	44
Whitchurch United	40	12	6	22	57	80	42
AFC Totton	40	12	6	22	56	82	42
Portsmouth Royal Navy	40	10	10	20	52	83	40
B.A.T. Sports	40	9	9	22	59	83	36
Sholing Sports	40	7	10	23	46	94	31
East Cowes Victoria Athletic	40	8	4	28	52	106	28
Romsey Town	40	3	2	35	20	168	11

Romsey Town moved to the Hampshire League. Andover joined from the Southern League, Downton joined from the Hampshire League and Petersfield Town joined as a new club after Petersfield United had disbanded and resigned from the Isthmian League.

1993-94

Wimborne Town	42	34	5	3	126	41	107
Andover	42	27	8	7	137	48	89
AFC Lymington	42	27	5	10	83	33	86
Thatcham Town	42	25	7	10	96	51	82
Gosport Borough	42	23	10	9	87	55	79
Fleet Town	42	21	9	12	82	48	72
Bemerton Heath Harlequins	42	19	11	12	72	56	68
Brockenhurst	42	17	12	13	70	64	63
B.A.T. Sports	42	17	10	15	66	66	61
Christchurch	42	15	13	14	55	58	58
Bournemouth	42	16	6	20	67	78	54
Ryde Sports	42	14	10	18	61	77	52
Portsmouth Royal Navy	42	13	10	19	59	78	49
East Cowes Victoria Athletic	42	14	7	21	78	114	49
Eastleigh	42	12	12	18	47	54	48
Downton	42	12	10	20	59	82	46
Horndean	42	13	6	23	56	95	45
Petersfield Town	42	11	7	24	64	96	40
Aerostructures Sports & Social	42	11	6	25	41	84	39
Swanage Town & Herston	42	10	7	25	53	89	37
AFC Totton	42	9	9	24	43	90	36
Whitchurch United	42	11	2	29	51	96	35

Sholing Sports resigned from the League because of ground problems after playing just one game.
Whitchurch United moved to the Hampshire League, swapping places with Cowes Sports.

1994-95

Fleet Town	42	32	4	6	116	42	100
Bournemouth	42	31	5	6	109	33	98
Thatcham Town	42	29	9	4	105	44	96
Bemerton Heath Harlequins	42	24	8	10	75	48	80
Wimborne Town	42	21	15	6	100	53	78
Brockenhurst	42	24	4	14	87	59	76
Andover	42	23	5	14	122	69	74
AFC Lymington	42	17	10	15	85	67	61
AFC Totton	42	18	6	18	69	70	60
Gosport Borough	42	17	7	18	85	64	58
Portsmouth Royal Navy	42	16	8	18	65	66	56
Ryde Sports	42	16	6	20	81	88	54
B.A.T. Sports	42	15	8	19	62	82	53
Eastleigh	42	14	9	19	66	73	51
Cowes Sports	42	14	8	20	61	87	50
East Cowes Victoria Athletic	42	13	10	19	65	72	49
Aerostructures Sports & Social	42	12	10	20	62	79	46
Christchurch	42	12	8	22	58	95	44
Swanage Town & Herston	42	10	6	26	49	115	36
Downton	42	7	11	24	45	85	32
Petersfield Town	42	8	5	29	59	163	29
Horndean	42	6	4	32	49	121	22

Fleet Town moved to the Southern League and Horndean moved to the Hampshire League. Whitchurch United joined from the Hampshire League.

1995-96

Thatcham Town	40	28	8	4	73	27	92
AFC Lymington	40	28	7	5	100	31	91
Ryde Sports	40	25	8	7	92	41	83
Eastleigh	40	21	13	6	83	50	76
Christchurch	40	21	8	11	66	49	71
Wimborne Town	40	20	6	14	85	61	66
Bournemouth	40	17	13	10	85	40	64
Bemerton Heath Harlequins	40	18	8	14	67	63	62
Andover	40	18	7	15	101	70	61
East Cowes Victoria Athletic	40	17	8	15	60	60	59
Gosport Borough	40	16	9	15	59	58	57
Downton	40	16	6	18	65	73	54
Whitchurch United	40	12	13	15	66	76	49
AFC Totton	40	10	13	17	55	66	43
B.A.T. Sports	40	10	12	18	44	58	42
Cowes Sports	40	11	7	22	38	76	40
Portsmouth Royal Navy	40	10	8	22	52	84	38
Aerostructures Sports & Social	40	9	10	21	41	71	37
Brockenhurst	40	11	4	25	42	74	37
Petersfield Town	40	8	4	28	53	93	28
Swanage Town & Herston	40	6	4	30	32	138	22

Swanage Town & Herston moved to the Dorset Combination.
Romsey Town joined from the Hampshire League.

1996-97

AFC Lymington	40	35	5	0	112	22	110
Wimborne Town	40	26	7	7	97	42	85
Thatcham Town	40	26	5	9	91	45	79
Ryde Sports	40	25	4	11	77	50	79
Bemerton Heath Harlequins	40	23	9	8	69	45	78
Andover	40	19	12	9	80	42	69
Eastleigh	40	19	8	13	71	56	65
Downton	40	18	7	15	72	70	61
Cowes Sports	40	15	14	11	65	55	59
Portsmouth Royal Navy	40	16	4	20	65	79	52
Gosport Borough	40	15	5	20	56	66	50
Aerostructures Sports & Social	40	13	9	18	45	66	48
Bournemouth	40	14	5	21	50	72	47
Brockenhurst	40	13	7	20	54	73	46
Whitchurch United	40	12	7	21	58	81	43
Christchurch	40	13	4	23	49	72	43
East Cowes Victoria Athletic	40	10	7	23	53	72	37
Romsey Town	40	10	7	23	52	94	37
B.A.T. Sports	40	8	9	23	43	74	33
AFC Totton	40	8	8	24	54	87	32
Petersfield Town	40	8	5	27	42	92	29

Thatcham Town had 4 points deducted.
Petersfield Town moved to the Hampshire League.
AFC Newbury joined from the Hampshire League.

1997-98

AFC Lymington	38	29	5	4	94	27	92
Andover	38	24	9	5	99	46	81
AFC Newbury	38	22	7	9	72	35	73
Eastleigh	38	20	11	7	74	31	71
Bemerton Heath Harlequins	38	19	11	8	69	38	68
Cowes Sports	38	20	6	12	67	51	66
Wimborne Town	38	18	9	11	89	63	63
AFC Totton	38	15	10	13	58	41	55
Bournemouth	38	16	7	15	64	68	55
Thatcham Town	38	16	6	16	64	54	54
Christchurch	38	15	6	17	55	69	51
East Cowes Victoria Athletic	38	13	11	14	46	42	50
Portsmouth Royal Navy	38	13	7	18	64	79	46
B.A.T. Sports	38	12	7	19	60	82	43
Gosport Borough	38	9	10	19	48	65	37
Aerostructures Sports & Social	38	9	10	19	50	77	37
Brockenhurst	38	9	9	20	43	83	36
Downton	38	7	10	21	36	66	31
Whitchurch United	38	7	8	23	37	78	29
Romsey Town	38	5	5	28	40	134	20

Ryde Sports resigned from the League and their record was deleted when
it stood as follows:

	17	0	2	15	16	69	2

AFC Lymington merged with New Milton Town of Division Two of the
Hampshire League to form Lymington & New Milton. Aerostructures Sports
& Social changed their name to Hamble Aerostructures Sports & Social
Club. Andover moved to the Southern League and Romsey Town moved to
the Hampshire League. Fareham Town joined from the Southern League
and Moneyfields joined from the Hampshire League.

1998-99

Lymington & New Milton	38	27	6	5	92	31	87
Thatcham Town	38	23	9	6	92	46	78
AFC Newbury	38	22	11	5	81	39	77
Eastleigh	38	22	8	8	69	43	74
Christchurch	38	22	7	9	72	53	73
Wimborne Town	38	18	14	6	81	34	68
Cowes Sports	38	19	8	11	77	54	65
Moneyfields	38	17	8	13	69	62	59
AFC Totton	38	15	10	13	60	50	55
Bemerton Heath Harlequins	38	17	4	17	59	54	55
Brockenhurst	38	14	7	17	52	61	49
Bournemouth	38	12	10	16	46	63	46
Fareham Town	38	11	12	15	58	67	45
Gosport Borough	38	11	11	16	66	71	44
B.A.T. Sports	38	10	13	15	55	65	43
East Cowes Victoria Athletic	38	10	4	24	48	103	34
Hamble Aerostructures S.S.C.	38	6	9	23	37	68	27
Portsmouth Royal Navy	38	6	9	23	42	81	27
Whitchurch United	38	5	11	22	36	76	26
Downton	38	4	7	27	40	111	19

Andover joined from the Southern League.

1999-2000

Team	P	W	D	L	F	A	Pts
Wimborne Town	40	32	4	4	126	33	100
Lymington & New Milton	40	31	7	2	115	27	100
Andover	40	25	7	8	147	60	82
AFC Totton	40	24	8	8	93	30	80
B.A.T. Sports	40	24	8	8	88	48	80
Moneyfields	40	22	9	9	76	64	75
Eastleigh	40	20	8	12	67	46	68
AFC Newbury	40	17	12	11	67	51	63
Cowes Sports	40	17	11	12	73	55	62
Bemerton Heath Harlequins	40	17	9	14	75	66	60
Fareham Town	40	14	14	12	72	71	56
Christchurch	40	16	7	17	68	67	55
Thatcham Town	40	15	7	18	62	69	52
Gosport Borough	40	8	12	20	40	70	36
Downton	40	10	6	24	74	113	36
Hamble Aerostructures S.S.C.	40	7	11	22	44	89	32
Whitchurch United	40	7	10	23	53	89	31
Brockenhurst	40	7	7	26	43	114	28
Bournemouth	40	7	8	25	54	110	27
Portsmouth Royal Navy	40	5	10	25	47	114	25
East Cowes Victoria Athletic	40	5	5	30	43	141	20

Bournemouth had 2 points deducted.
East Cowes Victoria Athletic moved to the Hampshire League. Fleet Town joined from the Southern League, Swanage Town & Herston joined from the Dorset Combination and Blackfield & Langley joined from the Hampshire League.

2000-01

Team	P	W	D	L	F	A	Pts
Andover	44	37	5	2	153	33	116
Lymington & New Milton	44	34	6	4	106	29	108
Wimborne Town	44	28	9	7	111	52	93
Fleet Town	44	29	3	12	91	56	90
AFC Totton	44	26	9	9	87	47	87
Thatcham Town	44	24	9	11	81	58	81
Eastleigh	44	23	10	11	87	48	79
Gosport Borough	44	23	8	13	74	44	77
Brockenhurst	44	23	7	14	93	72	76
Cowes Sports	44	22	4	18	80	70	70
Bemerton Heath Harlequins	44	15	9	20	63	70	54
AFC Newbury	44	15	8	21	71	78	53
B.A.T. Sports	44	14	10	20	52	75	52
Bournemouth	44	13	12	19	51	65	51
Fareham Town	44	12	10	22	48	74	46
Moneyfields	44	12	9	23	52	76	45
Christchurch	44	11	12	21	55	80	45
Hamble Aerostructures S.S.C.	44	10	14	20	39	70	44
Whitchurch United	44	8	13	23	37	72	37
Swanage Town & Herston	44	11	4	29	52	123	37
Blackfield & Langley	44	7	8	29	32	95	29
Downton	44	6	8	30	45	103	26
Portsmouth Royal Navy	44	4	11	29	37	107	23

Portsmouth Royal Navy moved to the Hampshire League and Portland United joined from the Dorset Combination.

2001-02

Team	P	W	D	L	F	A	Pts
Andover	44	30	6	8	138	53	96
Fleet Town	44	29	9	6	107	59	95
AFC Totton	44	29	7	8	104	50	94
Gosport Borough	44	26	11	7	101	41	89
Lymington & New Milton	44	26	6	12	94	47	84
Brockenhurst	44	27	2	15	99	57	83
AFC Newbury	44	22	12	10	87	51	78
Wimborne Town	44	21	14	9	82	53	77
Moneyfields	44	23	7	14	98	64	76
Fareham Town	44	21	13	10	72	54	76
Bemerton Heath Harlequins	44	18	11	15	103	84	65
Thatcham Town	44	19	8	17	94	77	65
Eastleigh	44	18	9	17	91	71	63
Portland United	44	17	8	19	81	66	59
Christchurch	44	16	7	21	61	80	55
Cowes Sports	44	15	9	20	66	73	54
Blackfield & Langley	44	16	5	23	82	121	53
Bournemouth	44	14	7	23	61	84	49
B.A.T. Sports	44	13	8	23	46	67	47
Whitchurch United	44	5	5	34	27	116	20
Downton	44	5	5	42	139	19	
Hamble Aerostructures S.S.C.	44	4	4	36	33	119	16
Swanage Town & Herston	44	3	6	35	31	174	15

Fleet Town had 1 point deducted.
Fleet Town moved to the Southern League and Swanage Town & Herston moved to the Dorset Combination. Alton Town joined from the Hampshire League.

2002-03

Team	P	W	D	L	F	A	Pts
Eastleigh	42	32	7	3	115	32	103
Gosport Borough	42	27	7	8	94	43	88
AFC Totton	42	27	6	9	96	47	87
Wimborne Town	42	26	7	9	113	44	85
Fareham Town	42	22	9	11	78	47	76
Lymington & New Milton	42	22	8	12	89	56	74
Andover	42	22	7	13	95	63	73
Portland United	42	20	8	14	81	62	68
Thatcham Town	42	18	13	11	68	58	67
Moneyfields	42	18	6	18	73	68	60
B.A.T. Sports	42	18	6	18	57	65	60
AFC Newbury	42	17	6	19	77	72	57
Christchurch	42	15	10	17	58	68	55
Bournemouth	42	15	9	18	57	67	54
Cowes Sports	42	13	13	16	57	55	52
Hamble Aerostructures S.S.C.	42	13	12	17	58	60	51
Alton Town	42	14	9	19	71	80	51
Bemerton Heath Harlequins	42	13	5	24	59	83	44
Downton	42	10	7	25	41	105	37
Brockenhurst	42	7	5	30	50	118	26
Blackfield & Langley	42	4	6	32	37	134	18
Whitchurch United	42	4	3	35	27	124	15

Eastleigh moved to the Southern League and Winchester City joined from the Hampshire League.

2003-04

Winchester City	42	35	3	4	151	35	108
Wimborne Town	42	31	6	5	105	45	99
Gosport Borough	42	29	5	8	96	40	92
Lymington & New Milton	42	29	3	10	98	38	90
AFC Newbury	42	26	4	12	94	53	82
Andover	42	25	4	13	100	65	79
Fareham Town	42	24	6	12	71	38	78
AFC Totton	42	18	10	14	76	55	64
Brockenhurst	42	19	7	16	49	74	64
Thatcham Town	42	16	10	16	70	72	58
Christchurch	42	17	6	19	63	62	57
Bemerton Heath Harlequins	42	16	7	19	77	79	55
Hamble Aerostructures S.S.C.	42	16	7	19	51	76	55
Cowes Sports	42	15	8	19	51	59	53
B.A.T. Sports	42	13	7	22	57	68	46
Portland United	42	14	4	24	58	86	46
Moneyfields	42	11	8	23	51	83	41
Alton Town	42	12	2	28	55	110	38
Downton	42	8	7	27	43	106	31
Bournemouth	42	8	6	28	41	86	30
Blackfield & Langley	42	7	7	28	51	99	28
Whitchurch United	42	7	5	30	38	117	26

VTFC (ex-Hampshire League Premier Division) and Hamworthy United (ex-Dorset Premier League) joined the League.

The League was re-organised into 3 divisions, by adding the 2 divisions of the Hampshire League. The existing Wessex League clubs formed the new Wessex League – Division One, apart from Blackfield & Langley and Whitchurch United.

These last two went into the new Division Two, which also included the other 17 clubs from the Hampshire League Premier Division, which were: AFC Aldermaston, Amesbury Town, Andover New Street, Bishops Waltham Town, Brading Town, East Cowes Victoria Athletic, Fawley, Horndean, Hythe & Dibden, Liss Athletic, Locks Heath, Lymington Town, Petersfield Town, Poole Town, Ringwood Town, Stockbridge and United Services Portsmouth (ex-Portsmouth Royal Navy). Division Two also included Alresford Town (Hampshire League Division One), Romsey Town (Hampshire League Division Two) and Shaftesbury (Dorset Premier League).

Division Three was formed by the other 13 members of the Hampshire League Division One and 9 from Division Two. From Division One: AFC Portchester, Clanfield, Colden Common, Farnborough North End, Fleet Spurs, Fleetlands, Hayling United, Laverstock & Ford, Micheldever, Overton United, Paulsgrove, Tadley Calleva and Verwood Town. From Division Two: Dave Coleman, Hamble Club, Ludgershall Sports, Netley Central Sports, Ordnance Survey, Otterbourne, QK Southampton, RS Basingstoke and Yateley Green.

Clubs promoted and relegated between divisions are shown in bold type. The remaining 5 clubs from the Hampshire League Division Two: Broughton, Durley, East Lodge, M & T Awbridge and Mottisfont, helped to form a new Hampshire League for 2004-05.

2004-05

Division One

Lymington & New Milton	42	31	6	5	123	41	99
Winchester City	42	31	4	7	134	38	97
Thatcham Town	42	24	13	5	95	51	85
Gosport Borough	42	25	9	8	75	49	84
Andover	42	24	8	10	100	67	80
AFC Newbury	42	23	8	11	80	45	77
Wimborne Town	42	20	12	10	82	53	72
AFC Totton	42	19	10	13	69	59	67
B.A.T. Sports	42	17	12	13	63	60	63
Moneyfields	42	14	14	14	62	57	56
Bournemouth	42	16	8	18	54	65	56
VTFC	42	16	7	19	69	80	55
Cowes Sports	42	16	6	20	70	69	54
Bemerton Heath Harlequins	42	15	6	21	64	72	51
Hamworthy United	42	14	9	19	51	72	51
Fareham Town	42	13	9	20	50	63	46
Christchurch	42	12	8	22	64	80	44
Brockenhurst	42	12	5	25	52	79	41
Alton Town	42	9	10	23	50	90	37
Portland United	42	8	6	28	35	104	30
Hamble Aerostructures S.S.C.	42	6	7	29	36	121	25
Downton	*42*	*7*	*3*	*32*	*50*	*113*	*24*

Fareham Town had 2 points deducted.
Lymington & New Milton moved to the Isthmian League – Division One.

Division Two

Lymington Town	**42**	**35**	**3**	**4**	**121**	**28**	**108**
Poole Town	**42**	**33**	**4**	**5**	**123**	**29**	**103**
Locks Heath	42	24	10	8	79	43	82
Romsey Town	42	23	8	11	84	55	77
Petersfield Town	42	21	10	11	77	49	73
Liss Athletic	42	21	8	13	106	77	71
Blackfield & Langley	42	20	9	13	89	61	69
Stockbridge	42	19	9	14	91	71	66
Horndean	42	18	12	12	85	76	66
Alresford Town	42	20	4	18	85	74	64
Ringwood Town	42	20	3	19	89	84	63
Whitchurch United	42	17	5	20	72	77	56
Shaftesbury	42	15	9	18	65	85	54
Hythe & Dibden	42	15	7	20	75	105	52
Amesbury Town	42	14	7	21	76	99	49
Brading Town	42	13	8	21	75	84	46
East Cowes Victoria Athletic	42	12	9	21	71	85	45
Andover New Street	42	12	6	24	45	100	42
United Services Portsmouth	42	9	6	27	58	103	33
Bishops Waltham Town	42	7	12	23	46	104	33
Fawley	42	9	4	29	54	111	31
AFC Aldermaston	*42*	*7*	*3*	*32*	*50*	*116*	*24*

Division Three

Colden Common	38	28	4	6	123	39	88
Hayling United	38	26	8	4	104	30	86
Farnborough North End	38	26	7	5	111	38	85
Fleetlands	38	23	6	9	115	42	75
Paulsgrove	38	22	7	9	93	46	73
Otterbourne	38	23	3	12	88	36	72
Overton United	38	22	6	10	88	52	72
Tadley Calleva	38	21	7	10	84	43	69
Micheldever	38	18	11	9	82	49	65
Clanfield	38	16	12	10	72	70	60
Laverstock & Ford	38	14	10	14	73	59	52
Netley Central Sports	38	13	7	18	71	66	46
Ordnance Survey	38	11	9	18	44	55	42
AFC Portchester	38	11	6	21	65	83	39
Hamble Club	38	9	11	18	51	86	38
Verwood Town	38	8	6	24	54	95	46
Fleet Spurs	38	6	11	21	59	98	29
Ludgershall Sports	38	7	3	28	48	118	24
QK Southampton	38	4	4	30	41	178	16
Yateley Green	38	2	2	34	30	213	8

Tadley Calleva had 1 point deducted.
Dave Coleman resigned from the League and their record was deleted
when it stood as follows: 7 3 0 4 12 24 9
RS Basingstoke resigned from the League and their record was deleted
when it stood as follows: 21 4 7 10 24 51 19
Ludgershall Sports moved to the Hampshire League and Yateley Green also
left the League.

2005-06

Division One

Winchester City	42	34	5	3	112	31	107
Thatcham Town	42	29	7	6	92	37	94
Andover	42	27	5	10	120	64	86
AFC Totton	42	25	9	8	101	40	84
Gosport Borough	42	23	10	9	85	44	79
Hamworthy United	42	21	12	9	65	40	75
Bournemouth	42	21	10	11	72	45	73
Poole Town	42	21	8	13	79	60	71
Fareham Town	42	19	10	13	74	61	67
Christchurch	42	17	9	16	72	62	60
Moneyfields	42	14	16	12	48	49	58
Wimborne Town	42	15	10	17	60	61	55
VTFC	42	13	15	14	65	66	54
Bemerton Heath Harlequins	42	14	8	20	70	86	50
Hamble Aerostructures S.S.C.	42	14	7	21	50	56	49
Cowes Sports	42	12	10	20	48	67	46
Lymington Town	42	10	14	18	42	71	44
B.A.T. Sports	42	10	6	26	61	109	36
AFC Newbury	42	9	8	25	35	96	35
Alton Town	42	8	9	25	51	99	33
Brockenhurst	42	4	6	32	42	93	18
Portland United	42	2	6	34	32	139	12

B.A.T. Sports and AFC Newbury were both relegated to Division Two for the
next season (formerly Division Three).
Winchester City, Thatcham Town and Andover moved to the Southern
League and Portland United moved to the Dorset Premier League.

Division Two

Locks Heath	42	31	5	6	96	28	98
Hayling United	42	27	8	7	99	39	89
Brading Town	42	27	7	8	96	50	88
Downton	42	27	6	9	108	64	87
Liss Athletic	42	26	5	11	99	57	83
Horndean	42	22	6	14	95	67	72
Fawley	42	20	9	13	76	53	69
Stockbridge	42	18	13	11	82	52	67
Ringwood Town	42	20	6	16	81	71	66
United Services Portsmouth	42	18	11	13	86	72	65
Farnborough North End	42	19	6	17	93	76	63
East Cowes Victoria Athletic	42	16	10	16	76	70	58
Romsey Town	42	15	11	16	59	61	56
Blackfield & Langley	42	14	13	15	81	69	55
Petersfield Town	42	12	8	22	58	91	44
Shaftesbury	42	10	10	22	53	96	46
Hythe & Dibden	42	11	7	24	50	98	40
Andover New Street	42	10	9	23	61	96	39
Amesbury Town	42	10	4	28	55	109	34
Alresford Town	42	8	9	25	49	86	33
Bishops Waltham Town	*42*	*7*	*7*	*28*	*57*	*112*	*28*
Whitchurch United	*42*	*5*	*8*	*29*	*44*	*137*	*23*

Warminster Town joined from the Wiltshire League.

Division Three

Paulsgrove	30	20	6	4	91	34	66
Laverstock & Ford	30	19	6	5	62	37	63
Verwood Town	30	19	3	8	73	42	60
Colden Common	30	17	5	8	86	45	56
Netley Central Sports	30	16	5	9	62	41	53
Fleetlands	30	15	7	8	59	36	52
Tadley Calleva	30	16	4	10	52	40	52
Otterbourne	30	14	6	10	56	45	48
AFC Aldermaston	30	12	5	13	64	68	41
Overton United	30	11	7	12	54	53	40
AFC Portchester	30	11	4	15	57	61	37
Ordnance Survey	30	10	6	14	69	68	36
Clanfield	30	11	3	16	56	62	36
Fleet Spurs	30	8	3	19	60	75	27
QK Southampton	30	2	3	25	24	123	9
Hamble Club	30	1	3	26	17	112	6

Micheldever resigned from the League and their record was deleted when
it stood as follows: 23 3 1 19 24 102 10
Ordnance Survey changed their name to Stoneham. Netley Central Sports
left to join the Hampshire League and Wellow joined from the
Southampton League.

**The Divisions were renamed to become the Premier
Division, Division One and Division Two from the
next season.**

2006-07

Premier Division

Gosport Borough	38	27	8	3	87	27	89
AFC Totton	38	27	8	3	89	31	89
VTFC	38	24	8	6	76	44	80
Poole Town	38	23	4	11	88	41	73
Bournemouth	38	20	10	8	69	38	70
Wimborne Town	38	19	10	9	82	54	67
Moneyfields	38	21	3	14	69	46	66
Fareham Town	38	18	12	8	95	57	65
Cowes Sports	38	17	9	12	61	50	60
Brading Town	38	15	7	16	74	80	52
Bemerton Heath Harlequins	38	13	9	16	55	73	48
Lymington Town	38	13	8	17	49	48	47
Brockenhurst	38	10	11	17	52	66	41
Christchurch	38	9	10	19	47	63	37
Hamworthy United	38	9	10	19	49	70	37
Horndean	38	11	1	26	51	104	34
Alton Town	38	9	7	22	59	87	33
Downton	38	7	10	21	48	89	31
Ringwood Town	38	5	8	25	34	85	23
Hamble Aerostructures S.S.C.	38	5	3	30	24	105	18

Fareham Town and Alton Town each had 1 point deducted.
Gosport Borough were promoted to the Southern League from which Lymington & New Milton were relegated, changing their name to New Milton Town.

Division One

Hayling United	**36**	**27**	**4**	**5**	**116**	**32**	**85**
Alresford Town	**36**	**23**	**8**	**5**	**53**	**28**	**77**
Romsey Town	**36**	**22**	**6**	**8**	**68**	**36**	**72**
Locks Heath	36	21	7	8	78	40	70
Fawley	36	18	7	11	78	57	61
Verwood Town	36	17	9	10	73	46	60
Stockbridge	36	17	8	11	64	54	59
Warminster Town	36	16	9	11	63	48	57
Shaftesbury	36	15	9	12	58	47	54
United Services Portsmouth	36	12	10	14	76	68	46
Farnborough North End	36	11	13	12	40	56	46
Laverstock & Ford	36	12	9	15	55	65	45
Liss Athletic	36	11	10	15	59	73	42
Hythe & Dibden	36	9	9	18	54	81	36
East Cowes Victoria Athletic	36	10	6	20	49	101	36
Blackfield & Langley	36	9	5	22	66	104	32
Petersfield Town	36	7	6	23	50	98	27
Amesbury Town	36	5	10	21	57	78	25
Andover New Street	36	5	5	26	37	82	20

Liss Athletic had 1 point deducted.
Locks Heath moved to the Hampshire Premier League.

Division Two

Fleetlands	30	25	2	3	101	18	77
Tadley Calleva	**30**	**23**	**5**	**2**	**103**	**33**	**74**
Wellow	30	19	6	5	77	36	63
AFC Portchester	**30**	**16**	**4**	**10**	**68**	**45**	**52**
B.A.T. Sports	**30**	**15**	**6**	**9**	**61**	**49**	**51**
Otterbourne	30	15	6	9	60	50	51
Overton United	30	14	6	10	66	55	48
Paulsgrove	30	14	3	13	69	63	45
Clanfield	30	10	7	13	60	59	37
Colden Common	30	11	3	16	66	76	36
Fleet Spurs	**30**	**10**	**5**	**15**	**55**	**58**	**35**
Whitchurch United	**30**	**10**	**4**	**16**	**48**	**61**	**34**
AFC Aldermaston	**30**	**10**	**4**	**16**	**61**	**78**	**34**
Stoneham	30	9	6	15	51	76	33
Hamble Club	30	1	4	25	29	130	7
QK Southampton	30	0	5	25	18	106	5

AFC Newbury resigned from the League and their record was deleted when it stood as follows: 7 1 2 4 7 23 7
Bishops Waltham Town resigned from the League and their record was deleted when it stood as follows: 7 1 0 6 4 28 3

BAT Sports changed their name to Totton & Eling, Stoneham added AFC to their name and Wellow left the league. 6 clubs (shown in bold) were promoted from Division Two.

Division Two then disbanded before reforming as the Hampshire Premier League for the 2007-08 season.

2007-08

Premier Division

AFC Totton	44	33	7	4	120	39	106
VTFC	44	32	6	6	106	35	102
Wimborne Town	44	30	6	8	125	33	96
Poole Town	44	29	9	6	120	35	96
Bournemouth	44	27	12	5	92	40	93
Brockenhurst	44	23	11	10	87	55	80
Moneyfields	44	24	7	13	82	45	79
Fareham Town	44	22	9	13	87	65	75
Cowes Sports	44	20	13	11	91	59	73
Hamworthy United	44	19	8	17	55	54	65
Horndean	44	15	13	16	76	73	58
Hayling United	44	15	9	20	66	101	54
Bemerton Heath Harlequins	44	15	8	21	74	101	53
Alton Town	44	15	7	22	66	89	52
Brading Town	44	13	12	19	67	85	51
Christchurch	44	15	5	24	67	80	50
Hamble Aerostructures S.S.C.	44	11	14	19	47	72	47
Romsey Town	44	12	7	25	68	98	43
New Milton Town	44	11	8	25	58	88	41
Lymington Town	44	11	7	26	63	103	39
Alresford Town	44	9	8	27	48	88	35
Ringwood Town	**44**	**5**	**9**	**30**	**45**	**124**	**24**
Downton	**44**	**1**	**3**	**40**	**29**	**177**	**6**

Lymington Town had 1 point deducted.
AFC Totton moved to the Southern League, swapping places with Newport (IOW).

Division One

Tadley Calleva	40	33	3	4	134	45	102
Laverstock & Ford	**40**	**29**	**3**	**8**	**124**	**59**	**90**
Farnborough North End	40	26	9	5	101	30	87
Verwood Town	40	23	6	11	94	63	75
Totton & Eling	40	22	8	10	80	50	74
Fawley	40	22	5	13	94	44	71
Warminster Town	40	20	11	9	89	48	71
Petersfield Town	40	21	7	12	90	53	70
United Services Portsmouth	40	21	6	13	98	65	69
Blackfield & Langley	40	18	10	12	70	57	64
Amesbury Town	40	16	5	19	100	86	53
Shaftesbury	40	14	9	17	73	63	51
Stockbridge	40	11	12	17	47	61	45
Fleet Spurs	40	12	6	22	64	95	42
AFC Portchester	40	11	9	20	59	86	42
Liss Athletic	40	8	10	22	58	95	34
Whitchurch United	40	8	10	22	51	97	34
East Cowes Victoria Athletic	40	8	10	22	50	103	34
Andover New Street	40	9	5	26	54	117	32
Hythe & Dibden	40	6	9	25	42	125	27
AFC Aldermaston	40	4	3	33	31	161	15

Liss Athletic moved to the Hampshire Premier League.

2008-09

Premier Division

Poole Town	42	38	2	2	144	34	116
VTFC	42	31	8	3	141	35	101
Moneyfields	42	29	4	9	99	44	91
Wimborne Town	42	26	9	7	115	41	87
Brockenhurst	42	24	10	8	71	41	82
Newport (IOW)	42	24	5	13	87	64	77
Christchurch	42	22	8	12	77	48	74
Hamworthy United	42	21	5	16	77	73	68
New Milton Town	42	18	10	14	72	55	64
Fareham Town	42	16	13	13	64	53	61
Romsey Town	42	16	12	14	65	75	60
Bemerton Heath Harlequins	42	16	5	21	56	67	53
Cowes Sports	42	13	11	18	65	78	50
Brading Town	42	13	8	21	62	70	47
Bournemouth	42	12	8	22	60	89	44
Hayling United	42	11	8	23	66	96	41
Alresford Town	42	11	7	24	53	88	40
Lymington Town	42	10	8	24	58	104	38
Alton Town	42	9	9	24	56	105	36
Laverstock & Ford	42	8	7	27	49	106	31
Hamble Aerostructures S.S.C.	*42*	*5*	*6*	*31*	*30*	*121*	*21*
Horndean	*42*	*5*	*5*	*32*	*45*	*125*	*20*

VTFC moved to the Southern League, swapping places with Winchester City.

Division One

Totton & Eling	**40**	**31**	**8**	**1**	**124**	**34**	**100**
Blackfield & Langley	**40**	**28**	**7**	**5**	**102**	**35**	**91**
United Services Portsmouth	40	23	8	9	119	66	77
Petersfield Town	40	22	10	8	86	56	76
Warminster Town	40	22	8	10	98	47	74
Whitchurch United	40	21	10	9	102	62	73
Hythe & Dibden	40	19	10	11	101	78	67
Farnborough North End	40	18	12	10	66	49	66
Fawley	40	18	8	14	84	59	62
Stockbridge	40	16	12	12	68	66	60
Ringwood Town	40	17	6	17	86	80	57
Amesbury Town	40	15	8	17	83	90	53
Verwood Town	40	14	9	17	65	75	51
AFC Aldermaston	40	12	6	22	64	91	42
Shaftesbury	40	11	9	20	61	92	42
Tadley Calleva	40	11	6	23	66	102	39
Downton	40	9	10	21	56	91	37
East Cowes Victoria Athletic	40	8	8	24	48	109	32
AFC Portchester	40	6	11	23	49	106	29
Andover New Street	40	7	6	27	58	111	27
Fleet Spurs	40	3	6	31	36	123	15

Totton & Eling had 1 point deducted.

2009-10

Premier Division

Poole Town	42	35	4	3	128	40	109
Wimborne Town	42	29	4	9	113	43	91
Bemerton Heath Harlequins	42	28	7	7	84	48	91
Bournemouth	42	27	7	8	87	49	88
Christchurch	42	22	12	8	91	66	78
Fareham Town	42	23	7	12	72	53	76
Totton & Eling	42	22	8	12	69	52	74
Blackfield & Langley	42	20	6	16	74	68	66
Newport (IOW)	42	15	14	13	61	55	59
Romsey Town	42	15	13	14	64	57	58
Winchester City	42	13	18	11	66	59	57
Moneyfields	42	15	8	19	60	72	53
Brockenhurst	42	13	12	17	62	77	51
Brading Town	42	14	7	21	54	68	49
Hayling United	42	11	11	20	51	84	44
Hamworthy United	42	11	9	22	49	62	42
Alresford Town	42	9	11	22	54	81	38
Alton Town	42	10	8	24	50	91	38
New Milton Town	42	9	9	24	45	70	36
Lymington Town	42	9	7	26	52	81	34
Laverstock & Ford	42	7	7	28	53	111	28
Cowes Sports	*42*	*6*	*9*	*27*	*54*	*108*	*27*

Wimborne Town moved to the Southern League

Division One

Hamble Aerostructures S.S.C.	**40**	**26**	**7**	**7**	**102**	**43**	**85**
Fawley	**40**	**25**	**7**	**8**	**125**	**63**	**82**
Fleet Spurs	40	24	4	12	102	63	76
Downton	40	22	10	8	96	57	76
Ringwood Town	40	22	8	10	79	55	74
AFC Portchester	40	22	7	11	85	60	73
Verwood Town	40	21	5	14	72	57	68
Petersfield Town	40	20	6	14	88	74	66
United Services Portsmouth	40	19	8	13	96	73	65
Whitchurch United	40	16	13	11	85	50	61
Amesbury Town	40	17	10	13	92	84	61
Horndean	40	18	6	16	92	74	60
Stockbridge	40	16	10	14	81	75	58
Warminster Town	40	15	4	21	66	85	49
Tadley Calleva	40	12	11	17	68	75	47
Hythe & Dibden	40	14	5	21	72	84	47
East Cowes Victoria Athletic	40	11	9	20	70	88	42
Farnborough North End	40	9	12	19	63	76	39
Andover New Street	40	7	8	25	75	141	29
Shaftesbury	40	5	5	30	53	151	19
AFC Aldermaston	40	1	1	38	29	163	4

Shaftesbury had 1 point deducted.
AFC Aldermaston moved to the Hampshire Premier League and
Farnborough North End moved to the Combined Counties League.
Pewsey Vale joined from the Wiltshire League.

2010-11

Premier Division

Poole Town	42	33	5	4	132	44	104
Bemerton Heath Harlequins	42	26	6	10	89	52	84
Winchester City	42	25	8	9	84	52	83
Brading Town	42	24	10	8	87	56	82
Bournemouth	42	23	11	8	100	43	80
Christchurch	42	21	12	9	86	60	75
Moneyfields	42	21	7	14	75	62	70
Fareham Town	42	19	10	13	76	69	67
Hamworthy United	42	19	9	14	88	70	66
Newport (IOW)	42	17	9	16	70	65	60
Lymington Town	42	18	5	19	77	79	59
Hamble Aerostructures S.S.C.	42	16	8	18	91	75	56
Alton Town	42	16	8	18	80	86	56
Blackfield & Langley	42	16	7	19	55	62	55
Alresford Town	42	13	6	23	82	84	45
Romsey Town	42	11	11	20	59	87	44
Laverstock & Ford	42	12	7	23	68	105	43
Totton & Eling	42	11	9	22	67	88	42
New Milton Town	42	10	7	25	56	104	37
Fawley	42	10	4	28	45	112	34
Hayling United	42	9	4	29	69	130	31
Brockenhurst	***42***	***8***	***5***	***29***	***56***	***107***	***29***

Poole Town moved to the Southern League. Hamble Aerostructures S.S.C. changed their name to GE Hamble.

2011-12

Premier Division

Winchester City	42	33	5	4	138	39	104
Bemerton Heath Harlequins	42	28	6	8	104	39	90
Christchurch	42	26	7	9	78	45	85
Moneyfields	42	26	6	10	105	62	84
GE Hamble	42	27	3	12	90	53	84
Downton	42	24	4	14	80	65	76
Hamworthy United	42	21	8	13	69	62	71
Romsey Town	42	21	4	17	77	66	67
Bournemouth	42	18	10	14	61	54	64
Alton Town	42	19	4	19	74	83	61
Totton & Eling	42	17	8	17	80	77	59
Fareham Town	42	14	14	14	77	68	56
Newport (IOW)	42	17	5	20	59	80	56
Lymington Town	42	16	5	21	63	78	53
Alresford Town	42	14	8	20	62	80	50
Blackfield & Langley	42	12	7	23	63	79	43
Horndean	42	10	8	24	47	68	38
Hayling United	42	10	8	24	59	104	38
Fawley	42	10	7	25	56	81	37
New Milton Town	42	10	6	26	64	108	36
Brading Town	42	10	6	26	54	102	36
Laverstock & Ford	***42***	***7***	***5***	***30***	***59***	***126***	***26***

Winchester City moved to the Southern League. Brading Town resigned and took their reserves' place in the Isle of Wight League.

Division One

Downton	**36**	**27**	**7**	**2**	**106**	**29**	**88**
Horndean	**36**	**25**	**4**	**7**	**104**	**53**	**79**
AFC Portchester	36	20	9	7	85	52	69
Pewsey Vale	36	20	9	7	77	44	69
United Services Portsmouth	36	20	7	9	90	57	67
Ringwood Town	36	18	5	13	61	60	59
Whitchurch United	36	17	4	15	77	54	55
Cowes Sports	36	15	8	13	59	62	52
Verwood Town	36	13	11	12	70	66	50
Fleet Spurs	36	15	3	18	82	85	48
Petersfield Town	36	12	9	15	68	73	45
Warminster Town	36	13	6	17	72	79	45
Amesbury Town	36	14	3	19	62	90	45
Hythe & Dibden	36	9	9	18	60	72	36
East Cowes Victoria Athletic	36	9	9	18	52	77	36
Tadley Calleva	36	11	3	22	69	101	36
Andover New Street	36	10	6	20	60	93	36
Stockbridge	36	5	9	22	44	95	24
Shaftesbury	36	4	9	23	39	95	21

Cowes Sports had 1 point deducted.
Shaftesbury moved to the Dorset Premier League. Team Solent joined from the Hampshire Premier League.

Division One

Verwood Town	**34**	**25**	**5**	**4**	**91**	**38**	**80**
AFC Portchester	**34**	**24**	**4**	**6**	**114**	**52**	**76**
Team Solent	34	19	7	8	75	52	64
East Cowes Victoria Athletic	34	19	6	9	82	46	63
Brockenhurst	34	18	9	7	72	41	63
Cowes Sports	34	15	5	14	62	45	50
Fleet Spurs	34	14	7	13	45	46	49
Whitchurch United	34	13	8	13	50	45	47
Ringwood Town	34	13	7	14	62	59	46
Andover New Street	34	13	10	11	53	56	46
Pewsey Vale	34	12	8	14	51	61	44
Petersfield Town	34	12	3	19	67	74	39
United Services Portsmouth	34	11	6	17	59	69	39
Amesbury Town	34	9	7	18	55	93	34
Stockbridge	34	7	12	15	34	63	33
Warminster Town	34	8	8	18	56	83	32
Tadley Calleva	34	8	4	22	39	82	28
Hythe & Dibden	34	6	4	24	47	109	22

Andover New Street had 3 points deducted.
Warminster Town moved to the Western League.

2012-13

Premier Division

	P	W	D	L	F	A	Pts
Blackfield & Langley	40	31	6	3	100	31	99
Alresford Town	40	29	2	9	124	51	89
Christchurch	40	26	6	8	106	49	84
Moneyfields	40	22	8	10	85	50	74
Bemerton Heath Harlequins	40	22	8	10	91	57	74
Newport (IOW)	40	19	11	10	76	63	68
GE Hamble	40	19	9	12	87	73	66
Downton	40	19	8	13	81	61	65
Fareham Town	40	19	5	16	77	72	62
Hamworthy United	40	15	9	16	76	73	54
Horndean	40	15	7	18	79	93	52
Totton & Eling	40	14	8	18	66	81	50
Bournemouth	40	14	7	19	72	95	49
Verwood Town	40	11	13	16	63	68	46
AFC Portchester	40	13	7	20	69	85	46
Hayling United	*40*	*13*	*5*	*22*	*74*	*112*	*44*
Fawley	40	12	5	23	62	91	41
Alton Town	40	12	4	24	67	92	40
Lymington Town	40	9	11	20	47	69	38
Romsey Town	40	7	1	32	38	137	22
New Milton Town	*40*	*6*	*6*	*28*	*51*	*88*	*24*

Alton Town moved to the Combined Counties League. Sholing and Winchester City both joined from the Southern League. GE Hamble changed their name to Folland Sports.

2013-14

Premier Division

	P	W	D	L	F	A	Pts
Sholing	42	33	5	4	134	29	104
Alresford Town	42	31	4	7	125	52	97
Folland Sports	42	27	7	8	100	48	85
Newport (IOW)	42	25	9	8	105	47	84
Winchester City	42	25	6	11	93	41	81
Blackfield & Langley	42	23	9	10	81	57	78
Bemerton Heath Harlequins	42	22	5	15	99	65	71
AFC Portchester	42	21	13	8	86	43	70
Moneyfields	42	21	10	11	75	53	67
Fareham Town	42	18	8	16	78	81	62
Brockenhurst	42	17	8	17	72	82	59
Hamworthy United	42	16	9	17	78	78	57
Whitchurch United	42	16	7	19	57	69	55
Lymington Town	42	15	5	22	71	99	50
Bournemouth	42	12	7	23	66	89	43
Christchurch	42	11	7	24	56	112	40
Horndean	42	10	7	25	55	95	37
Totton & Eling	42	12	0	30	54	117	36
Verwood Town	42	8	10	24	45	78	34
Fawley	42	7	9	26	49	108	30
Downton	*42*	*6*	*8*	*28*	*49*	*121*	*26*
Romsey Town	*42*	*6*	*7*	*29*	*43*	*107*	*25*

AFC Portchester and Moneyfields both had 6 points deducted. Folland Sports had 3 points deducted. Sholing moved to the Southern League.

Division One

	P	W	D	L	F	A	Pts
Brockenhurst	**30**	**22**	**3**	**5**	**82**	**26**	**69**
Whitchurch United	**30**	**22**	**3**	**5**	**76**	**23**	**69**
Team Solent	30	20	4	6	65	37	64
Cowes Sports	30	20	2	8	77	36	62
Pewsey Vale	30	15	8	7	72	41	53
Petersfield Town	30	16	5	9	76	46	53
Tadley Calleva	30	15	3	12	69	45	48
East Cowes Victoria Athletic	30	14	7	9	70	55	48
Ringwood Town	30	10	4	16	48	71	34
Fleet Spurs	30	10	3	17	49	55	33
Stockbridge	30	10	2	18	48	80	32
United Services Portsmouth	30	9	4	17	56	76	31
Laverstock & Ford	30	8	7	15	41	71	31
Amesbury Town	30	7	4	19	31	76	25
Andover New Street	30	4	8	18	40	93	20
Hythe & Dibden	30	3	3	24	27	96	12

East Cowes Victoria Athletic had 1 point deducted. Andover Town joined as a newly formed club.

Division One

	P	W	D	L	F	A	Pts
Petersfield Town	**30**	**23**	**5**	**2**	**118**	**36**	**74**
Andover Town	**30**	**23**	**4**	**3**	**108**	**28**	**73**
Cowes Sports	30	22	3	5	84	36	69
Hythe & Dibden	30	19	5	6	85	37	62
Tadley Calleva	30	15	7	8	64	43	52
Team Solent	30	16	5	9	82	51	50
United Services Portsmouth	30	14	5	11	61	53	47
Pewsey Vale	30	14	4	12	59	52	46
Laverstock & Ford	30	12	2	16	46	54	38
Amesbury Town	30	12	2	16	56	66	38
New Milton Town	30	10	2	18	69	71	32
Fleet Spurs	30	8	3	19	50	79	27
Ringwood Town	30	7	1	22	41	104	22
Hayling United	30	6	4	20	47	106	21
Andover New Street	30	7	0	23	33	111	21
East Cowes Victoria Athletic	30	4	4	22	32	108	16

Team Solent had 3 points deducted. Hayling United had 1 point deducted. Stockbridge resigned from the League on 18th February 2014 as their ground was badly flooded and they were unable to fulfil their fixtures. Their record was deleted: 13 5 1 7 25 34 16 They subsequently joined the Hampshire Premier League for the 2014-15 season. Hayling United also moved to the Hampshire Premier League.

2014-15

Premier Division

Petersfield Town	40	29	9	2	118	42	96
Winchester City	40	28	5	7	120	38	89
AFC Portchester	40	25	7	8	91	45	82
Moneyfields	40	22	9	9	92	42	75
Blackfield & Langley	40	21	10	9	83	44	73
Whitchurch United	40	20	7	13	80	76	67
Newport (IOW)	40	20	5	15	69	52	65
Folland Sports	40	20	5	15	74	74	65
Lymington Town	40	19	5	16	70	57	62
Hamworthy United	40	15	10	15	71	65	55
Horndean	40	16	7	17	62	69	55
Andover Town	40	16	4	20	66	70	52
Bemerton Heath Harlequins	40	15	7	18	65	81	52
Brockenhurst	40	15	5	20	72	89	50
Verwood Town	40	13	5	22	57	79	44
Alresford Town	40	11	6	23	64	82	39
Fawley	40	10	8	22	44	81	38
Bournemouth	40	9	8	23	61	126	35
Fareham Town	40	7	11	22	50	92	32
Totton & Eling	*40*	*8*	*7*	*25*	*53*	*107*	*31*
Christchurch	*40*	*7*	*8*	*25*	*60*	*111*	*29*

Petersfield Town and Winchester City both moved to the Southern League. Sholing joined from the Southern League and Salisbury joined as a reformed club after Salisbury City had disbanded.

Division One

Team Solent	**28**	**22**	**1**	**5**	**83**	**38**	**67**
Cowes Sports	**28**	**20**	**4**	**4**	**78**	**32**	**64**
Tadley Calleva	28	20	3	5	86	33	63
Amesbury Town	28	18	0	10	85	41	54
United Services Portsmouth	28	16	3	9	68	46	51
New Milton Town	28	15	4	9	70	49	49
Hythe & Dibden	28	14	2	12	42	48	44
Laverstock & Ford	28	12	3	13	39	54	39
Fleet Spurs	28	11	5	12	50	63	38
Pewsey Vale	28	9	4	15	44	48	31
Ringwood Town	28	9	4	15	42	53	31
Downton	28	6	9	13	33	48	27
Andover New Street	28	7	4	17	37	66	25
Romsey Town	28	4	4	20	40	81	16
East Cowes Victoria Athletic	28	1	2	25	18	115	5

AFC Stoneham joined from the Hampshire Premier League, Alton Town joined from the Combined Counties League and Portland United joined from the Dorset Premier League.